On Beginning an Analysis

ON BEGINNING AN ANALYSIS

Edited by

Theodore J. Jacobs, M.D. & Arnold Rothstein, M.D.

INTERNATIONAL UNIVERSITIES PRESS, INC.
Madison Connecticut

Library of Congress Cataloging-in-Publication Data

On beginning an analysis / edited by Theodore J. Jacobs & Arnold Rothstein.
p. cm.
Includes bibliographical references.
ISBN 0-8236-3750-6
1. Psychoanalysis. I. Jacobs, Theodore J. II. Rothstein, Arnold, 1936- .
[DNLM: 1. Psychoanalytic Therapy—methods. WM 460.6 058]
RC506.05 1990
616.89'17—dc20
DNLM/DLC 90-4427
for Library of Congress CIP

Manufactured in the United States of America

Contents

Contributors

Sander M. Abend, M.D., Training and Supervising Analyst, New York Psychoanalytic Institute; Editor-in-Chief, *Psychoanalytic Quarterly*.

Adrienne Applegarth, M.D., Training and Supervising Analyst, San Francisco Psychoanalytic Institute; Clinical Professor of Psychiatry, University of California Medical School, San Francisco.

Henry M. Bachrach, Ph.D., Member, New York Psychoanalytic Society; Clinical Professor of Psychiatry, New York Medical College at St. Vincent's Hospital of New York.

Harold P. Blum, M.D., Clinical Professor of Psychiatry and Training Analyst, New York University; Executive Director, The Sigmund Freud Archives; Past Editor, *Journal of the American Psychoanalytic Association.*

Charles Brenner, M.D., Training and Supervising Analyst, New York Psychoanalytic Institute; Past President, American Psychoanalytic Association; author, *An Elementary Textbook of Psychoanalysis* (2nd. ed.), *Psychoanalytic Technique & Psychic Conflict* and *The Mind in Conflict.*

Judith Fingert Chused, M.D., Clinical Professor of Psychiatry and Behavioral Sciences at George Washington University School of Medicine; Training and Supervising Analyst (in child, adolescent and adult analysis) at the Washington Psychoanalytic Institute.

Charles C. Hogan, M.D., D. Med. Sc., Assistant Clinical Professor, Department of Psychiatry, Albert Einstein College of Medicine/Montefiore Medical Center, Bronx; Lecturer, Columbia University College of Physicians and Surgeons; Faculty, Columbia University Center for Psychoanalytic Training Research.

Milton H. Horowitz, M.D., Training and Supervising Analyst, New York Psychoanalytic Institute; Clinical Professor of Psychiatry, New York University School of Medicine.

Theodore J. Jacobs, M.D., Clinical Professor of Psychiatry, Albert Einstein College of Medicine; Training and Supervising Analyst, New York Psychoanalytic Institute and at The Psychoanalytic Institute at New York University.

Wayne A. Myers, M.D., Clinical Professor of Psychiatry, Cornell University Medical Center; Training and Supervising Psychoanalyst, Columbia University Center for Psychoanalytic Training and Research.

Mortimer Ostow, M.D., Attending Psychiatrist, Montifiore Medical Center; President, Psychoanalytic Research and Development Fund; author, *Drugs in Psychoanalysis and Psychotherapy* and *The Psychodynamic Approach and Drug Therapy.*

Michael S. Porder, M.D., Training and Supervising Analyst, New York Psychoanalytic Institute; Associate Editor, Psychoanalytic Quarterly; Associate Clinical Professor of Psychiatry, Mt. Sinai School of Medicine.

Arnold Rothstein, M.D., Member, New York Psychoanalytic Society; Editor, No. 1-4, Workshop Series of the American Psychoanalytic Association; author, *The Narcissistic Pursuit of Perfection* (2nd ed.) and *The Structural Hypothesis: An Evolutionary Perspective.*

Estelle Shane, Ph.D., Founding President, Center for Early Education and College for Developmental Studies; Training and Supervising Analyst in Adult and Child Analysis, Los Angeles Psychoanalytic Society and Institute; Faculty, University of California, Los Angeles.

Morton Shane, M.D., Training Analyst and Supervising Analyst in Adult and Child Analysis and Director of Education, Los Angeles Psychoanalytic Society and Institute; Associate Clinical Professor, Department of Psychiatry, University of California, Los Angeles.

Martin H. Stein, M.D., Training and Supervising Analyst, New York Psychoanalytic Institute, Former Chairman, Board on Professional Standards, American Psychoanalytic Association.

C. Philip Wilson, M.D., Member of the Faculties of the Psychoanalytic Institute, New York University Medical Center and the Columbia University Center for Psychoanalytic Training and Research; Senior Attending Psychiatrist and Lecturer in Psychosomatics, St. Luke's-Roosevelt Hospital Center, New York; Assistant Clinical Professor of Psychiatry, Columbia College of Physicians and Surgeons, New York.

Preface

In 1977 Shapiro (1978), reporting to the annual meeting of the American Psychoanalytic Association on a survey of psychoanalytic practice, noted: "a sizeable group of graduated members are conducting relatively few psychoanalyses. Twenty-two percent reported that patients in analysis in the survey week in April 1976 made up 10 percent or less of their private office patients; 19 percent reported that they then had only one patient in analysis or none at all" (p. 619).

Shapiro continued: "Two-thirds of those who experienced a decline attributed it to decreased referral of *suitable analytic patients*" (p. 619; emphasis added).

I left that meeting impressed with the statistics and wondering what these colleagues meant by "a suitable analytic patient." I remember thinking that Leo Stone would probably suggest that a patient had to prove he or she was *not* suitable for analysis, and not analyzable after a trial of analysis. I wondered if analytic training contributed to engendering an evaluative attitude toward prospective analysands and whether the search for the "good" case does justice to the realities of practice in the contemporary world. It is rare today for "good" cases to present themselves for analysis. Rather, to develop a practice most analysts today must see the possibilities in individuals who seek treatment, allow them to begin the way they can begin, work systematically with resistances, and thus help patients get into analysis.

Some time later, while chatting with a group of recent graduates at a dinner party, the question of the number of their analytic cases came up for discussion. After sharing their difficulties, one colleague turned to me and said, "And how many cases do you have?" My answer "ten" was met with a mixture of awe and incredulity; one colleague commented, "it must be because you have written some papers and a book." I said I did not think so, and added, somewhat presumptuously, that I thought I knew something about how to begin an analysis. Shortly thereafter I began to collect clinical data from unusual opening phases of analyses that I had conducted.

Many colleagues are vitally interested in discussing clinical data that might help them more successfully begin analyses and develop analytic practices. In response to this perceived need, Dr. Jacobs and I decided to develop this book. Our plan was to invite distinguished analysts with expertise in particular areas to discuss the way that they begin analyses in a variety of clinical situations. Our intention has been to emphasize the reporting of case material so as to best demonstrate what experienced analysts actually do in their analytic practices.

Arnold Rothstein, M.D.

Introduction

Theodore J. Jacobs, M.D.

This is a book about beginnings. It is about the ways in which analyses get started and about the ways in which analysts go about starting them. It is also a book about the changing face of analysis. Increasingly, colleagues are called upon to treat individuals whose pathology falls outside the range of the classical neuroses. In consultation analysts are often asked to assess a wide range of problems including borderline cases, affective disorders, severe character pathology, and psychosomatic conditions. In addition, a number of analysts are seeing patients who are currently taking medication or for whom its use for shorter or longer periods of time may be indicated. The analysis of the older patient, too, is no longer a rare occurrence, and increasingly, individuals in the sixth and seventh decades seek analytic treatment.

Analysts working with younger people will, at some time, have the task of evaluating patients suffering from eating disorders, behavioral problems, and other conditions common to that age group. Those working with older patients also encounter with some frequency those action-prone individuals for whom the acting out of emotional conflicts has become a deeply engrained feature of their character.

While analysis is the appropriate therapeutic approach for only a small percentage of patients whose pathology lies outside the range of neuroses, for certain such individuals it is in fact the treatment of choice. The identification and selection of such patients from among the great variety of individuals with whom he consults presents the analyst with a formidable task.

Equally difficult, however, and in many instances more so, is the task of getting the analysis of such patients off on the right foot. In initiating analytic work with them, the usual, well-established techniques for handling the opening phase may have to be modified. In the chapters that follow a number of experienced clinicians will discuss the special problems involved in selecting analysis and beginning the treatment of this group of patients. Their emphasis will be not only on clarifying the pathology involved and the resistances encountered, but on the particular techniques that they have found useful in launching the treatment. The kinds of cases selected for discussion are those seen with some frequency by analysts. They also present the kinds of difficulties that make navigation of the opening phase a difficult and sometimes perilous journey.

It is not only in the case of the more disturbed patient, however, that some modification in the usual manner of beginning an analysis may be necessary. It is not rare today for patients in need of analysis to balk at the idea of undertaking such treatment. Long-standing resistances, buttressed by culturally supported attitudes, and practical problems of time, money, and scheduling, often combine and lead to rejection of the recommendation for analysis.

The analyst must then begin his work in some other way. Often he does so by seeing the patient in analytic psychotherapy or modified analysis with a reduced schedule of appointments. Conducted carefully, with proper attention to the resistances that underlie the patient's inability to commit himself to analysis, such treatment may prove to be of the greatest value in helping him clear away the obstacles to making such a commitment. Beginnings of this kind, which in today's analytic world are more the rule than the exception, may serve as a useful and often essential introduction to the more intensive analytic work which is to follow. These considerations are spelled out in detail in chapter 10 which takes up the question of beginning treatment work with a reluctant patient.

In every analysis the opening phase of therapy is important, setting the tone for all that is to occur, but with certain patients, whose anxiety about beginning analysis is high, whose resistances are strong, and in whom the difficulties in establishing a working alliance are formidable, the way in which they experience the opening days and weeks of treatment will determine in large measure their accessibility to further analytic work.

Freud (1913) was well aware of the importance of beginnings in analysis and he likened the initial phase of treatment to the opening moves of a chess game. The analyst's task was to know the game well and to master the strategies which, varying only slightly from patient to patient, became part of his standard operating technique. If he applied his technique skillfully, conducted himself properly, and maintained the appropriate analytic stance, he could be reasonably assured of a satisfactory beginning. Thus, in Freud's mind the opening phase of analysis, as contrasted with the midgame, followed certain well-established rules and patterns.

Although his analytic cases covered a wide spectrum of diagnostic categories and many of the individuals whom he treated were quite troubled, Freud made few distinctions between patients with regard to beginning the treatment. Today the situation is very different. Although much of what Freud had to say about the opening phase of analysis remains valid and useful, the advances in theory and technique that have taken place in recent years have made it possible for the contemporary analyst to refine his method of beginning an analysis and attune it to the requirements of the individual case.

Traditionally, analysts have been taught certain principles in the handling of the opening phase. These include such technical matters as analyzing from the surface downward, interpretation of fluid defenses before those embedded in character, and interpretation of affects before content. While the modern analyst understands the value of such precepts, and has them in mind as he begins work with a new patient, he also recognizes the importance of approaching analytic work with flexibility. He knows that there are situations when, from early on, interpretations must be deep and incisive, when character defenses must be confronted at the outset, and when the interpretation of affects must be deferred. For what he has come to understand is that technique cannot be made rigid or formalized in rules but must be adaptable and responsive to the needs of the patient. This is particularly so in the opening phase when the analyst's capacity to grasp and respond to the communications and metacommunications being transmitted between himself and the patient is so critical a factor in the establishment of the kind of rapport that fosters the unfolding of an analytic process.

The beginning of any analysis is a time of becoming acquainted, of testing, of experimentation, and of validation. The two members of the analytic team are getting to know each other, trying one another on for size, testing out their sending and receiving equipment, and making adjustments in their communication systems. Although transferences are beginning to exert an influence on perceptions, patient and analyst alike are also taking accurate readings of the other. The analyst's initial impressions of his patient, obtained in the consultation period, are reviewed, edited, and revised. He begins to develop a feel not only for the intricacies of the patient's symptoms and pathology, but for those unique qualities that convey the essence of a person.

The patient, too, is taking the measure of the analyst. While, overtly, his curiosity may appear to be limited to certain factual questions about his therapist, he actually wants to know more. Anxious at the beginning of treatment and concerned to know just who this person is to whom he has entrusted himself and his deepest secrets, the patient searches for clues to the personal qualities of his analyst. Within a short time he forms an impression of the analyst's honesty, integrity, skill, and capacity for empathy. In myriad and often subtle ways he puts the analyst's character to the test and the frankness with which he is willing to reveal himself depends in large measure on what he discovers. If he perceives the analyst to be a devious person or a self-serving one, if he gains the impression that the analyst is unduly concerned with money, position, or prestige, or if he senses that he is not truly interested in the patient's welfare, he will respond by holding back aspects of himself. While on the surface he may seem to be associating freely and to be adhering to the basic rule, in fact much material relating to certain critical areas of vulnerability will unconsciously be kept out of awareness. More guarded than he himself may know, the patient will avoid painful self-exposure and in other important ways will not allow the analysis to touch him deeply.

While impressions formed at the outset of treatment often have enduring effect on the ensuing process, recognition of just what those effects are, and the manner in which they have colored the interaction between patient and analyst, may be long delayed. In one instance, a young man in analysis failed after several years to show evidence of progress despite the keenness of his analyst's understanding of him and the correctness of his interpretations. It was not until he was well into his third year of analysis that this patient could permit a troubling idea to rise to consciousness. He believed that from the outset his analyst did not really like him and that he regarded certain aspects of his character to be fixed and unchangeable. When the patient revealed this, the analyst became aware of the truth of this perception. Certain qualities of the patient had, initially, put him off and he had not been optimistic about change taking place in certain characterological traits. He acknowledged the correctness of the patient's perceptions and with the air now cleared, they explored what it was about the patient's initial presentation of himself that had been off-putting. This exploration was the first truly joint undertaking between patient and analyst. It heralded a new beginning and a new dimension in the work. The patient's wariness, previously present in subtle forms, was now dissipated. In its place had developed a more trusting and enthusiastic attitude which contributed to more productive analytic work.

In the opening phase of some analyses, transferences develop with surprising rapidity and effectively color all that ensue. Such transferences may arise not only in the patient, but in the analyst as well. This was the case in the analysis of a young businessman who began treatment with an analyst who was the same age as the patient's thoroughly disliked older brother. The patient immediately experienced hatred, rage, and envy toward the analyst, making the initial analytic hours tense and difficult. To complicate matters, the analyst had a younger brother with whom recent tensions had arisen. The patient's age and general manner, together with the powerful feelings he was expressing toward his analyst, evoked strong affects in the analyst and promoted in him a rapidly developing transference. With distorted perceptions on both sides of the couch holding sway, the analysis could not be properly launched. It took understanding of what was happening, together with early and repeated interpretations of the transference interactions between patient and therapist, to set the analysis on the proper course.

Sometimes transferences are preset and have come into existence months or years before the analysis has actually begun. In a number of such instances, the patient has seen the analyst in other settings, and has formed an impression of him in his role as teacher, lecturer, author, or committee member. He may have known someone who was in treatment with the analyst and from this or other sources have heard a good deal about him.

Patients who are initially seen is psychotherapy inevitably develop perceptions of the therapist based not only on transference distortions, but on accurate observation. Such perceptions will inevitably color the opening phase of a subsequent analysis undertaken with these patients, but unless the analyst is aware of the importance of these perceptions and makes efforts to bring them to the surface, they may remain concealed and act as silent, though powerful, influences on the analytic work. In one instance a patient's initially strong negative feelings toward her analyst contrasted sharply with her attitude toward him when, at an earlier time, she was in psychotherapy with him. Analysis of her reaction showed that although she had decided to end the therapy some years before in order to marry and move to a new community, she never forgave her therapist for allowing her to do so and for turning her over to another man. This sequence of events unconsciously connected with a central trauma of her childhood. After her mother's sudden death when she was four, she was sent by her distraught father to live with an aunt. The girl experienced this change in her life as a total betrayal, and years later the ending of her therapy reactivated a storehouse of memories. It took much reconstructive work in analysis before the patient could fully understand the meaning of the change that had taken place in her feelings and the experiences of childhood that lay behind them. And it was only the early and active interpretation of the long-buried memories enacted in the transference that allowed the analysis to proceed.

It is not only the "widening scope" patient who presents formidable challenges at the beginning of analysis. Analytic work with adolescents and young adults poses special problems, and whilst it is essential to engage such patients at the outset of treatment it is often a difficult task to do so. The young person seeking to find his place in life is oriented toward action and toward the outer world. The regressive pull of the transference and the need in analysis to reopen old wounds constitute threats that are often avoided through concentration on reality issues and through the extensive use of externalization. Exploration of these problems are taken up in the chapters that discuss the special considerations involved in beginning an analysis with young people.

Special problems occur, too, in beginning analytic work with candidates, with individuals who have had previous analyses, with patients who suffer from psychosomatic disorders, and with those who have experienced severe traumas in childhood. Although each of these situations requires careful handling in the opening phase, little has been written about the theoretical and technical issues involved in the management of this critical period of treatment. It is for this reason that separate chapters in this book have been devoted to an overview of the difficulties and opportunities involved in beginning an analysis with these groups of patients.

It is our hope that by sharing the experiences of seasoned clinicians as they describe the way they go about beginning analysis under a wide variety of circumstances, readers will enlarge the range and scope of their understanding of this crucial period. We hope, too, that they will become acquainted with techniques and ways of thinking about the opening phase that will prove useful as they initiate analytic treatment with their own patients. For it is by sharing the knowledge and experience gained in the crucible of the therapeutic encounter that advances in analytic treatment are made.

PART I
THEORETICAL CONSIDERATIONS

Chapter 1

The Analyst's Thinking and Attitude at the Beginning of an Analysis: The Influence of Research Data at the Beginning of an Analysis

Henry M. Bachrach, Ph.D.

When a patient and analyst begin to meet, is what follows a largely unpredictable venture? Many analysts believe it is, because of the multitude of factors that govern the fate of analyses. Freud (1913), as we know, likened analysis to a game of chess where only the opening and closing moves could be prescribed, and in 1920, after twenty years of experience with the psychoanalytic method proper, he suggested:

> Even supposing that we have a complete knowledge of the aetiological factors that decide a given result, nevertheless what we know about them is only their quality, and not their relative strength. Some of them are suppressed by others because they are too weak, and they therefore do not affect the final result. But we never know beforehand which of the determining factors will prove the weaker or stronger. We only can say at the end that those which succeeded must have been the stronger. Hence

> the chain of causation can always be recognized with certainty if we follow the line of analysis, whereas to predict it along the line of synthesis is impossible [1920b, p. 168].

Freud held to this view to the very end of his psychoanalytic career. In *Analysis Terminable and Interminable* (1937), he spoke to the indeterminability, at the beginnings of analyses, of subtle alterations of the ego, and the quantitative factors associated with trauma, the variability of the instincts, the castration complex, and libidinal, aggressive, and masochistic compromise formations. Waelder (1963), coming to psychoanalysis from physics, marshaled an argument on the basis of the general principles of determinism and predictability. He suggested that the variability inherent in the human organism is such that dynamic forces continually remain in flux, and there is, therefore, no way of knowing beforehand how they will affect later situations. Moreover, "this state of affairs is not just due to the 'youth' of our science or to the alleged failure to adhere to rigid standards of investigation and verification, but to the factors [quantitative] which appear inherent in the subject and therefore are, on the whole, unalterable" (p. 40). Contemporary inquiries of highly experienced analysts have not altered these views (Firestein, 1978, 1984). Does this mean that every analyst is confronted with the *ultimate* uncertainties in beginning each new case? Hardly, for every analysis begins in a preliminary consultation. Whether anxious, depressed, or offering rationalized presentations, most patients consult an analyst in order to seek relief for one or another form of mental suffering. From the very beginning, the task of the analyst is to gather psychological data to construct a hypothetical working model of the patient to rationally recommend the form of treatment likely to be most helpful.

In days past, it was possible to recommend psychoanalysis on a trial basis because there were few viable treatment alternatives. But in the past several decades a wide variety of alternative treatment modalities has been developed based upon behavioral, biological, cognitive, psychodynamic, and social models, each making its own claims for efficacy. Insofar as any helpful analysis is likely to be a time-consuming venture making considerable demands upon both analyst and analysand, questions always stand out in the analyst's mind in undertaking any given case. Given the patient's circumstances, does analysis seem to be *indicated,* and if so (by virtue of recalcitrantly debilitating compromise formations), what is the likelihood that the patient will benefit more by application of the psychoanalytic method than by other treatment procedures, and what resources does the patient bring to the psychoanalytic undertaking? Essentially, how *suitable* a candidate is the patient for psychoanalysis? Truly, the essential questions were adumbrated by Oberndorf (1943) when he asked what type of treatment is best suited to what kind of patient, suffering what kind of illness, at what point in his or her life, when treated by what kind of analyst, in what manner?

In one form or another the accumulated wisdom of the entire clinical psychoanalytic literature bears upon these questions insofar as clinical discussions speak to the fates of different kinds of cases, considerations of understanding, and clinical management required by the vast array of patients consulting analysts; varied understandings of different forms of symptoms in varied characterological settings; the scope and limitations of the psychoanalytic method; and ultimately, to the central issue of the indications for psychoanalysis and the qualities of patients which render them suitable to the psychoanalytic undertaking. The degree to which one might expect a patient's conflicts to be most beneficially altered by psychoanalysis, or the indications for psychoanalysis and the patient's suitability for the psychoanalytic undertaking, remain among the major questions in the mind of all analysts throughout every analysis. In beginning an analysis they are among the most central questions.

Over the years many panels (1960, 1963, 1968) and critical discussions (Waldhorn, 1967; Tyson and Sandler, 1971; Bachrach and Leaff, 1978; Erle and Goldberg, 1979; Firestein, 1984) have reviewed the accumulated clinical wisdom of a century of practice about the issues of analyzability, but it is remarkable how Freud's (1920b) early observations have stood the test of time.

> [T]he ideal situation for an analysis is when someone who is otherwise his own master is suffering from an inner conflict which he is unable to resolve alone, so that he brings his trouble to the analyst and begs for help. The physician then works hand in hand with one portion of the pathologically divided personality against the other party in the conflict. Any situation which differs from this is to a greater or lesser degree unfavorable for psychoanalysis and adds fresh difficulties to the internal ones already present [p. 150].

Within the past several decades a new form of systematic, extra-analytic, methodologically informed research has entered the discussion. The aim of this essay is to critically review this research, and to explore how it might and might not influence the analyst's thinking and attitude in beginning an analysis.

THE RESEARCH STUDIES

Contemporary systematic research on analyzability might be said to have begun with the Menninger Foundation Psychotherapy Research Project. It is clearly the most clinically and methodologically ambitious study of psychoanalysis that has been undertaken. Begun in 1954 under the leadership of Louis Robbins and Robert Wallerstein, it was designed to clarify what kinds of changes take place in psychoanalysis and psychotherapy, and how they come about. Twenty-one cases of psychoanalysis and twenty-one cases of psychotherapy were to be studied from the point of first contact through a follow-up period of two years. The routine clinical practices of the Foundation made it possible to study these cases naturalistically because careful case records were kept every step along the way. The initial outpatient evaluation process was the most comprehensive in the world, and consisted of ten clinical interviews, interviews with family members, and a complete battery of psychological tests anchored in psychoanalytic ego psychology, all guided by a senior analyst. Process notes with regular summaries were part of the routine clinical record for all cases. It was possible, therefore, for teams of experienced analysts to review these records and come to their own independent assessments, without the need for potentially influential research probes into the treatments. At termination and follow-up, the patients were reexamined by the research teams, including psychological testing. An incredible 100 percent follow-up was achieved (extended in many cases, including up to thirty years). In its history the project gave rise to five books and more than sixty papers (including Kernberg's seminal papers on personality disorders), but it was not until 1986, nearly thirty years after the inception of the project, that a final, integrative account was published (Wallerstein, 1986). True to the spirit of the project, Wallerstein's account is a virtual clinical treasure trove that provides detailed summaries of all the cases, the courses, and ultimate fate of their treatments. In the face of Wallerstein's clinical accounting, it is simply not possible to do more than adumbrate the outlines of the methodology and findings—for more the reader must turn to Wallerstein's (1986) account.

Originally, thirty-five patient qualities were selected for study which were reduced (because of redundancy) to twelve carefully defined clinical dimensions (e.g., ego strength, level of anxiety, motivation, psychological mindedness). Twenty-one treatment qualities were similarly reduced to eight (e.g., interpretative techniques, transference, therapist's skill in this case), and fourteen situational factors were reduced to seven (e.g., stress, conflict triggers, degree of interpersonal support). Treatment outcomes were studied primarily along three dimensions: amount of global improvement, increase in ego strength, and transference resolution. A unique, high-level clinical exercise was employed to reduce complex clinical judgments to quantitative dimensions. Independent research teams wrote a paragraph about each of the variables for each of the patients at the beginning of treatment, termination, and follow-up. These write-ups were then passed on to other research teams, which compared every patient on a one-to-one basis with every other patient on each of the variables to determine which of the two was higher on a given dimension. In this way it was possible to rank all of the patients on all the dimensions at the three points in time, and transform complex clinical judgments into reliable, quantitatively paired comparisons for statistical analysis. At the same time the clinical records were studied by experienced analysts who formed their own independent, working models of the patients, the suitability for the treatments they received, the events of the treatments, and their ultimate outcomes.

All too often the best laid plans have a way of taking unanticipated directions. In the case of the project, while the cases were selected on a random basis, there were also specific criteria for exclusion. Most pertinent among the latter were patients whose status was restricted because of their close relationship to the Foundation (e.g., staff, family members, training analyses). As such cases were typically treated by training analysts, the amount of time senior analysts had available for treating other cases was limited. As a consequence, most of the analyses wound up being conducted by candidates, while most of the psychotherapies wound up being conducted by other more experienced clinicians.

By the time of the study the Menninger Foundation had established an international reputation as a psychoanalytic sanatorium of singular merit. Patients traveled to Topeka from far and wide, many as a "court of last resort" having failed in past treatment efforts. As a consequence many of the study patients were severely ill (twenty-two required concomitant hospitalization), and many cases treated by psychoanalysis were far more ill than is usual for contemporary psychoanalytic practice. In many ways the project turned out to be a study of patients taken into psychoanalysis for "heroic" reasons (Ticho, 1970), and yet treated by the least experienced analysts. For example, one patient was taken into analysis while hospitalized at the urging of his family because of several chronic alcoholism, inability to work, and impulsive, violent outbursts. The patient did not see much need for treatment, rapidly developed a paranoid transference psychosis, and died of an alcohol related physical illness shortly after he had employed legal means to extricate himself from the hospital and his analysis of one year's duration. A highly intelligent, but severely action bound analysand with a long history of uncontrolled drinking, perverse homosexuality, and a lifelong passive–masochistic posture, was unable to commit himself to anything, including his analysis, which ended in a severe negative therapeutic reaction. Lest it be thought that the Menninger Foundation had become a hotbed of therapeutic misadventure, it must be recalled that the inception of the project coincided with the challenge of a "widening scope" for psychoanalysis (e.g., Stone's classic paper had appeared in 1954), and if ever there was a place where the scope of these ideas could be tested, it was the Menninger Foundation. Less severely ill, more suitable cases were, of course, also included in the study.

What became of these patients? First, because of the vagaries of case assignment twenty patients were assigned to analysis and twenty-two to psychotherapy. Nearly all the analytic cases required modifications, six analyses had to be converted to psychotherapy early on, one-third were reckoned as outright failures, with the rest achieving varying degrees of therapeutic benefit. Of ten relatively unmodified analyses, two were judged to have a "very good" result and four a "moderate" result. In contrast, two-fifths of the therapy cases were seen as achieving good results and only one-third as failures. The results of psychoanalysis seemed, at least on the face of it, similar to the results of psychotherapy or modified analysis, with *these* patients. However, in Wallerstein's retrospective clinical review of the cases, only 45 percent taken into analysis seemed suitable, and 27 percent, in fact, were undertaken on the basis of heroic indications, all of which failed. Also, in retrospect, 45 percent of the cases appeared to have been misdiagnosed, all in the direction of underestimating their pathology, in part due to concealment of major areas of psychopathology despite the unparalleled comprehensiveness of the evaluation process.

All this considered, it may come as no surprise that the predictability of the clinical outcomes of these cases was disappointing. From the statistical report of the study (Kernberg, 1980) we learn that the number of factors assessed at the beginning of treatment significantly associated with the three measures of outcome was less than might be expected on the basis of chance alone! Only initial ego strength was significantly related to global improvement (but not transference resolution and increased ego strength), and initial level of anxiety to global improvement and increased ego strength (but not transference resolution). The therapist's skill was related to global improvement (but not transference resolution and increased ego strength); however, even this finding is open to question as the research teams were aware of the outcome when they were rating the "Therapist's skill in this case." Not only is it possible that these few significant correlations could readily be attributed to chance alone, but the magnitude of the few relationships that did appear was quite small. On the average, only one-fifth of the outcomes of these cases could be associated with initial level of anxiety and ego strength; four-fifths of whatever was tapped by the measures of global improvement and ego strength was related to factors other than the patients' qualities as understood at the beginning of treatment.

Another approach employed in the Menninger Project was to study the relationship between patient qualities and outcomes as assessed from psychological test data (Appelbaum, 1977). On the basis of these data alone, and uncontaminated by any other knowledge of the patients, two psychoanalytically trained psychologists made predictions based upon the test data. When compared with clinical judgments, judgments based upon the test data alone were superior in predicting outcome (Appelbaum, 1977), but the magnitude of the relationships was still not substantial—correlations were in the 0.2 range (Coyne, 1978, personal communication).

Just as the Menninger Project was getting under way, the Columbia University Psychoanalytic Clinic launched its own research project under the stewardship of John Weber in which all cases continuing for more than six sessions from 1945 to 1971 were to be studied. During this time extensive data were collected, coded, and stored on computer tape about the characteristics and outcomes of seven hundred cases of supervised psychoanalysis and 885 cases of supervised psychoanalytic psychotherapy. The treatments were conducted by candidates and, until 1972, training in psychotherapy was included in the basic curriculum of the institute. Data were collected from case records, patients, treating analysts, supervisors, and institute records about the candidates. Patients were assigned to psychoanalysis or psychotherapy, generally on the basis of one screening interview by an experienced analyst, after a history had been taken by a psychiatric social worker, with the final determination being made by the clinic chief.

At the point of initial evaluation, nine graduate analysts evaluated each case according to thirty-eight demographic variables, thirty-six clinical variables (e.g., diagnosis, social relations, areas of disturbance), nine ego strength scales, and the clinic chief's prediction of outcome. The cases were evaluated once again on the same dimensions by the graduate analyst judges from the clinic record at termination, or the analyst's graduation, whichever came first (the clinic record was closed upon the analyst's graduation). The reliability of these judgments was evaluated and found consistent with levels generally obtained in psychotherapy research. In cases where treatment continued beyond the candidates' graduation, a twenty-eight item questionnaire (including clinical rating scales) was sent to the graduates for a retrospective assessment of their cases. The outcomes of these cases were judged according to the degree to which an analytic process had developed (as judged from a combination of three scales in the questionnaire: handling of psychological data, use of resources at termination, and transference manifestations during treatment), and three measures of therapeutic benefit: circumstances of termination, direct clinical judgments of improvement, and change scores (based upon the difference between beginning and end evaluations of the graduate analyst judges). For methodological reasons the final study was divided into several parts.

In the first part (Weber, Bachrach, and Solomon, 1985a) only cases treated between 1945 and 1961 were included for which there was complete and unequivocal information regarding the cases and their circumstances of termination: 295 analyses, 172 psychotherapies, and 114 psychosomatic patients treated by psychotherapy. These patients were middle class with an approximately equal distribution between sexes and marital status. They ranged in age from eighteen to fifty-nine, with a large majority falling in the twenty to thirty-four range. Analytic patients were characterized as functioning within a neurotic range in initial examination, and patients referred for psychotherapy were considered more impaired in terms of motivation, psychopathology, and ability to participate in an analytic process. One hundred fifty-nine candidates conducted these analyses, with ninety-eight treating one case, thirty-four treating two, and the rest between three and five. Among the psychotherapy cases, one hundred and five candidates treated one case, thirty-five treated two, and the rest between three and five.

To what extent were these analyses found beneficial? The greatest therapeutic benefit was associated with analyses continuing beyond the analyst's graduation (and therefore the longest); 52 percent terminated by "mutual agreement that maximum benefit had been achieved," 91 percent were judged "improved," with an equally substantial improvement rate in terms of primary and secondary areas of disturbance, *even though only 43 percent were judged to have developed an analytic process.* In contrast, analyses terminating before the analyst's graduation (and therefore the shortest) showed less benefit. Only 26 percent terminated with maximum benefit, more than half terminated unilaterally with 41 percent unimproved, and 44 percent were rated unchanged or worse. In many ways the clinical outcomes of this group resembled those of psychosomatic patients treated by psychotherapy, about half of whom terminated unilaterally as unimproved and were judged unchanged or worse by their therapists.

Overall, analyzability was modestly associated with all measures of therapeutic benefit (i.e., correlations in the 3–4 range). However, of the analyzable patients, 89 percent terminated with maximum benefit, 78 percent were judged "much improved" and 91 percent were diagnosed as functioning within a neurotic range. In contrast, only 47 percent of the patients who did not develop an analytic process terminated with maximum benefit, and only 40 percent were judged "much improved." Clearly, patients judged analyzable achieved greater therapeutic benefit than patients who did not develop an analytic process, but only two-fifths of patients who remained in analysis were characterized as having developed an analytic process at termination. Neither analyzability or therapeutic benefit turned out to be more than marginally predictable from the clinic chiefs' expectations, the patients' qualities evaluated at the beginning of treatment, rudimentary characteristics of the candidate analysts (e.g., demographic, faculty ratings), or combinations of these factors. Viewed retrospectively from the perspective of the treating analyst at termination, however, there was a stronger relationship between patient qualities and clinical outcomes (i.e., correlations in the .4–.5 range).

In the second part of the study (Weber, Bachrach, and Solomon, 1985b), designed in part as a cross-validation of the first, thirty-six analyses and forty-one psychotherapies, for which there was complete and reliable data, conducted between 1962 and 1971, were studied. These cases were similar to the first sample, though they were seen as functioning at slightly higher levels in initial evaluation. The cases were treated by forty-three candidates. Detailed questionnaires, including rating scales, were distributed to candidates, patients, and supervisors; data about the analysts were obtained from institute records and faculty ratings. Essentially the same variables were studied as in the first study, though now the data were collected by a modified method (i.e., questionnaires to analysts instead of independent judges). It was found that while 96 percent of the analytic cases were considered improved (with one-third terminating with "maximum benefit" and another quarter terminating mutually but without "maximum benefit"), only 50 percent of the analytic cases were judged as having developed an analytic process. Analyzability was again associated with therapeutic benefit: 78 percent of the analyzable cases were judged "much improved" in contrast to 29 percent of the cases where an analytic process had not developed, and 75 percent terminated with maximum benefit, in contrast to 38 percent of the unanalyzable cases. However, the fate of these treatments was again no more than marginally predictable from the perspective of initial evaluation, either from individual patient or analyst characteristics, or the direct predictions of supervisors (i.e., correlations in the .10 range), though the magnitude of the relationship between analyzability and therapeutic benefit was enhanced by the level of insight at termination (Bachrach, Weber, and Solomon, 1985).

In 1960, Knapp et al. reported on a project conducted at the Boston Psychoanalytic Institute investigating the suitability of one hundred supervised analytic cases, but the cases were only studied through the first year of treatment. The momentum of the project gave rise to an additional series of studies of terminated cases at the

Boston Institute (Sashin, Eldred, and van Amerongen, 1975; Kantrowitz, Singer, and Knapp, 1975).

Sashin et al. (1975) studied one hundred thirty control cases treated by sixty-six candidates between 1959 and 1966. Patients were initially seen by one or two experienced analysts for screening interviews, and they then presented their findings to an intake committee which made the final recommendation for analysis. All cases were initially seen as functioning within a neurotic range and suitable for analysis by a candidate; fifty-nine cases were diagnosed as hysteric, thirty-seven were obsessive compulsive, and seventeen were mixed neuroses. The outcomes of the cases were judged retrospectively by the treating analysts (sometimes years after the cases had terminated) according to overall global change, circumstances of termination, and six clinical scales: symptom restriction, symptom discomfort, work productivity, sexual adjustment, interpersonal relations, and insight. Sharp distinctions between therapeutic benefit and analyzability were not made. Of the one hundred thirty cases, 75 percent were judged to have improved at least moderately, 4 percent to be unchanged, and 6 percent to be worse. In terms of circumstances of termination, 69 percent terminated by mutual agreement, 27 percent were premature terminations, and 4 percent became interminable. Thus, it appeared that well over half of the cases improved. The authors then attempted to determine which factors in the initial evaluation might have been predictive of clinical outcomes. Because of concerns about the reliability of the analysts' ratings of change, circumstances of termination was used as the main criterion for prediction.

To assess the initial evaluation materials, two experienced analysts and one advanced candidate/senior research fellow were trained. They independently studied the evaluation materials and filled out a questionnaire designed to assess factors considered predictive of psychoanalytic outcomes. Originally one hundred and three initial patient qualities were reduced to forty-six reliable predictive factors, and the judges made outcome predictions. How possible was it to predict the circumstance of termination from these patients' initial characteristics? In only eight instances did any of the predictors differentiate between the four circumstances of termination. All of the other predictors, including anxiety tolerance and diagnosis, did not differentiate between the circumstances of termination. Following the published report of the project, further statistical analyses were conducted. Fifty-one individual predictors were correlated with all twelve outcome measures. Hence, a total of 612 possible relationships between initial patient qualities and outcomes were scrutinized; only sixteen (less than 3 percent) achieved conventional levels of statistical significance, and the magnitude of the relationships that did appear was small (i.e., correlations in the .2 range), on the average accounting for only about 5 percent of the outcomes. The few relationships, which might have appeared on the basis of chance alone, were studied to determine if they could be meaningfully understood in clinical terms, but the groupings "made little clinical sense" (Sashin, 1979, personal communication). Hence, it was not possible to effectively predict the outcomes of these control analyses from the analysand's initial characteristics. The authors suggested that the poor predictive showing might have been a function of the variability of the screening reports, more thorough evaluations might have yielded more effective prediction, and that a highly selected group of patients was studied limiting the possibilities for discrimination in this narrow band.

Kantrowitz, Singer, and Knapp, (1975), Kantrowitz, Paolitto, Sashin, Solomon, and Katz (1986), Kantrowitz, Katz, Paolitto, Sashin, and Solomon (1987a,b) employed psychological testing as a means of evaluating psychoanalytic outcomes and their predictability. Twenty-two cases treated by twenty-two candidates were studied. Each case was evaluated by one screening analyst and an intake committee as functioning within a neurotic range, and suitable for analysis by a candidate. Each case was also judged by clinic interviewers on 7-point scales of reality testing, object relations, motivation, affect availability, and tolerance, and, at the beginning of analysis, each analysand was given a battery of psychological tests (Rorschach test, TAT, DAP, Cole Animal, selected WAIS verbal subtests) from which reliable ratings of the same variables were made by a psychoanalyst or psychoanalytically informed psychologists. One year after termination the initial test battery was repeated, a brief follow-up interview was conducted with the patient, and a more extended follow-up interview with the analyst focused on the change processes of each case and the study variables. While these cases showed a wide range of therapeutic benefit, only 41 percent were judged to have developed an analytic process according to the treating analysts' follow-up interviews, and pretreatment assessments based upon psychological testing or clinical interview failed to predict analyzability or level of therapeutic benefit. The findings of this study partially confirm those of the Menninger

Project (partially in that the test battery employed was more limited than the comprehensive Menninger test battery).

At the New York Psychoanalytic Institute, Erle (1979) and Erle and Goldberg (1984) reported another series of studies relating to the predictability of psychoanalytic outcomes. Erle (1979) studied forty control cases treated between 1967 and 1969; 37.5 percent were initially diagnosed as mixed character neuroses, 27.5 percent as hysterical, and 15 percent as obsessional characters. Each patient was initially interviewed by two or three experienced screening analysts with some cases taken to an intake committee; in all cases the final recommendations were made by the medical director of the treatment center. In each case the investigator studied the full clinic record and the case was discussed with the analyst and supervisor. Sixty percent of the cases were judged to have benefited substantially, though only 42.5 percent were judged to have developed an analytic process. Fifteen of the seventeen cases where an analytic process developed were rated as having substantial therapeutic benefit, while only nine of the twenty-three unsuitable cases received substantial benefit. The final diagnoses differed from the initial impressions in nearly half the cases, all in the direction of more severe pathology. When the pooled judgment of the intake committee was studied, it was found that only eight of fourteen cases where there was substantial question actually turned out to be unsuitable.

In a second part of the study, Erle (1979) surveyed seven graduate analysts about their cases during the same time period. The analysts reported forty-two private analytic cases and made judgments about analyzability and therapeutic benefit in their own customary manner. Fifty-five percent were judged as having achieved substantial therapeutic benefit and 60 percent as having developed an analytic process. However, these figures must be taken tentatively because 40 percent of the cases were still in analysis at the time of data collection. Of the twenty-five cases where the analyses had ended, only six were considered to have "satisfactory" terminations and nineteen were considered premature; at termination eighteen of twenty-five cases were considered to have more severe pathology than initially believed.

Aware of the pressing need for data about analyses conducted by experienced analysts, Erle and Goldberg (1984) studied the work of sixteen experienced analysts more than five years postgraduation with predominantly analytic practices. During the study period (1973–1977) they ranged in reporting three to fifteen cases, with an average of ten cases. Altogether, one hundred sixty cases were reported with a wide range of generally neurotic level symptomatology, some patients seeming "ideal," but others taken into analysis for "heroic" reasons. Nineteen cases began in psychotherapy and were converted to analysis between one month and two years. The longest had been in analysis for 12.5 years. A semistructured questionnaire was distributed to the analysts who made judgments about the suitability and level of therapeutic benefit of their own cases. At the time of final data collection, 61 percent of the cases had terminated. Twenty-six percent of the terminated cases were considered to have developed a classical analytic process, 28 percent required modifications or had a more limited result, and 35 percent were unanalyzable. (Among the cases still in treatment, 56 percent were reported as having developed an analytic process, 31 percent required modifications or had limitations, and 13 percent were considered unanalyzable.) All the cases judged analyzable at termination were also judged as having received at least moderate therapeutic benefit, but sixteen unanalyzable cases were also judged to have achieved "good–excellent" therapeutic benefit. All fifteen cases receiving ratings of no significant therapeutic benefit were also seen as unanalyzable. About such figures the authors wisely caution that the categories might reflect different types or degrees of change, comparable only to the previous level of functioning for a given case.

Another series of studies pertinent to the predictability of psychoanalytic outcomes derives from a *clinical* methodology developed by Pfeffer (1959). This method consists of a series of four to six once-a-week relatively unstructured interviews with terminated cases, conducted by an analyst other than the treating analyst, several years after termination. The interviews are scrutinized for data relating to symptomatology, transference manifestations, and resolution. A summary is written by the follow-up analyst which is compared to an account independently prepared by the treating analyst. In nine cases reported by Pfeffer (1959, 1961, 1963) there was a consistent finding; in each a brief recrudescence of transference phenomena appeared to emerge, microscopically representative of the analysis, from which it was possible to construct a picture of the course of the analysis highly similar to the treating analyst's independent account. Pfeffer (1959) concluded that: "Those aspects of the transference neurosis that are unanalyzed remain organized as transference residues which are available for neurotic reactions in certain life situations. These highly organized residues are also readily available for emergence in follow-up studies . . ." (p. 437).

Sixty-two cases have been subsequently reported essentially employing this methodology conducted by three additional sets of investigators. All confirm Pfeffer's findings. From San Francisco, Ormeland, Blacker, and Norman (1975) reported two "successfully" analyzed cases (i.e., patient and analyst agree there has been significant alleviation of presenting and uncovered pathology by an analytic process, with confidence that the process will continue, and there is mutual agreement about termination); in both cases areas of incompleteness were found, especially involving analysis of the transference. Norman, Blacker, Oremland, and Barrett (1976) reported five cases, including three who were now graduate analysts. Again, areas of incompleteness were found leading the authors to conclude that the transference neurosis is not obliterated by psychoanalysis, but the analysand gains mastery over prior areas of conflict, the transference neurosis becomes a structure that comes under control of the unconscious ego, and the resulting capacities reflect growth. From Chicago, Schlessinger and Robbins (1974) reported six cases with an augmented methodology. The analyst of a successfully completed case submitted case material about the beginning of the analysis, the period of the decision to terminate, and the final sessions to a group of advanced candidates. The group microscopically studied the material and a series of unstructured follow-up interviews was conducted by a senior analyst two to five years after the termination. In all cases areas of incompleteness were found, despite the development of an analytic process and substantial therapeutic benefit. Schlessinger and Robbins (1975) reviewed another case in detail and the findings confirmed the prior report; they suggested that all the cases demonstrated a mastery of conflict, and the development of a self-analytic function as a significant outcome of the analysis. Schlessinger (1987) subsequently reported that a total of fifty-five cases had been studied since the group began its work, and in all of them the method developed by Pfeffer (1959) and the findings regarding incompleteness in successful analyses had been confirmed. These studies, therefore, caution against perfectionistic expectations.

A third line of research, exemplified most recently by the work of Bradlow (1987), takes important psychoanalytically related data from the beginning of analyses as its point of departure. In an effort to "validate the hypothesis that the presence of certain specific overt elements in the initial manifest dream report in psychoanalysis may be useful in predicting a limited therapeutic outcome, a limited capacity for analyzability, and could point as well to the presence of severe character pathology and certain types of ego organization" (p. 155), Bradlow (1987) reported a series of studies conducted concerning the presence of undisguised references to deliberate murder (Bradlow, 1971), nonviolent death (Bradlow, 1987), undisguised sexual activity between family members (Bradlow, 1973), and the undisguised presence of the analyst in the manifest content of initial dreams (Bradlow and Coen, 1975), and late first dream reporters (i.e., 40th session or later) (Bradlow, 1973). The data were taken from the cases collected by the Columbia Project, and analyzability was defined by a four-point scale of *improvement.* Control groups were employed consisting of the next case in the project record.

Murder in the manifest content of the initial dream appeared in seven cases, 2 percent of the cases randomly sampled. Six of these seven cases showed no significant change from the standpoint of conflict or transference resolution, and one was considered partially analyzable, in contrast to the control group which showed a more favorable result. Four of the six cases, however, were schizophrenic and the other two were also quite disturbed. Reports of nonviolent death in manifest contents, the undisguised presence of sexual activity between family members (4 cases), the undisguised presence of the analyst (13 cases), and very late dream reporters (8 cases), did not show statistically significant differences between the control group or were predictive of clinical outcomes. Of interest, however, is that nearly all the cases where "unusual" dream reports appeared turned out to be severely ill, and the nature of their dreaming activity was entirely consistent with clinically expected conflict (e.g., murder dreams in relation to severe conflicts in modulating aggression, late dream reporters in relation to distrust). Therefore, the question must be raised whether it is the presence of unusual dream activity or the degree of psychopathology that is the determining factor.

In sum, six systematic, clinical–quantitative studies of terminated classical analyses have been completed in recent times involving five hundred fifty patients largely suffering from a broad range of psychopathology, treated by three hundred seventy relatively inexperienced analysts at four different psychoanalytic training centers. Two provisional clinical–quantitative studies (Erle, 1979; Erle and Goldberg, 1984) have also been reported in which one hundred and thirty nine completed analyses were conducted by twenty-three experienced psychoanalysts with primarily psychoanalytic practices. Seventy-one cases have also been studied with Pfeffer's clinical methodology at three psychoanalytic centers. Though these studies are not free from methodological fault, and what study is, they are all more clinically informed than is typical of most psychotherapy research (see Garfield and Bergin [1978] for comparisons), and they all converge on similar findings. What are the implications of these findings for clinical practice, especially in beginning an analysis? The implications relate mainly to general expectations.

DISCUSSION

Case Selection

With the exception of cases taken on for "heroic" reasons, the patients in the studies were selected for psychoanalysis overwhelmingly on the basis of their pretreatment level of functioning, the higher the level the more likely they were considered suitable. As Freud (1904) put it, they were intelligent patients of good character capable of psychically normal conditions (i.e., they functioned within a neurotic range). This should come as no surprise because the patients in most of the studies were selected for pedagogic reasons (i.e., suitability for analysis by a candidate), and stringent efforts were made to eliminate more difficult or unsuitable cases. While assessments are not reported for cases thought unsuitable, or what eventually became of them, studies by Karush (1956), Knapp et al. (1960), Berk, Ouker, Goldart, Swerdloff, and Wolf (1964), Feldman (1968) and Lazar (1973), for example, report that unsuitable cases generally presented with severe character and/or ego pathology, as understood in initial evaluation. A comprehensive review of the characteristics of patients who "drop out" of the broader range of psychotherapies is consistent with this finding (Baekeland and Lundwall, 1975). Clearly, more data from the work of experienced analysts is required.

Therapeutic Benefit

The findings derived from these studies show the majority of *suitably* selected patients treated by psychoanalysis achieve therapeutic benefit, with the general exception of cases taken on for heroic reasons; improvement rates are typically in the 60 to 90 percent range, depending upon how improvement is measured. However, the findings of the clinical studies caution against perfectionistic expectations, and remind us of Freud's (1937) final statement of what is to be expected of psychoanalysis: "Our aim will not be to rub off every peculiarity of human character for the sake of a schematic 'normality', nor to demand that the person who has been 'thoroughly analyzed' shall feel no passions and develop no internal conflicts. The business of the analysis is to secure the best possible psychological conditions for the functions of the ego; with that it has discharged its task" (pp. 249–250).

In many of the studies the treating analyst was employed as the final arbiter of clinical processes and outcomes, and while one might ask who is in a better position to make such judgments, the analyst is always biased. Ideally, one would want the treatments independently evaluated by experienced analysts based upon more public data. However, the methodology developed by Pfeffer (1959) reveals a considerable correspondence between the treating and research analysts' accounts. Studies by Berzins, Bendar, and Severy (1975) and Mintz, Luborsky, and Christoff (1979) have shown that therapists' judgments of outcomes are surprisingly reliable; such judgments correspond highly with statistically reliable measures of outcome obtained independently, at times as highly as the most reliable statistical measures correspond with one another. If anything, studies of Pfeffer (1959), Klein (1960), Firestein (1984) and Weber et al. (1985b) suggest that analysts are likely to be more critical about their results than patients or outside analytic observers. But the strategy of the statistical studies has largely been built around the method of large scale, multivariate analysis in which it is necessary to *predetermine* selection and outcome criteria, leaving little room for the precise accounting of the *individual* nature of change. Moreover, most of the studies do not provide for an in-depth exploration of the contribution of the analyst to the treatment process, with the possible exception of Wallerstein's summaries and Kantrowitz's clinical vignettes. These studies therefore speak to *general* trends, and their findings largely confirm the accumulated clinical wisdom.

Analyzability

The studies show a substantial relationship between the development of an analytic process and therapeutic benefit, though only about half of the cases selected as suitable develop a psychoanalytic process.

The distinction between therapeutic benefit and analytic process is important for theoretical as well as clinical reasons. The conceptual structure of psychoanalysis is built upon observable *analytic* data as the empirical referents of psychoanalytic concepts, independent of therapeutic benefit. Theories and concepts derived from other sources of observation, including "analyses" where analytic processes do not develop, may *not* be pertinent to psychoanalytic models. Despite the import of this distinction, few studies provide a precise, clinical–operational definition.[1] Moreover, while many analysts find the concept useful, others have pointed to its potentials for ambiguity, magical conceptions, methodological difficulties, and varied narcissistic investments in paradigms (Erle and Goldberg, 1979; Rothstein, 1982; Abend, 1986; Abrams, 1987). Whatever individual analysts mean, the psychoanalytic process is hardly an all-or-nothing affair as the methodology of the studies tend to imply.

The studies also suggest that it is necessary to wait until a case is terminated before a true assessment of analyzability can be meaningfully made (Erle, 1979; Erle and Goldberg, 1984). Bachrach et al. (1985), for example, compared judgments made by candidate analysts about their cases at termination with judgments made while the case was still in progress, and found only marginal correspondence about the same factors. This finding raises questions about the meaning of studies of analyzability in which assessments of analyzability are made while cases are still in progress (e.g., Knapp et al., 1960; Feldman,

[1]The definition offered in the Columbia project may capture what many analysts mean:

> By analytic process we refer essentially to a collaborative endeavor between analyst and analysand in which the increasingly intense and cyclic analysis of resistance and transference in free-association evolves into the development of a transference neurosis and transference phenomena, and where analysis leads toward enhanced awareness and mastery of intrapsychic conflict which we conceptualize as structural change. The process is one in which the analyst leaves no stone unturned in removing obstacles to communication as they occur in free-association [Bachrach, Weber, and Solomon, 1985, p. 382].

The extent to which this meaning was captured by the operational measure is, however, an open question.

1968; Weber, Bradlow, Moss, and Ellison, 1974; Huxster, Lower, and Escoll, 1975), or the *psychoanalytic* utility of studies (e.g., Bradlow, 1987) attempting to find signs of unanalyzability in manifest contents of unknown *individual* meaning at the beginnings of analyses.

Predictability of Outcomes

Despite careful efforts at selection, whether by clinical interview, intake committee evaluations, psychoanalytically informed diagnostic testing, or combinations of these methods, the studies show that levels of therapeutic benefit and analyzability are no more than marginally predictable from the vantage point of initial evaluation. (This, in part, no doubt resulted from the elimination of the seemingly less suitable cases; for example, only 10 percent of the patients applying to the Columbia and New York Institute clinics during the study periods were accepted for analysis.) While the selection process varied from one to two screening interviews to the most comprehensive Menninger Clinic evaluation, the trend in all the studies was toward more severe levels of impairment in final, retrospective assessments of the cases at termination. The situation of experienced practitioners does not seem substantially different (Erle and Goldberg, 1984). It may be that there are insurmountable limits to the predictive value of the data elicited in the consultation process, spanning, on the one hand, from the effects of transference–resistance configurations inherent in all consultations (see Erle and Goldberg [1979] for an excellent discussion), to the possibility that crucial data (i.e., quality of trust, potential for alliances) may not be available at the beginning of analyses (Kris, 1957). It is in this sense that all analyses may be, in actuality, trial analyses.

Problems of Generalizability

While guided by general trends, our concern, as analysts, is *not* with general trends but with *individual* cases. This is what concerned Freud (1933) about summaries of large numbers of cases:

> At one time a complaint was made against psychoanalysis that it was not to be taken seriously as a treatment since it did not dare to issue any statistics of its successes. Since then, the Psycho-

> Analytic Institute in Berlin, which was founded by Dr. Max Etington, has published a statement of its results during its first ten years. Its therapeutic successes give grounds neither for boasting or being ashamed. But statistics of that kind are generally uninstructive; the material worked upon is so heterogeneous that only very large numbers would show anything. It is wiser to examine one's one individual experience [p. 152].

Freud's concern was with *heterogeneity*, irrespective of the number of heterogeneous cases assembled per se, with the ability of analysts to assemble data about large numbers of *like cases* in the manner suggested by Oberndorf (1943).

When a patient consults us and we become impressed that *this* patient's conflicts will only yield to analysis, what can we take from these studies to help us decide whether or not we, *not* as the ever ubiquitous "average expectable analyst," but as an individual analyst with unique talents, experiences, preferences, and tolerances, should undertake analysis with *this* patient? That is, what is it that makes a patient *unanalyzable* with any given analyst? On this point the studies are relatively silent with the exception of Bradlow's (1987) effort, in part because they have not specifically addressed the question, have explored the analyst's contribution to the treatment process only in the most limited terms, and have largely been more concerned with analyzability as a patient quality rather than as a consequence of a dyadic procedure. The issue can be brought into sharpest focus with regard to the matter of heroic indications. It will be recalled that *all* of the patients taken into analysis for heroic reasons in the Menninger project did poorly. These patients, however, were treated by inexperienced analysts and drawn from the ranks of patients with severe alloplastic character pathology, severely alcoholic, addicted, sociopathic in unreflective, paranoid, borderline–psychotic settings. While such patients may indeed have been unanalyzable with *any* analyst to judge from Wallerstein's (1986) detailed clinical descriptions, there are groups of very ill patients with autoplastic pathology that can and have been analyzed even though the findings of the analyzability studies would lead one to expect they are unanalyzable. Here patient (e.g., motivation, psychological mindedness, determination, primary and secondary gains) and analyst (e.g., special talents, interests, tolerances) qualities combine with the organizing aspects of the psychoanalytic situation. Abend, Porder, and Willick (1983) and Richards

(1980, 1988) have recently described successful analyses of such patients (e.g., severely ill, hypochondrical, and self-mutilating).

Paradoxically, there are also cases that *should* be analyzable according to the research findings that are not. Some highly functioning neurotic characters (e.g., obsessional–masochistic) do not yield readily to analysis, and even within a broad spectrum of neurotic level cases, secondary gains and the absence of motivation, for example, may leave some patients unanalyzable at a given point in their lives. While the clinical rule of thumb that the influence of the analyst's personal qualities is proportionate to the ego weakness of the patient does hold generally, there are also cases where the simple match between a reliable, well-functioning analysand and a reliable, talented, and experienced analyst can take on significances unanticipatable at the outset (Firestein, 1984). Freud (1937), Viederman (1976), and Jacobs (1986), for example, have commented upon the effect of the analyst's personality on the analytic process, and Nunberg (1969) noted instances where patients have been accepted for analysis despite the fact that they initially seemed too disturbed to succeed, and yet where it was possible to obtain access to healthy portions of the ego paving the way to successful analyses. Similarly, a period of extended consultation or preparatory psychotherapy, addressed particularly to resistances (Rothstein, see chapter 10) may evolve into productive analyses.

Matters of definition and conceptualization also limit the generalizability of the findings insofar as there was no clear consensus regarding the meanings of terms, or the method of measurement of clinical concepts. Whether it is a working definition of psychoanalysis, or the meaning of terms such as *improvement, therapeutic benefit, analytic process,* or even *circumstances of termination,* all such terms exist within varied conceptual and institutional frameworks, and were measured differently in all studies.

All analysands begin in their own unique ways. Some begin and continue in what manifestly appear as ideal ways, only for it to be found that such ways conceal the most intractable of resistances (Stein, 1981). Others begin with a panic or paranoia which makes us doubt the wisdom of our effort, only to find some analysands assuming reflective attitudes within a matter of weeks or months, though in some cases regressions do not subside in the analytic situation. While from the very beginning the analyst's task is to analyze, such instances may give rise to a wish for readily observable, reliable indicators of what is to follow. Comforting as the idea of such indicators may be, there is a regressive danger in reliance upon signs unless their reliability is *unerringly* established. The danger is that the analyst may become swayed from the task of analyzing, and as a result assume attitudes that are more descriptive than analytic. The 1960 panel on analyzability cautioned against rote application of research findings to the clinical situation. The analyst's task is to analyze, and he or she must continue in this task until the analysis is terminated, in one way or another.

SUMMARY AND CONCLUSIONS

At the time of writing, the data of the analyzability research speaks mainly to general expectations and has yielded confirmation of the general clinical wisdom. Namely that: (1) it is important to make distinctions between the indications for analysis and a patient's suitability, and between therapeutic benefit and analyzability; (2) most patients who function within a neurotic range, for whom analysis is indicated, and where careful selection suggests they are suitable, will derive therapeutic benefits; (3) therapeutic benefits are no more than marginally predictable from a beginning perspective among carefully selected cases; (4) only half will go on to develop an analytic process; (5) analytic process can only be determined after termination; (6) areas of incompleteness are found in even the most successful analyses. Number 6 cautions us against perfectionistic expectations and reminds us that the work of analysis results in enhanced mastery over conflict, shifts in compromise formations rather than the obliteration of conflict. These findings should not be underestimated. The psychoanalytic undertaking by its very nature is not open to public scrutiny. The studies inform us that what we have learned in the crucible of our own, individual and inevitably restricted clinical experiences, supervision, study groups, and necessarily condensed clinical literature, is representative of the wider psychoanalytic community, and moreover stands confirmation by extra-analytic methods. The fiber of findings can be strengthened when confirmed by different, applicable methods.

However, the data of the analyzability research is limited by the fact that most studies have been restricted to the work of candidate analysts, defined measures in different ways, have not carefully explored the analyst's contribution to the treatment process, and have not clarified when, and under what circumstances, the work of experienced analysts (with what qualities?) differs in terms of consequences from that of less seasoned analysts. These caveats in mind, if there is any single message that might be conveyed from the data of the analyzability research to the analyst in beginning an analysis, it is that we may remain confident that once we have selected a patient as potentially suitable for analysis by ourselves, therapeutic benefits are likely, though the eventual fate of the case will be relatively indeterminate, beginnings (as well as middles and endings) will continue with ambiguity, there are no substitutes for analysis in determining analyzability, and we must respect the necessary tolerance for uncertainty required of psychoanalysis.

Chapter 2

The Opening Phase: A Developmental Perspective

Estelle Shane, Ph.D.
Morton Shane, M.D.

Before beginning an analysis a deliberate assessment of analyzability must take place. Analysts may differ as to what this constitutes, but everyone has a set of criteria by means of which the patient is scrutinized to determine whether analysis is the treatment of choice as opposed to some alternative form of psychotherapeutic intervention (Werman, 1984). Thus, analysts select their patients consciously and deliberately, however much unconscious factors in the analyst may contribute to this process. Who is considered analyzable by a particular analyst is often closely related to the theory he holds. A Kleinian analyst would not necessarily be deterred by evidence of psychotic thinking and functioning, any more than a self psychologist would be deterred by severe narcissistic features in the personality organization. A classical analyst, on the other hand, would be more likely to find either of these sets of diagnostic features contraindications for beginning an analysis.

But regardless of the diagnostic limitations perceived in the patient, it is our conviction that analyzability can be enhanced by an opening phase informed by a creative and flexible developmental perspective. To our view, a developmental perspective is not defined by a particular set of theoretical constructs; rather, what its proponents have in common is the contention that the analytic process, and the relationship itself, have significant developmental valence. That is, we recognize the psychological growth potential inherent in the analytic milieu; we seek to address the patient where he or she is; and we expect that the analysis, properly applied, will potentiate maturation away from skewed or arrested lines of development into more normal channels.

This perspective has particular relevance for the opening phase. Some patients who want and require deep structural change in their personality organization may not on the face of it appear to the analyst to have the capacities required to engage in analysis. Or, if analysis is begun, they may be unable, despite ordinary analytic interventions, to be contained in the process. But if the analyst takes the position that his or her relationship with the patient can serve new-object functions, and that such functions may be necessary for improvement over and above the interpretation of the transference relationship and the defenses against it, then the seemingly unanalyzable patient can become more amenable to the analytic procedure.

As for the point that a developmental perspective need not be limited by any particular theoretical framework, it is our view that the analyst must achieve the fullest understanding possible of the developmental status of the patient, particularly the more difficult patient, and that such a full understanding may require concepts advanced from a variety of theoretical perspectives. As will become apparent, the approach with the patient to be described made use of concepts contributed by Loewald, Winnicott, Anna Freud, Erikson, Mahler, and Stern, as well as the self psychological contributions of Kohut.

Finally, inherent in a developmental perspective is the idea of a normal developmental progression, into and through adulthood, described in the concept of the developmental line. Pathology then becomes understood as arrests, delays, regressions, or skewing along particular lines, and analyzability can be determined by the patient's status in relation to those lines deemed relevant to the analytic venture. These include object constancy, self constancy and cohesiveness, true self consolidation, self regulation and self righting, and reality testing. Interpretations that relate to conflict and conflict resolution can free an individual to progress developmentally, but it is well established that the relationship to the analyst not only facilitates the uncovering of such conflict but also more directly potentiates development through the establishment of a new object relationship. It is through this relationship that the patient's capacities for engaging in the analytic process are promoted; object constancy, self constancy and cohesiveness, self regulation and self righting, and reality testing are improved, and the analysis can progress. And in fact, the new object relationship between patient and analyst can be more important for initiating and facilitating the analytic process than the effect of the interpretation per se. This is what distinguishes the developmental approach: an assessment which reveals arrested or skewed development, even in important capacities, is not necessarily considered a contraindication for analysis; analysis becomes a process which works in the direction of furthering this very same development.

The classical literature has included discussion of aspects of the analyst–patient relationship which promote the analytic process, most often in nondevelopmental terms, such as in Greenson's germinal papers on the working alliance (1965, 1967). And while Strachey (1934) and Alexander (1956) contributed to an understanding of new object potential in the analytic relationship, it was Loewald (1960) who pioneered the idea from a developmental perspective with the COPER Report (1974) defining and elaborating on it. More recently, Kohut (1977, 1984) specifically outlined ways in which the analytic relationship potentiates development through the medium of the selfobject transference. Also, Modell (1988), using Winnicott's concepts of the holding environment and the authenticity and inauthenticity of the true and false self, has contributed his own developmental perspective. In the clinical material which follows, we borrow freely from all of these concepts in our conceptualization of an opening phase with a difficult to analyze patient. It is our contention that without the developmental perspective provided by this integration of views, this patient might not have been able to engage in and sustain an analytic process. (For ease of presentation the case will be described in the first person.)

Mrs. T. was a thirty-eight-year-old freelance writer, married for fifteen years and the mother of two children, when she was referred for therapy having previously had three unsuccessful attempts at analysis with three different analysts. Her most recent experience immediately preceded her referral to me. She had left the previous analyst because she felt the woman did not understand her, that, in particular, she did not comprehend the patient's experience of being the daughter of Holocaust victims. Actually, Mrs. T. had revealed when she first came in her uncertainty as to whether she wanted to be in therapy at all, much less analysis; her disappointments with previous analysts left her feeling pessimistic about ever being able to get any help for herself.

There were many reasons for Mrs. T.'s pessimism, not the least of which was the difficulty she found in clearly formulating her complaints. It was only after several sessions that I was able to understand the many reasons for her unhappiness. I learned that she had no sexual life whatsoever with her husband, being unable, because of her deep antagonism toward him, to allow herself the necessary closeness that sexuality for her entailed. She was not even certain that she wanted to remain married to him. Moreover, Mrs. T. was aware of her inability to be close to anyone other than her two children. She told me she could not, and did not, trust others, had not trusted her parents, did not trust her previous therapists, and did not trust her husband. Friends were nonexistent, though she had acquaintances among her husband's professional contacts and the mothers of her children's friends. She and her husband were currently alienated from even these rather distant relationships, their lives together seeming to have wound down to almost nothing, leaving her feeling excluded from the lives of everyone but her two children.

Mrs. T.'s mother and father were both Holocaust victims who met in the displaced persons' camp in France to which they were both sent after rescue. Each arrived there alone, knowing no one, impoverished, and feeling isolated. Apparently choosing one another to marry did not involve deep trust or love; they lived in mutual suspicion growing to hatred at some point in the patient's life, remaining locked together in an alien environment. The patient was born during their time in France, and then the family moved to Argentina, where there was an enclave of wealthy relatives. While her parents perceived this extended family network as demeaning, warning her against trusting her relatives, and advising her to be secretive, the patient felt comforted by their presence, her time with them experienced as a relief from the cold isolation that being with her angry, frugal, and silent parents entailed. When the patient was seven, a brother was born, and when she was eleven, the family moved to Los Angeles. Her mother and father, having saved some money, embarked on a catering business. The new business involved desperately long hours, kept her parents away from home, and chronically concerned with finances. At age eleven, then, the patient was left to herself to struggle with the new environment and the new language. While there was an aunt and an uncle in Los Angeles, they lacked the warmth of the Argentinian branch of the family, and for the most part she herself had to care for her brother after school until her parents, tired, impatient, angry with one another, and worried, would return. Dinner would be a silent, cheerless affair, bedtime would follow, and then the new day would bring nothing new.

Mrs. T. continued to feel alienated throughout high school. While successful academically, she found herself without friends. She turned to sexual experiences with boys to compensate for her loneliness. She was able to have pleasure in her sexuality, but only with boys she did not know well. Upon graduating from high school she was accepted by a local university with a partial scholarship. Her father adamantly refused to pay the balance of her tuition. A huge fight ensued, resulting in Mrs. T.'s moving out of the house and into her own apartment where she supported herself, working her way through college. For many years she did not see her father at all. Her mother maintained contact with her, and, without her father's knowledge, supplied her with funds from time to time. The bitterness toward her father has never abated, and she remains disdainful of her mother for remaining with him.

Shortly after graduating from college, Mrs. T., having had numerous short and meaningless affairs, and rebounding from a hurtful, humiliating relationship, met and subsequently married her current husband, a young man also from a cold and distant family who had attached himself to her and seemed to need her desperately. During the first years of their marriage she discovered that her husband was addicted to cocaine. She experienced much misery with him, but after five difficult years, he successfully completed a drug rehabilitation program and has not used drugs since. She still carries the resentment of the long period she had to care for him and nurse him back to health and sanity. He remains, from her perspective, impulse-ridden, unreliable, and intemperate. Their sexual life, never satisfactory from her point of view, had deteriorated to nothing.

The only satisfying aspect of Mrs. T.'s life when she first came to see me was her relationship with her children. Surprisingly enough, she was a confident, empathic mother from the start whose young sons had flourished under her care. She worried that her relationship with her husband, so similar to that of her parents, would destroy her children's happy childhoods; on the other hand, she felt divorce would be even more unsettling to them.

As I said, this history emerged slowly, the patient revealing great difficulty in putting her feelings into words and in trusting me to understand and sustain interest in what she was attempting to tell me, describing her fear that I would "trivialize her experiences." However, she came to rely on seeing me to diminish the unpleasant states of excitement which punctuated her day-to-day existence. The irritability, tension, anxiety, and proneness to upper respiratory illness which had characterized her life gradually receded, without her really being aware of it or being able to put these feeling states or their absence into words. Mrs. T. pressed to see me more often, expressing disappointment in me that I didn't arrange for more time quickly enough. However, I hadn't yet decided what the most appropriate course of treatment would be for this woman. Her difficulty in expressing herself at first seemed to indicate a lack of psychological mindedness. Moreover, her obvious proneness to mistrust me as she had mistrusted the other analysts who came before me, together with her previous treatment failures, warned me to go slowly and not leap to the conclusion that yet another analytic foray was indicated for this woman.

A dream which occurred about this time allowed us to address the pervasive nature of her pessimistic suspiciousness and mistrust, and the extent to which it was unconsciously being expressed in the transference. She is alone in a foreign country where no English is spoken. She herself cannot understand anyone nor make herself understood. She realizes that she is under threat from some man whom she discovers is talking to a crowd of people. She is in the crowd, too. She suddenly perceives that if he is able to capture her attention and look into her eyes, he will enter her soul, taking her over. It is only with great difficulty that she resists the temptation to look into his eyes, fearful always of giving in, and she awakens in terror.

In discussing the dream, the patient first made the obvious connection to her move at age eleven to a foreign country. She then associated to her husband, who is always telling her what she should think and what she should do. With loathing she described the disgust and underlying fear she associates with making love to him, feeling she must protect herself from her husband out of an intense conviction that if she gives in sexually, it will be as if she is yielding control of herself over to him, as in the situation with the threatening man in the dream. Her further associations led to her lifelong feeling with her parents that she couldn't be open with them for fear that she would be submerged by them and would lose a sense of her own self as an entity. I then connected her fear of being controlled by others whom she could not trust with a similar fear of me. She agreed, telling me of her frequent wishes to flee from me, as she had done in the past from her other analysts, when she felt I had let her down or had not understood her.

But despite these palpable proclivities on her part to pull away, I gradually noticed that being with me seemed to both calm and soothe my patient, a sense that she spontaneously confirmed. She told me, with some hesitation and embarrassment, that on the nights following her appointments with me she was able to sleep; other nights, and particularly weekend nights, she found herself lying awake agitated, without apparent reason. Subsequent discussion of her sleepless nights allowed her to identify the agitated thoughts and feelings that had heretofore remained nameless. In time she expressed her gratitude for my patience, my interest, and my concern over these small details which seemed to her to have escaped the attention or interest of her previous analysts. The necessity for her to experience another as able to regulate her affect states, for the analyst to function, in effect, as a self-regulating other (Stern, 1985), had apparently not been noted before. The experience with me apparently allowed Mrs. T. to observe herself without feeling overwhelmed by anxiety, and to reveal herself to me without feeling the danger of being taken over and submerged by another. A small step in development was thus achieved, the developmental step being comprised of a strengthened sense of self constancy and self cohesiveness, advancement toward a true self formation, and an improved capacity to utilize the analyst for self regulation and self righting. In turn, the analyst became an object of greater constancy and increasing trustworthiness. We do not mean to suggest that four months spent with a patient in increasingly frequent therapeutic–analytic interviews could accomplish any more than a very small developmental change, but we do suggest that the changes in Mrs. T. were significant enough to make a difference in her capacity to successfully engage in analysis. It seems appropriate at this point to address the question, what was done and what was not done with Mrs. T. during this early phase that improved her capacity to work analytically?

To begin with, the analyst recognized that the patient began the therapeutic engagement with signs of both idealizing, and defending against idealizing, her analyst. Interpretations were directed toward the patient's fear of reexperiencing in the idealizing maternal transference being either overcontrolled or abandoned, the patient responding to these interpretations with reduced anxiety. The reduction in anxiety in turn facilitated the emergence of a less defended against idealizing selfobject transference mediated in part through the new object relationship with the analyst, an experience, we want to emphasize, with developmental impact, contrasting as it did with previous and current object relationships. It was via this idealizing selfobject transference that the patient's self regulation was increased through a soothing and calming experience with an admired parentlike figure. Such an experience had been lacking in the patient's childhood, leaving her with a conflictual wish for such gratification. Mrs. T. could sense the difference between the analyst's trustworthiness and the untrustworthiness of her parents, her husband, and other significant people in her life. She could respond to the analyst's consistently being there with her in contrast to her parents' continual absences. She could admire the analyst's intuneness and capacity to verbalize the patient's feelings for her in contrast to her parents' indifference and insensitivity to her affect states and their unfamiliarity with nuances of the English language.

Such intense idealization had created in the analyst some mild discomfort, confirming via countertransference the nature of the transference relationship, and fostering a slip, very meaningful to the patient, when on one visit the analyst neglected to place a napkin on the couch for her ahead of time.

We want to make the point that it was through this aspect of the transference that the patient was enabled to work into and work within the opening phase of the analysis. She came to be able to tolerate seeing the analyst at times as both disappointing and disillusioning, making the connection with her mother and father, and yet, at the same time, keeping the distinction clear. Mrs. T. had not been able emotionally, or even, at times, cognitively, to keep this difference in mind, an inability which contributed to the failures of her previous attempts at analysis.

It does seem important to address more directly what went wrong in this patient's earlier attempts to get help in order to illustrate in what way a developmental perspective has more effectively engaged this patient in the analytic process. Despite the obvious difficulty in reconstructing with any certainty what transpires with another analyst, we do have Mrs. T.'s spontaneous reflections on what led to a disruption of the relationship in two of the three previous experiences. In the case of the last unsuccessful attempt, with Dr. A., it appears in retrospect that this woman analyst had not focused at all on the self regulating or idealizing aspects of the analytic relationship, nor, so far as we have been able to discern, on any other transference manifestations, but this last is more based on inference. Instead, Dr. A. appears to have too quickly and forcefully raised the issue of the patient's conflictual masochistic relationship with her husband and his lack of ability to satisfy her both emotionally and sexually. The patient, who was disdainful of the very same inability in her mother, heard this as a criticism, but did not have the ability to risk confronting the analyst with her feelings. A patient less fearful of object loss and with a greater capacity for self cohesiveness might have directly engaged Dr. A. This patient, feeling challenged to defend her own self-despising inability to leave her husband, unconsciously made the choice to leave her analyst instead.

Dr. B. was an analyst the patient had seen several years before Dr. A. The memory of the important exchange with this analyst, also a woman, occurred to Mrs. T. during the current analysis when she was describing a phone conversation with her father in which he once again was discovered to have an ulterior motive for calling her. Mrs. T. reflected that her conversations with her father were always like that. She then suddenly recalled an exchange with Dr. B. that had led her to leave the treatment peremptorily. She had only seen Dr. B. three times, but felt a dislike for her because she saw her as cold and remote. Though she wanted to leave immediately, she summoned up the courage to tell the analyst on her next visit that she found her cold, and to ask whether her other patients experienced her in the same way. Dr. B. did not answer directly the question regarding her own contribution to the current relationship between them. Instead she interpreted in the form of a question, who in Mrs. T.'s life had been cold? Mrs. T., knowing for certain now that she could not work with this woman, responded, "No one; just you." In recalling the incident in her current analysis, Mrs. T. said, "I guess it was my father who is cold." She added, "I can see now that in some way Dr. B. was right, it was a response to someone in the past, but it settled the issue for me that Dr. B., just like my father, could not be trusted to be on my side; she wanted something for herself more than she wanted to help me" (meaning she wanted to be analytically correct and to make the right interpretation rather than to look at what she herself might be contributing to the patient's impression of her).

Mrs. T. went on to maintain that she had not been mistaken about the analyst; Dr. B. was like her father in some important way and was unwilling to discuss the issue. Now, questions like whether Dr. B. was really cold and remote, whether she was actually like Mrs. T.'s father, or even the more obvious issue of whether Dr. B. should have explored the patient's perception of her first, are not relevant here. Errors in analysis are inevitable and ubiquitous, as Wallerstein (1986) points out, and patients capable of being analyzed must be able to endure, confront, and work these errors through with the analyst. What is relevant here is that Mrs. T. was unable to do just that; yet a vigorous capacity for maintaining a viable current object relationship with the analyst in the face of the analyst's apparent errors and her own aggressive response to them was taken for granted by Dr. B. Dr. B. assumed that Mrs. T. could benefit from the interpretation of the father transference and could perceive the contrast between the experience with her father and the experience with her analyst. However, Mrs. T. at that time lacked sufficient object constancy and self stability to make this important distinction.

At this point Mrs. T. has been in a five-times-per-week analysis for approximately a year and a half. While she continues to struggle with the wish to leave, she nevertheless remains engaged in the process, continuing to use the analyst's interpretations as well as utilizing the analyst to facilitate and enhance developmental attainments. One area that remains shaky is that of reality testing at those times when she must depend upon someone important to her whom she fears is unreliable. We have included the following clinical vignette to illustrate this issue, as well as to demonstrate how Mrs. T., now just past the opening phase, is currently working in the analytic situation.

The following two-day analytic sequence took place immediately after a recent midsummer week's vacation. It will be reported in the first person from notes made during the hours and from a summary completed just afterwards. On the first day following the brief holiday, Mrs. T. began describing some feelings about her mother. The patient, too, had been away from the city and her mother had stayed at her house, along with the housekeeper, to help with the children. Mrs. T. expressed great anger with her mother because her mother had, upon the patient's return, criticized the condition of her house, saying that the housekeeper doesn't keep it clean. Mrs. T. was incensed at this. Her house is much cleaner than her mother's, she told me, and in fact is really fine. She is quite aware of some disorganization, hates it, feels that she does not know how to correct it, that she had never had help growing up with how to keep order, and always worries about the disorder around her. But her mother is much worse. Her mother is in effect dishonest. She pretends, by criticizing others about this, that she is neat and organized and clean herself, but she is not. What most disturbs Mrs. T. is her mother's dishonesty.

Mrs. T., in an apparent digression, went on to describe all the ways she is feeling better, how much easier it is for her now, for the first time in her life, to engage in a group and to assert herself in a group. It helps to have joined a community organization, to involve herself with some political ideas that she thinks are really important. It allows her to feel part of something bigger than herself. She thinks it is because of this new involvement in the community organization that she is suddenly able, also for the first time, to feel okay about making friends in the new country club she and her husband have joined. She has already become close to Cynthia (a writer like herself), the first friend she has made since college. She notes that she hadn't had any friends when she started treatment. It had been one of her central complaints that she was unable to feel comfortable with anyone, and now she is better, because of joining the community group. (I am bristling, feeling unappreciated and belittled in my actions with her; it is as if I have no importance whatsoever. I feel her coldness and indifference to me. It is more than that she discounts my help; she actively disengages from me.)

Mrs. T. then tells me that she was able for the first time in years, literally, to have sex with John (her husband) without feeling disgust. No excitement, no orgasm, but she did feel close and good with him. She guesses it is because she and he can have friends together for the first time that they can be close enough to have sex. (Again, I and the importance of our work together are ignored. I continue to sit and listen and say nothing.)

Slowly, Mrs. T. gets to the sense that she didn't really want to come back to see me. I inquire about this and she says that she is feeling better, maybe she is sufficiently better to not need to see me at all. It is an interruption in her schedule, and it no longer seems important to her. I wonder with her whether she is aware of feeling angry with me or disappointed with me, suggesting that though she says it is because she feels better and it may not therefore be worth her time to continue, that maybe some of the disappointment and anger she feels with her mother, and even the sense of betrayal, might be connected with some feelings about me. She responds, for the first time with feeling, that she was really thrown when I left town suddenly, giving her very little warning. (I am startled and very confused as I don't know what she can possibly mean by this statement.) I say to her, I wonder if she is referring to the vacation I just took, and she says yes. On questioning her, I find to my complete surprise that she had not remembered that we had talked at length, for several months, in fact, about that vacation. I remind her that back in April I had told her I was probably going to be gone the first several weeks in August because she had been trying at that time to schedule her own time away, attempting to juggle the family's vacation with that of her husband's analyst. Her husband's analyst had told him that he planned to go away at the end of August, and I told her then that I was going away at the beginning of August. I recall saying aloud to her that we had had some discussion about who should have to miss analytic times, she or her husband. I then told her that I had subsequently corrected my original projection of several weeks in August, to one week, the first week only. As I talk, she remembers the discussions, but says she cannot remember my telling her the exact dates, and that she had not written the time down anywhere. She describes hearing me tell her for what she then thought was the first time about the vacation I was to take only a week before I left, though I couched it then as a reminder rather than as a first-time announcement. (I realized then that in her mind I had been dishonest—I am the dishonest person she was unconsciously referring to when she was talking ostensibly only about her mother.)

Mrs. T. went on to describe her state of shock when she heard for what she thought was the first time about the vacation, but acknowledged that she didn't mention it to me. She went home and searched every one of her journals and appointment books to discover if I had really told her I was going before that date when I said I was "reminding" her, but she could not find it recorded anywhere, and knew then that I had only said I had told her before, that in effect I was lying. Even as she reviews all of this with me in the present, it is clear that she is not convinced I have really told her the dates in advance. As she continues to talk, I become aware she still views me as having somehow lied, or at the least been imprecise about the dates. Though she can see, intellectually, that I am correct in the description of our discussion, emotionally she still feels I disappointed her and let her down. She tells me she is puzzled about this. I make the correlation with her feelings about her mother: that her mother is dishonest with her; that her mother pretends to be wanting to help her, so she trustingly lets her mother into her house, and once there, her mother criticizes what she sees. In the same way, I pretend to be there to help her, but like her mother I disappoint her; she is afraid that if she lets me in, I will not be able to listen and understand her; instead I will betray her by being critical of what I see (this is an old theme)—that she had better leave me while she can, before she gets too dependent on me. She responds by saying that she does not doubt I will listen to her, but she feels I will not understand. How can I be interested in her experiences? She is afraid I will trivialize her. The hour is up.

The next day she begins the session with the following dream:

> I go into Cynthia's house. Cynthia always talks about how clean and neat and organized she is, about how difficult it is for her, so often, to keep housekeepers because her standards are so high. But in the dream Cynthia's house is a complete and disgusting mess. I cannot believe how Cynthia has distorted and lied. Then there are four of us, Cynthia, Cynthia's husband, another man, and myself sitting and talking. Suddenly the two men are rolling around on the floor, making sexual noises. I try to ignore them, but Cynthia asks me if I think they are doing something sexual. I find myself having the unpleasant responsibility of gently confronting Cynthia with the truth: "Well, yes, Cynthia, I think they are having sex."

Mrs. T. tells me that she awoke from the dream very disturbed. It is as if the dream has a reality of its own for her, and the fact that Cynthia could live such a lie, and be so unaware, makes her feel that she has to get away from her. She finds herself having to call Cynthia right away, though it is very early, so that she can dispel the reality of the dream with another reality, but it still feels as if it is just a competing reality, on all fours, in some way with the dream, but no more real than the dream itself.

By way of background for the dream, Mrs. T. is a freelance writer who has had no time or energy, until quite recently, to work more than sporadically. Her husband, an advertising executive, is putting together, along with his several partners, a very large ad campaign for an important client. She has done work for her husband's firm in the past, and they have been satisfied with her work, though what is being proposed now is a considerably more ambitious task. The partners have agreed to hire her, but she feels reluctant to take all of this on herself, and proposes, first to her friend Cynthia, and then to her husband, that she work in a partnership with Cynthia. Her husband disapproves of this idea, saying that the partners had agreed to her, because they know her work, but if she were to include Cynthia as a partner, they might put the contract out to open bid. My patient understands, and decides she will make Cynthia her assistant, to be called upon only when the work seems overwhelming. Mrs. T. relates that she had wanted to begin work on the copy on the previous day. She had called Cynthia who seemed very preoccupied and busy and could not identify sufficient time in the day to work with her. Mrs. T. told Cynthia in response that she wondered how Cynthia could work with her at all; apparently she was too busy. She thinks to herself that Cynthia seems unreliable, and also seems flustered and disorganized. She ends up starting the work herself, decides herself upon an overall design and writes some significant copy. Mrs. T. begins to feel, she tells me, she can do it all on her own. Then that night she had the dream described above and woke up feeling very strange about Cynthia and her situation, as already described. Mrs. T. then said she feels she has to get away from Cynthia, to get away from a friend who has such a strange circumstance in her life, that her friend is strange and sick. When she calls Cynthia after the dream, she lets her know that she has already made a good start on the work. I reconstruct for her the process that led to the dream and its aftermath: that she had some initial doubts about Cynthia which were sown by John, and that Cynthia's unavailability that day had convinced her that she was not someone she could, or should, rely upon, that she had to separate herself from this woman.

The dream in which Cynthia is revealed to be strange and strangely out of touch with her own life thus serves to allow her to make the break that she feels she needs to make in order to preserve herself. I then connect this series regarding Cynthia to her concerns about me, that I am not reliable, that she needs to separate herself from me in order to avoid the risk of severe disappointment and betrayal—she has to leave me first before in some sense I leave her.

I add that she enacts this with Cynthia instead of me as it feels safer to be without Cynthia than to be without me. In response to my interpretation, Mrs. T. said that she remembered thinking about this herself immediately upon waking—that she felt really strange and disconnected from herself and very anxious. She knew that in some way the dream about Cynthia was like her feelings about me, that she has to get away from me. She could connect her fear that I was about to leave her, thereby demonstrating my unreliability, with the "forgetting" to write down the dates I would be gone and then the "forgetting" that I had told her I would be gone at all. Mrs. T. then told me that she understood she had handled her fear about Cynthia's unreliability in the same way, with the sense that Cynthia was inadequate and then attributing to Cynthia an unreliability because of her being busy that one day and because of the dream. Mrs. T. connected this to her experience with her mother. She ended the hour describing her distress at discovering that she takes a blueprint from the past, her experience with her mother, and then applies it to her relationships with others in the present.

We have included this vignette to demonstrate a particular developmental lag in this patient's capacity for reality testing. When made anxious in relation to threatened loss of object and/or selfobject support, Mrs. T. displays a shakiness in distinguishing the experience in a dream or a fantasy from that of her realistic and awake perceptions.

The misremembering concerning her analyst, like the dream concerning her friend, served to defend her against a dangerous, albeit sought-after closeness to important others who have signaled to her the potential for unreliable actions. With insight she can only partly correct for her fantasied view of the individual involved, holding both views parallel in her mind. She continues to function with Cynthia as if her dream about her were reality; and she continues to hold in doubt the fact she herself remembers, that her analyst had told her about her upcoming vacation, that she had even planned her own vacation based upon that information. Interpretation, therefore, does not seem to correct the faulty reality testing. The hope is that further interactions with a reliable new object will reduce the anxiety she experiences that all important others will prove to be unreliable. Such interactions in the analysis might improve the compromised reality testing already developmentally present in this patient. In addition, we contend that these repeated experiences with an important new other will foster for the first time new developmental attainments in this area; that is, a new capacity in this patient will be acquired that will allow her to face anxiety-provoking revelations about herself and to maintain that new vision of herself clearly and permanently. Self-object functions presently required of the analyst will become the developmental attainment of the self.

SUMMARY

It seems that Mrs. T. was not analyzable by the ordinary analytic approach. Capacities for analyzability, sometimes referred to as the capacity to form a therapeutic alliance, were not present. Specifically, Mrs. T. revealed difficulties with object constancy, self constancy and cohesiveness, true self consolidation, self regulation and self righting, and reality testing. Her capacity to trust another in the face of her own ambivalence was therefore severely compromised. In the absence of a developmental perspective, these capacities may be seen as either present or not present, and the patient as either analyzable or not analyzable.

A developmental perspective, however, provides the analyst with more flexibility, as we hope we have demonstrated with this patient.

Experiences with the analyst first during the extended evaluative stage, and then within the analysis proper, provided opportunities that enabled the patient to resume an arrested developmental thrust, further potentiating her capacities to engage in the analytic process into the middle phase. We believe such a developmental process goes on in all analyses, alongside of the ordinary interpretive work within the transference and concomitant conflict resolution. But for some patients the development-enhancing experiences seem to take center stage. They are often most effectively conceptualized as having experiences in the analysis that provide needed selfobject functions, or, using an alternative framework, as experiencing self authenticating transitional object phenomena within a holding environment (Modell, 1988). In more classical terms, this aspect of the analysis may be seen, nonpejoratively, as a corrective emotional experience (Alexander, 1956; Schlesinger, 1988), or corrective object relationship (Alpert, 1959). In terms of a developmental perspective, we can view this patient as having an arrested or skewed development related to self and object constancy, and a perpetuation of archaic selfobject needs to maintain self cohesion. A less than mature need for a self regulating other to support inadequate self righting capacities was notable. A tendency toward inauthenticity revealing a skewed false self formation was also evident, impeding sensual–sexual capacities, especially in the area of genital pleasure. All of this led to an inadequately joined and resolved Oedipus complex that reverberated into adolescence and adult life.

PART II
ON BEGINNING WITHOUT MODIFICATIONS

Chapter 3

On Beginning an Analysis

Charles Brenner, M.D.

Freud (1913) wrote at some length on the subject of beginning an analysis. His recommendations may be summarized as follows.

First of all, he recommended that patients be started in a trial analysis "to decide whether [the case] is a suitable one for psychoanalysis" (p. 124). One couldn't predict from any preliminary interview, however thorough, said Freud, whether a patient would be able to free associate well enough to be suitable for analysis. One had to see what happened when the patient lay down and was told that everything, without exception, that came to mind must be imparted to the analyst. In addition, Freud felt, should a patient unexpectedly prove to be psychotic on better acquaintance, so that analysis had to be abandoned for that reason, it was easier on the patient if it was understood in advance that it was only a trial analysis anyway.

There followed a number of recommendations that are best characterized as helpful hints; avoid lengthy preliminary discussions, if a patient has had previous therapy of other sorts, and if the analyst has known the patient previously, the transference will be more difficult to understand. Don't tolerate delay in starting analysis, however reasonable the excuse for doing so may sound. If you analyze someone who is a family member or a friend, be prepared to lose that friend. It doesn't matter whether a patient is skeptical about analysis in advance or an enthusiastic believer in its value. Patients should be allotted a specific time in one's daily schedule and be responsible for that time whether they show up or not. One should make a definite arrangement right at the start about fees and payment. It is the wisest and most honorable thing to make clear to every prospective patient that analysis is neither quick nor easy. Patients should be free to stop treatment at any time. If a patient is unable to continue treatment because of physical illness, it is best to stop analysis and resume when the patient has recovered. There are special difficulties associated with treating patients gratis. Patients should use the couch.

Freud apparently did not take a formal history before beginning analysis. Instead, if he proposed to begin a trial analysis, he had the patient lie down and said, "Tell me what you know about yourself." At the same time, however, he instructed the patient to follow what has come to be called the fundamental rule of psychoanalysis; to say everything without exception that comes to one's mind. This aspect of beginning an analysis was clearly the most important in Freud's opinion, since he devoted a full page to a verbatim account of what he said to patients about "free association" (pp. 136–137). In those years the idea of defense analysis was quite unknown. The essential task of an analyst, it was thought, was to interpret to a patient the unconscious, sexual meaning of the patient's "free associations." Anything else an analyst did was not thought of as analysis, but rather as clearing away resistance(s) that kept the patient from being "in analysis." In other words it was thought of as a prelude or adjunct to analysis. It might be an essential adjunct, to be sure, but it was not considered to be more than an adjunct. Thus, for example, Freud (1918) described most of the first three-and-a-half years of the Wolf Man's analysis as a period of education or training that preceded the few months of real analysis with which the treatment concluded. The prevalent view then and for many years thereafter was that one deals with defenses and resistance by education and persuasion rather than by analysis.

To return to his paper on beginning an analysis, Freud (1913) devoted the concluding section of it to a discussion of various aspects of transference, emphasizing that the analyst need do no more to permit a workable transference to develop than to give evidence of his "serious interest in [the patient], carefully clear away the resistances that crop up at the beginning," and avoid making mistakes like being moralistic, adversarial, or directive (p. 139). He advised also that premature, deep interpretations are to be avoided. Until "an effective transference has been established in the patient [one refrains from] disclosing to him the hidden meaning of the ideas that occur to him and . . . initiating him into the postulates and technical procedures of analysis" (p. 139).

The impression one has, then, is that in 1913 Freud saw the important tasks to be performed by an analyst on beginning an analysis to be to instruct the patient as to the fundamental rule and see how well the patient could follow it, while at the same time allowing a positive transference to develop and clearing away whatever resistance to the task of free associating could be cleared away.

The fact is that as late as the 1930s, one of the questions analysts frequently asked when discussing the suitability of a patient for analysis was, How well can he or she free associate? The realization that a patient's inability to talk freely while lying on an analyst's couch might be something to be analyzed had hardly penetrated the professional consciousness of most analysts. Even though the groundwork for defense analysis or, more generally, for ego analysis had been laid by Freud (1926) some years before, Anna Freud's *The Ego and the Mechanisms of Defence* appeared only in 1936, and the practice of analyzing defenses systematically did not become widespread, in the United States at least, until after 1950. That it did so was a result of the better understanding of conflict, symptom, and character that was inaugurated by Freud (1920a, 1923, 1926). The same improved understanding resulted also in considerable changes in how one begins an analysis and why one begins as one does. What Freud recommended in 1913 is certainly not common practice today, if, indeed, it is ever done. One does not at once tell a prospective patient to lie down on the couch, instruct him or her with respect to the fundamental rule, and judge suitability for analysis by setting a trial period during which one assesses the patient's ability to free associate.

Glover (1955) discussed the opening phase of analysis in a way intended both to inform and to encourage and reassure the beginning analyst. He emphasized that one should not be discouraged if a patient leaves analysis during its opening phase, since some failures are inevitable in every analyst's practice. He also stressed the importance of treating patients on an individual basis rather than on the basis of rules used to apply to all, although the reader has the impression at times that "individual" meant primarily "according to each patient's diagnosis," whether hysteric, obsessional, narcissistic, or depressive. As for the fundamental rule, although Glover, like Freud, thought of the opening phase as a time when one helps one's patient to overcome resistances against abiding by the rule, he recognized and illustrated the value of interpreting the patient's anxieties and defenses when necessary even in the initial sessions. He wrote that such interpretations are necessary throughout analysis, since "a large part of the analyst's work will up to the last moment consist in an endeavor to circumvent . . . evasion" of the fundamental rule (p. 27).

Thoma and Kächele (1985), like Glover, emphasized the importance of treating each patient individually in the initial interview(s), but in a very different sense. What is important in their view is to create for each patient an atmosphere of freedom and hope by being flexible. Thus, in the initial interview "we have to consider how the most favorable conditions for the patient's development can be created and which psychoanalyst is the best for this task. . . . Today treatment can be planned and structured to meet the individual patient's needs" (p. 189). Further, "the standard technique is very limited in its applicability" (p. 187); the term *standard technique,* meaning "silence and stereotyped nonanswering of questions" (p. 187). In sharp contrast with Glover's stress on diagnosis, Thoma and Kächele, in their discussion of the initial interview, don't even mention a concern with what brought the patient to the analyst in the first place: "the analyst creates a relationship between what the patient says and how he behaves in the analytic situation, and then uses this relationship diagnostically and therapeutically" (p. 179).

There are few extensive discussions in the analytic literature on the subject of beginning an analysis. The samples just given are representative of the variations to be found among analysts with respect to their opinions and practices. In the discussion that follows the reader will observe two guiding principles at work. The first is that rules of thumb are avoided as much as possible. The emphasis is on why one proceeds in a certain way, not on what to do when. The second is that an analyst's chief aim is to understand (and at the proper time to interpret) the nature and origins of the conflicts that underlie a patient's pathological compromise formations (neurotic symptoms and character traits). The better one understands a patient's conflicts, the better able one is to decide what is the best thing to say or do, both at the beginning of an analysis and at any later stage.

Is analysis the treatment of choice for this patient? and, What should I tell this patient about analysis in order to get optimal cooperation? are the two questions one should ask oneself before starting any analysis. Sometimes a patient comes asking for analysis. Sometimes a patient is referred by a colleague for analysis. Even in such cases, however, where one is asked to accept a patient for analysis, one should decide for oneself whether the patient is one whose best interests are served by being in analysis.

As we have seen, there have been those who said that one can best decide whether a patient should be in analysis by a period of trial analysis. The fact is, however, that a short period of trial analysis during which the analyst says little or nothing can only demonstrate whether a patient can or cannot talk freely at the start. Some patients who can talk freely turn out not to have very successful analyses. Others, who cannot talk freely, turn out to have successful ones. The correlation is too uncertain to establish trial analysis as an especially good way to answer question number one.

Another device that has been recommended as a help in answering the question is that of offering one or more tentative interpretations during the diagnostic interview. The idea is that a patient who reacts to such a trial balloon with acceptance, interest, and the production of confirmatory ideas, affects, and/or memories is a better prospect for analysis than one who doesn't. This device, like the device of trial analysis, seems less than wholly satisfactory. For one thing what seems at the time like a safely superficial interpretation may in fact be one that is fraught with far more guilt and anxiety for a patient than one can possibly know to be the case. An interpretive intervention during a diagnostic interview may well do more harm than good. For another, a patient's response to any intervention may be chiefly determined by a desire to please or favorably impress the prospective analyst with the result that it is an unreliable indicator on that account.

There is, in fact, no sure way to answer the first question. One does the best one can on the basis of all the information one can gather from whatever sources. Should one decide that analysis is indeed the treatment of choice, that is what one says to the patient, simply and straightforwardly. Should the patient agree, one proceeds as described below. Should the patient disagree and take him- or herself elsewhere, there is no more one can do. There are some patients, however, who want to stay, but not in analysis. They want some other form of treatment. What is one to do then? One is convinced that the patient should be in analysis, that analysis is the treatment of choice, and that there are no obstacles to beginning analysis except the patient's own reluctance. How should onc proceed?

If one is willing to accept the patient into treatment, one should proceed as one does in dealing with resistance in any analytic situation. One tries to learn the reasons for the resistance, to understand the determinants of the patient's behavior. On the one hand the patient has confidence in the analyst's professional ability, as witnessed by the desire to take the analyst as his therapist. On the other hand the patient refuses to take the advice of the very person to whom he is ready to entrust responsibility for his treatment. One must assume that the patient has reasons for not taking the advice he has been given that are related to conflicts, to wishes, fears, guilt feelings, of which he is unaware. If the analyst can learn what they are, if they can be correctly analyzed and suitably interpreted to the patient, the patient's resistance to analysis should be sufficiently diminished to make it possible for him to do what he has been advised to do.

In brief, one proceeds analytically. One encourages the patient to talk about what his or her expectations of analysis are. If the patient is able to do so, it may be possible to provide help such that the initial reluctance disappears as a result of the patient becoming sufficiently less anxious. One should not, however, expect that such a favorable result will necessarily occur in a session or two. It may well be that a few weeks or even months of psychotherapy are necessary before a patient is able to make a commitment to analysis *lege artis*. An analyst should be prepared to spend as much time as is necessary to understand the motives for such a patient's reluctance and to interpret them so the patient understands them as well.

Objections have been raised to the recommendations just outlined that take the following form. A patient, it is maintained, is an equal partner in the psychotherapeutic enterprise. He is free to come or go, and the analyst should make every effort to avoid acting in a way that is or may seem to a patient to be authoritarian. If a patient decides to come once or twice a week rather than four or five times weekly, that should be the patient's decision to make and the analyst should accept it.

It is true that every patient deserves to be treated by the analyst with the respect due a fellow human being. Respect for a patient is an essential part of every analytic situation. It should go without saying that an analyst will behave so toward every patient. There is, however, an area in which the analyst is in a position of authority, namely, the area in which he or she functions qua analyst. A patient comes for advice about what treatment is most likely to be of help. The very act of coming for consultation places the analyst who is consulted in a position of authority that cannot be avoided or denied no matter how hard he or she may try to do so. To refuse to assume one's responsibility as an analyst can only be detrimental to a patient. To give orders to a patient and insist they must be obeyed is authoritarian and unanalytic, whatever the orders may be. To abdicate authority by simply leaving it up to a patient what kind of treatment he or she receives is irresponsible. One should certainly not try to force a patient to follow one's advice, but if a patient has chosen one as a therapist, one must try to understand and to help the patient understand (=to analyze) whatever resistances appear as impediments to treatment.

Once a patient has decided to accept the analyst's advice and to undertake analysis, the answer to the second question is of paramount importance. How can one best instruct a patient how to proceed? To what extent are Freud's (1913) recommendations still applicable today?

The answer is that it depends on the patient. In 1913 there were very few prospective patients who had any idea what the procedure of analysis was like. Today the reverse is true. There are few prospective patients who don't know something about the procedure. The simplest thing to do with any new patient is to ask what they do know before giving any instructions.

When one does give instructions one should be guided by one's own understanding of the patient's role and of the reasons for it. What one is after as an analyst is to learn as much as possible about the nature and origins of the patient's pathogenic conflicts. Whatever information a patient can give about himself is potentially useful in attaining that end. It is particularly advantageous if a patient speaks as freely as possible; if a patient says whatever comes to mind, whether it seems at the moment to be pertinent or not. In addition, it is important, indeed, advantageous, to include under "whatever comes to mind" both emotions and physical sensations that form part of a train of thought as well as the thoughts themselves. To put the matter slightly differently, emotions and physical sensations are thoughts, too. They are among the thoughts that are useful in getting to understand a patient's pathogenic conflicts.

Some patients know in advance, from reading or from other sources, that psychoanalytic patients are supposed to say whatever comes to mind ("free associate"). Even if they do know this, it should be made clear that the recommendation is based on good reason: talking as freely as possible will help analyst and patient to understand what's causing the patient's problems and/or symptoms and will help the patient overcome what caused him or her to seek help in the first place. If a patient nonetheless views the recommendation as a command or as a demand made by the analyst, that's something to be analyzed. If a patient then or later decides to withhold some thoughts, that too is to be analyzed; why one should do something that one is told is to one's disadvantage becomes the question to be answered.

It is with all these considerations in mind that one should undertake to instruct a patient concerning "the fundamental rule of analysis." The "rule" began as a command with obvious roots in the hypnotic situation out of which psychoanalysis and the psychoanalytic situation developed. It has become a recommendation, not a command, a recommendation based on reasons that should be made clear to each patient in whatever way is suitable for that patient.

The same is true for the physical arrangements of the analytic situation. Freud himself pointed out that the idea of having analytic patients lie on a couch came from the time when he put patients in a recumbent position before hypnotizing them (Freud, 1913). He confessed also that he sat behind his analytic patients as a matter of personal preference (Freud, 1913). He went on to add what is important to us today, namely, that each of these aspects of the analytic situation has proved to be useful to the patient. It is to a patient's advantage to be in a relaxed position facing away from the analyst. If he is reluctant to lie down and/or face away, one should explain that to assume this position is to the patient's advantage, provided the patient doesn't already know this. Beyond that explanation, which should be brief and simple, one should try to understand the patient's motives for wanting to sit up and/or face the analyst and try to help the patient understand them as well. One should deal with such reluctance analytically, in other words.

One's attitude toward a patient is no different when it comes to arrangements about money and time, although the basis for those arrangements is different from the basis for the advice to patients we have just been discussing. One informs the patient, if necessary, about what he should know and one is interested to learn from a patient whatever he has to say about his thoughts concerning whatever is under discussion. In this case, what a patient should know is that, while the length and frequency of the visits are, in general, arranged for the patient's benefit, the size of the fee, the requirement that payment be timely, and the fact that the patient is responsible for any missed hours are primarily for the analyst's benefit. One charges a fee because one wishes to be paid for one's services, not in order to teach patients "the value of money." One sees patients by appointment rather than on demand for practical reasons that have to do with one's own convenience, not in order to teach patients the virtue of being punctual.

Freud (1913) remarked that in analysis as in chess one can learn the opening moves. As we have seen, he outlined a number of them in the paper referred to. Even in chess, however, it is a good idea to do more than just memorize moves. One should understand the reasons for the standard moves if one is to be able to deal properly with a player who begins with an irregular opening, one that isn't in the book. The same is true for analysis. It is important to know what experienced colleagues have to say about what to say and do at the start of an analysis. It is more important, however, to know why one says or does any particular thing. It is easy to begin an analysis with a suitable patient who comes into one's office ready to lie down and get started. It is when there are difficulties of whatever sort that it is good to understand rather than to proceed by rote, because no two patients are ever just alike. What is good to say or do for one may be bad for another.

After all, the goal of beginning an analysis is the establishment of an analytic situation. The two absolute essentials of any analytic situation are a patient and an analyst. The patient has come for help, whether or not he admits it at the start, and must be told, if he doesn't already know, what to do in order to get the help that is hoped for. The analyst has the responsibility of deciding whether the patient is suitable for analysis, of making a recommendation to the patient in accordance with that decision, and of instructing the patient if necessary as to what an analytic patient should try to do in order to get the most out of analysis. In addition the analyst sets certain conditions with respect to fee and schedule. Beyond that the analyst's role is to be analytic, nothing more. An analyst tries to understand the motives for a patient's thoughts and behavior, the nature and origin of the patient's conflicts, and to communicate that understanding to the patient in the best way at the best time (i.e., to offer correct and timely interpretations). That's what an analyst should do, or try to do, from the first to the last day of every analysis.

Chapter 4

The Influence of Patients' Previous Knowledge of Analysis on the Opening Phase

Sander M. Abend, M.D.

All patients come to analysis knowing more about it than they acknowledge. This is not to suggest that they mean to deceive their analysts about the extent of their familiarity with analysis, since what they know exists largely in the form of vague conscious and preconscious beliefs of which they may be only partly aware themselves. Much of this information is inaccurate, and is often fragmentary and impressionistic, since it is likely to have come from casual reading, media exposure, and what they may have heard from friends and relatives. This network of ideas about analysis often has some detectible influence on how patients behave in the early days of their treatment. While it is rarely if ever crucial, it may be technically advantageous for the analyst to keep this in mind as he becomes engaged in the establishment of an analytic relationship.

An example from one of my first cases will serve to illustrate the kind of technical problem I have in mind.[1] Several early sessions

[1]This and subsequent examples have been disguised to protect confidentiality, but should serve the illustrative purposes for which they are presented, despite the alterations I have made in the data.

commenced with the report of a dream. This would be followed by some tentative speculations about whom various dream figures might represent, and perhaps an interpretation of what the dream "really" meant, after which my patient appeared to lose interest in the dream material. My inexpert efforts to encourage further associations from her invariably fell flat. My supervisor suggested that my patient probably had a store of pseudoknowledge, and advised me to inquire about what she might have heard about analysis in general and dream analysis in particular.

It turned out that this young woman had several relatives who were either practicing therapists, or planning to enter the field. Furthermore, she had friends who had been in treatment, some in classical analysis. My patient had heard many stories about what analysis is like. She also harbored profound feelings of inferiority in respect to some of these people, one focus of which was her sense of being intellectually and educationally limited in comparison to them. Once she decided to enter analysis herself, she tried to prepare by reading parts of Freud's *The Interpretation of Dreams* (1900). From that effort she had gathered a sketchy idea about how dreams are analyzed, and her behavior in sessions reflected her wish to make a good impression on her analyst by giving only "correct" interpretations, as she imagined the best analysands are able to do. It is also true, but incidental to the point that I wish to emphasize, that other unconscious wishes were also involved in determining her unusual behavior; among them were the desire to compete with her analyst, and, in addition, to defeat her own ambitions despite her good intentions. These latter influences could not be understood at all, much less worked with effectively, until much later in the analysis. While it is always true that the analyst cannot possibly arrive at a full understanding of patients' initial responses to the analytic situation at the time these occur, gaining access to analysands' preexisting theories about how to behave may provide a very useful point of departure for the analytic journey.

Not every case provides a vivid example of how patients' ideas about analysis can affect their behavior, but my experience as a supervisor of other beginning analysts has shown me that they may be helped to find their way about in the early stages of work with some patients by being made aware of the possibility that these analysands may be acting in response to preconscious theories about how to behave in analysis. In one case, a new analysand who was a serious, promising, but not yet very well-known writer puzzled her analyst by making many incomprehensible references to her craft and her slim body of published work, without any effort to clarify these for her analyst. My hint about the patient perhaps having preformed ideas led the analyst to discover what had not previously been mentioned. The consultant who had referred the case had told the prospective analysand that she was being sent to an analyst who was especially suitable to work with her. The patient had taken this well-intentioned recommendation to mean that the treating analyst not only had a special knowledge of her branch of literature, but a prior familiarity with and interest in her work, and so believed it unnecessary to explain in detail references that she assumed her analyst already understood.

In both examples, what the patients knew, or thought they knew about analysis, was not the sole determinant of their unusual behavior. In each case their own specific conflicts influenced what they made of what they had heard or read, as well as the shape of its manifestations in sessions. What is more, the complex network of those conflicts and their resulting compromise formations supported the structure of transference wishes and resistances that were displayed in the early hours. These underlying influences could barely be glimpsed at that stage of the treatment. The technical advantage of the analyst's bearing in mind that patients hold a background matrix of beliefs about analysis is admittedly a minor one, since there are other ways to get at the meaning of its derivatives. It may sometimes be helpful, though, for the analyst to consider how he might explore such a possibility, whenever he finds himself faced with oddities of patients' behavior at the beginning of an analysis.

The early stage of analysis is a learning period for both participants. The analyst studies how his patient responds to the analytic situation, and the patient, while trying to take his analyst's measure, is also learning how the analytic work is supposed to proceed. Until not so long ago many analysts gave patients a certain amount of explicit advice or instruction about analysis at the beginning of treatment. They often added further bits of education as commonplace technical issues arose for the first time in each case. A familiar example of the latter would be a patient's bringing up some detail about the scheduling arrangements of the analysis as if it were merely an administrative question, and not really a part of the analysis proper. Such a separation seems natural enough to inexperienced patients, but analysts have long recognized it as a form of resistance, and know that they need to make patients realize that unconscious significance is attached to what may seem like trivial matters.

We are no longer so prone to explain procedural matters to new patients, since we have learned that remarks intended merely to educate or advise patients about how to work in analysis are experienced by them in more complicated ways. Like the way we now think about patients' artificial separation of what is inside the analysis and what appears to be outside it, analysts' informative activities are seen to have complex unconscious ramifications that must be taken into account. At the very least we are alert to the impact of such interventions on our patients: the unconscious resonances may be far removed from the well-meant pragmatic surface interactions. Under the best of circumstances we avoid giving instructions altogether, in favor of more analytically sophisticated approaches to the technical problems we wish to address. One such approach might be to utilize a more neutral form of calling patients' attention to the phenomena we notice, one designed to elicit their associations; another, better still, to offer an interpretive explanation of the surface behavior, if we understand it. Either would obviously be preferred modes of response. Our hope is that patients will thereby learn more than how best to work in analysis; they may, at the same time, gain a measure of understanding of why they tend to do things in some fashion that is less advantageous for analysis, as well. They also are exposed to the still more important principle that every aspect of the analytic situation and relationship can be studied with profit, and that the analyst is fully committed to that position. By example, rather than by exhortation, analysands are invited to adopt the same attitude.

Helping the patient at the very start of analysis to become aware that he has ideas in his mind that he hardly knew were present, that these exert an influence on his behavior in sessions, and that uncovering these beliefs can help explain why he behaves as he does, is a useful introduction to what lies ahead. There is no one special technique recommended for bringing out the preexisting ideas about analysis. Merely by keeping in mind that patients probably possess theories and ideas about analysis, analysts will be more likely to take that possibility into account in formulating interventions during the opening phase of analysis, especially when patients' idiosyncratic reactions to the analytic situation make their appearance.

If the analyst succeeds in getting the patient to think about what he might have heard or read about analysis, and then obtains confirmation that such influences help explain some of the patient's behavior, it may not immediately abolish what has been illuminated. The reason for this is that the sorts of idiosyncratic response to the analytic situation we are considering are generally derived from important unconscious sources of resistance, as well as from the preconscious ideas that patients bring to analysis. As is true of resistances in general, they are bound to recur, in similar if not identical forms, as long as their unconscious determinants continue to play an important part in the analysis. My patient's way of working with her dreams remained somewhat constricted for several years, even at times reverting to the extreme limitation of responses noted in the opening days. The main value of exposing the preexisting beliefs lies in its demonstration of the principle of analytic inquiry, on a relatively nonthreatening level, at the very beginning of treatment.

I make it a point to ask prospective analysands during preliminary evaluation sessions what they may know or believe about analysis. This is often called for, since these days patients are less likely than in the past to come for consultation with their intention to enter analysis already formed. Part of the consultation process includes a determination of whether analysis or some other form of treatment is to be recommended, and learning about the patient's preferences, prejudices, and fears is a necessary part of that endeavor. In that context, it seems natural to me to inquire about what patients may have heard about analysis, and how it is conducted. Even when such a discussion is productive, only a small fraction of patients' preconscious beliefs comes forward, as subsequent experience with those who become analysands quickly demonstrates.

For example, a young graduate student who was the child of an analyst entered analysis after a series of evaluatory sessions in which some of her apprehension about analysis had been explored. Her parents had strongly encouraged her to enter analysis because they were concerned that certain features of her behavior posed a danger to her well-being and her future prospects. In the opening days of her analysis she described many episodes that, it soon became clear, were covertly designed to test her analyst's reactions. Although it had never come up in the consultation sessions, she readily confirmed my conjecture that she had often heard all about how analysts are supposed to be nonjudgmental, but had long since formed the opinion that her mother was not that way in respect to her patients' values and behavior, any more than she was in response to her daughter.

My patient's not quite conscious mission was to prove that this estimate could also justifiably be applied to her analyst, to which end she closely monitored my responses to her provocative accounts. Her manifest behavior in sessions was also intended to conform to other things she had heard about analysis, such as that she was conscientiously to bring all problematic issues to the analysis for a thorough airing. Her silent skepticism about my objectivity was part of her unconscious predisposition to invite a transference repetition of the complex, gratifying struggle with her mother, the dimensions of which could only be explored much later on in the treatment.

The children of analysts are a special class of patient who pose unusual technical problems, of which their prior exposure to analytic talk is but one facet. Another category whose previous experience raises special problems is that of patients who have been in analysis before. A detailed exploration of the issues involved lies well beyond the scope of this presentation, but it is certainly common for the new analyst to have occasion to explore what the patient came to believe about analysis and its procedures based on his work with the other analyst or analysts. It should not be necessary to add that here, too, important patterns of resistance may be detected as contributing to patients' syntheses of their previous analytic experience; these naturally reappear as technical problems, even though the present analyst's contributions to the analytic interchange may be different in some respects from those of the previous therapists.

What I wish to underline is that while children, spouses, or other relatives of analysts, and individuals with previous experience of analysis, are assumed to have a substantial body of information (and perhaps misinformation as well) about analysis, the same is true in some degree of all analysands. Special attention to the impact of their conscious and preconscious knowledge is widely recognized as useful when commencing analysis with the former classes of patients; I advocate a comparable attentiveness when commencing analytic treatment with those analysands whose prior exposure is less obvious.

The full extent of the impact of patients' beliefs about analysis on their reactions to the analytic situation may not always become evident to the analyst in the opening phase of treatment. One analysand did not get around to disclosing a particularly important preexisting conscious idea about analysis, one which had great influence on her behavior, until well into the second year of her treatment. This woman came for a consultation because she was unhappy about a series of relationships with men who took advantage of her tendency to attach herself to them with a slavish, submissive devotion that invited exploitation. She was quite determined to get into serious treatment, but was very reluctant to accept my opinion that analysis offered her the best prospect for a satisfactory result. As we explored her hesitation in an extended series of vis-à-vis sessions, several influential factors became clarified. One was a consequence of her father encouraging her to enter analysis. He made no secret of his appreciation of the benefits he thought his analysis had brought to him, and of his consequent conviction about its advantages over less intensive therapies. My patient loved, admired, and respected her father, whom she saw as a brilliant and successful entrepreneur; his good opinion mattered more to her than anything in her life. She also saw him as still frighteningly explosive and erratic in his personal life, and as emotionally abusive to her mother, her siblings, his business associates, and even to service personnel like waiters and taxi drivers when they failed to please him. This evaluation of his residual pathology left her profoundly skeptical about the benefits of analysis that he extolled so much.

In the course of my inquiries I also learned that her father had continued to see his former analyst over the years to seek his advice about family crises, and he had even sent various other members of the family, including my patient, to see this man for consultation and even brief therapy. The analyst, quite well known locally, had permitted himself to become a kind of psychological guru to this wealthy and socially prominent family. All of this emerged gradually over a number of weeks, in the course of which she also provided me with details of her complex history, and of the pattern of unsatisfactory relationships that had brought her to decide for herself that treatment was indicated.

A recurrent theme during this exploratory period was her fear of "commitment." She thought of this as an obstacle to making better relationships with men, even though on the surface it usually looked as if the men were even more leery of commitment than she was; the same phrase was offered as an explanation of her reluctance to enter analysis. It became possible to show her that her fear of committing herself to analysis expressed her dread that analysis would turn into yet another relationship in which she would come to feel helpless, trapped, frustrated, hurt, and exploited. She could begin to see that this fear was a reflection of the role her father played in her emotional life, and in the masochistic pattern of her relationships with men. As this became clarified she was able to drop her resistance to the idea of analysis, the extended consultation period ended, and a formal analysis was begun.

Up to this point in the evolution of the case one might well regard it as illustrating the thesis that previous knowledge about analysis may affect the problem of getting a patient into analysis, rather than of posing difficulties in the opening phase proper. As will become clear, what had come forth so far was only a derivative layer of her resistance; the essential beliefs that supported its more subtle and profound effects were still hidden, their presence entirely unsuspected by both of us. As my patient settled into analysis, she displayed a frequently encountered obsessional style of working in her sessions. She attended conscientiously, and spoke with some measure of candor even about difficult subjects, but also revealed a clear need to retain some editorial control over what she would discuss. While I learned a great deal about her current activities, her family and personal history, her emotional reactions, her dreams and fantasies, two areas of avoidance gradually became apparent. For one thing, she invariably referred to me only as "the doctor." She insisted on holding to an interpretation of our relationship that was limited to its professional nature, and denied having any thoughts or fantasies about me as an individual with a life outside the office, much less as a man. This was rationalized for many months as strictly realistic on her part. The second area of omission was that of her sexual life. While she discussed her past and current interactions with boyfriends, as these were central to her reason for being in treatment, she was self-conscious about talking about sexual experiences, feelings, and fantasies. She was both conscious of and apologetic about this censorship, but she felt unable to overcome her discomfort. Slowly she came to realize that her constricted view of me was not just realistic, but was defensively motivated, and that it was related to her unwillingness to talk to me about sexual matters.

During a session well into the second year of her analysis, in which this aspect of her resistance was the focus of attention, she revealed for the first time an idea about analysis she had held all along; it proved crucial to the unravelling of this behavior. One of the things she had heard, either from her father or his analyst, she was never sure which one, was that every analytic patient must fall in love with the analyst for the process to work properly. She not only dreaded this prospect, she had also made a conscious resolution that it would not happen to her. She had never before connected these ideas with her initial reluctance to accept my recommendation for analytic treatment. It was now possible in retrospect to make more specific sense of her worry about the meaning of commitment to analysis, and to see that the work done during the consultation period, although sufficiently accurate to free her to start an analysis, was an incomplete approximation of the true source of her resistance. Of course it was now also very much more clear why she had fought off acknowledging her transference reactions, and why she had been so reluctant to talk to me about her sexual life.

As is typical, the revelation of her ideas about analysis, although providing transient and partial relief of her constriction, did not completely abolish their influence on her behavior. It did advance our understanding, and it proved to be an important step forward in the analysis of her recurring cycles of resistance and transference fantasy, a task which, as it always does, characterized the entire analysis up to the closing days of a lengthy and successful treatment. In a manner of speaking, one might say that this example demonstrates that the opening phase of analysis may be of many months' duration, rather than consisting only of the early days or even weeks of treatment. At any rate, the particular idea about analysis held by this patient had a profound impact on her behavior in treatment, one which neither she nor I could comprehend fully until it was finally revealed, in part as a consequence of the months of analytic work that preceded its acknowledgment. Certainly, my inquiries during the consultation period were insufficient to help her to bring it forward. This case served to impress upon me the potential importance patients' ideas about analysis can have, even when their presence is not so clearly suggested by highly unusual or idiosyncratic behavior in the early sessions.

In summary, every patient who considers entering analysis does so under the influence of a set of conscious beliefs about what the procedure entails. These are formed by his or her previous contacts with others who may have been patients, practitioners, or merely more or less knowledgeable individuals; this list of sources also includes writers and the like who promulgate information about analysis. The knowledge such prospective analysands possess inevitably consists of much misinformation, as well as some realistic understanding, and is selectively shaped by its correspondence with that individual's relevant unconscious fantasies. At least in part because of the latter connection, the patient-to-be is usually not quite aware of the extent of his or her store of data about analysis, and is not able to reveal all of it, even if the analyst makes inquiries during the course of conducting an evaluation. Nevertheless, this background matrix may have an influence on the patient's willingness to accept a recommendation for analytic treatment, a point that should be kept in mind when doing consultations.

When a patient comes into analysis, this store of previous knowledge is liable to have an effect on his or her responses to the analytic situation. In my experience, this shows up in the form of patterns of resistance, and consequently the conscious ideation is merely a surface contributor to the behavior observed. All the same it may be technically useful for the analyst to explore such possible sources for resistant behavior that makes its appearance in the opening phase. One should anticipate that the amelioration of its effect will only be partial and temporary, since resistances are not abolished as long as their unconscious determinants remain active. Even so the benefit of looking for preexisting conscious sources of patients' behavior in analysis extends beyond its value as an initial stage of resistance analysis. It can also serve as a valuable and relatively unthreatening introduction to the analytic rationale, in that the analyst's curiosity about possible sources in the patient's experience and ideation for explanations of his or her behavior and attitudes is thereby aptly demonstrated.

Relatives of professionals, as well as members of the profession who become patients, like analysands who have had prior experiences in analytic treatment, are all correctly assumed to be in possession of some knowledge of analysis, and experienced analysts automatically search for its influence when commencing treatment with these classes of patients. The same practice should be applied even in those other analysands in whom previous exposure to analysis may not be as obvious.

Chapter 5

The Influence of Trauma on the Opening Phase of Analysis

Harold P. Blum, M.D.

The opening phase of psychoanalysis has both general characteristics and individual features. The analytic process which is set in motion during the opening phase continues throughout the analysis, but certain issues of adaptation to the analytic situation and process are common to all patients, while others vary with the individual patient's personality organization and psychopathology. Every patient reacts to the couch, the rendering of the fundamental rule, and the analyst's relative selective silence. There may be great variations in freedom of association; for example, affective expression in hysterical patients with overdramatization, or in obsessive patients with isolation of thought and affect. Traumatic experience has its own particular impact upon the opening phase, and free association. The imprint of trauma may reappear with far greater clarity and meaning in the terminal phase of analysis, but the recognition, correct clarification, and interpretation of derivatives of trauma in the opening phase may be crucial to the inception of the analytic process. The significance and emphasis to be attached to traumatic experience as a major determinant of both the patient's psychopathology and the opening phase varies considerably.

This chapter will emphasize the importance of trauma in the opening phase of analysis of many patients. Trauma will influence the patient's motivations for treatment, the ability to free associate, the initial transference and formation of the transference neurosis, the recognition of internal conflict and transference, the therapeutic alliance, including the therapeutic split of observing and experiencing ego, and problems of resistance and regressison. Very severe trauma may preclude a manageable transference and progressive analytic process.

The opening phase, which may last from two months to up to twelve months with resistant patients, provides an initial period of gradual adaptation and participation in the analytic process. It also permits analytic evaluation by the analyst and an initial understanding of the patient's central difficulties and problems. The opening phase is no longer, in the main, a time of trial analysis, but the patient's ego resources and the analyst's therapeutic skills are reciprocally evaluated by the two partners in the analytic work. While Glover (1955) stated that the opening phase is "determined less by the conditions of analysis than by the spontaneous reactions of the patient" (p. 19), the spontaneous reactions of the analyst must also be considered. The analyst's style; the manner in which he explains such matters as the framework, including times of sessions, frequency, fee, cancellations or missed appointments, and vacations; the way in which the fundamental rule is formulated; and the invitation or command to use the couch are all significant variables.

A transference–countertransference field can be defined from the outset of treatment, and this may be particularly important to the patient who has been sensitized by previous traumata. The analyzable, previously traumatized patient, whether the trauma took place recently or in the remote past, does not need any special alteration of the usual conditions of the analysis or any change in technique. The analyst has to comprehend the patient's associations and has to deal with resistances in the patient and sometimes within himself through interpretation. An analytic attitude of benevolent neutrality, of calm, patient tolerance is essential to the unfolding of derivatives of the trauma in the analytic process. The analyst need not attempt to proselytize, to specially educate or indoctrinate, nor to artificially cultivate a positive transference. In my opinion, a neutral analytic attitude is to be differentiated from psychotherapeutic maneuvers such as direct reassurance. Therapeutic intent is implicit, and analysis does not require a diatrophic, supportive attitude (Spitz, 1956). Neutrality encompasses impartiality, objectivity, and remaining nonjudgmental and nonintrusive; the analyst remains unbiased and with attention equidistant from the psychic structures and external reality. The analyst's dedication, empathy, and commitment to analytic work and goals will be continually demonstrated and tested as the analysis proceeds. The maintenance of an analytic attitude and correct interpretation is especially important if severe trauma is not to be provoked and repeated without understanding in the analytic situation.

As the opening phase unfolds, a therapeutic alliance develops and deepens. This arises from the patient's conscious wishes for help and mastery, as well as irrational and often magical motives for seeking analysis. Though the alliance is initially founded upon the unconscious transference relationship, it also has elements of a new object relationship and ego identification. The patient identifies with the observing ego of the analyst, and a therapeutic "split" will be crucial in order for the patients to be able to both observe and reexperience the repetition of trauma in the transference. Anna Freud (1965) regarded the therapeutic alliance as based upon ego attitudes that go with later stages, namely upon self observation, insight, oedipal object relationship, and secondary process function (p. 40). The stability of the patient's ego and of the therapeutic alliance will greatly assist the analytic work during times of turbulent traumatic transference recapitulations and in the face of intense negative transference and resistance. It must be noted that the capacity for self observation as well as verbalization was absent during the period of traumatic overwhelming of the ego. The opening phase facilitates emergence of derivatives of the traumatic situation along with some affective abreaction and the beginning of autonomous ego distance from the trauma and associated transference conflicts. The patient can be encouraged to verbalize and cautioned against impulsive action, but ordinarily, nonanalytic encouragement or interdictions, promises of obedience to the analytic rules, exhortations, or instructions should be unnecessary. With the patient who is suitable for psychoanalysis, and who has a sufficient, relatively intact ego, despite trauma, parameters should not be necessary.

In the opening phase in the analysis of both adults and children, defense analysis usually takes precedence over the analysis of unconscious content. Symbolic interpretations and excessive attention to any one form of material such as slips, dreams, or fantasies about the analyst would generally be secondary to the careful scrutiny of the patient's resistance and modes of defense. During the opening phase of analysis, the patient adapts to the relative sensorimotor deprivation and the lack of the usual social amenities and conversation. The analyst's silence will gradually be understood as a further invitation for the patient to associate without undue external interference. Both patient and analyst listen to verbalization and silence, and the patient begins to reflect on his own style and content of association. Dealing with initial resistances, the analyst may note hints of past trauma when an important object or time period is conspicuously absent in the patient's associations, or a protracted silence often occurs prior to the weekend separation, or through overenthusiastic attachment to the analysis, masking great distress and anxiety. Since trauma tends to be fixated and repeated, its imprint will be present in the opening phase, although not necessarily recognized. The patient who has been seduced in childhood may attempt to seduce the analyst and, similarly, the patient who has been traumatized by violent assault may attempt to attack or repel the aggressor, or to seduce, ingratiate himself with, and propitiate the potential attacker. The analytic situation itself will be perceived, at some point, as dangerous, because it both beckons and threatens a return of the traumatic situation. While in a patient whose trauma has remained repressed, silence may clearly be understood to derive from fear of being overwhelmed by traumatic anxiety, the same may be said of patients who cannot stop talking about their traumatic experience. These latter patients may be living in a chronic traumatic situation, forever attempting to master unconscious dimensions of the trauma and the dangers of recurrence of traumatic anxiety (Freud, 1939).

In the original traumatic situation, the patient's ego was relatively or totally unable to cope. Obligatory regression is absolutely characteristic of trauma, with a return to more primitive defenses and modes of ego function. There is always a tendency toward fixation to trauma, repetition in thought and action, and variably persistent anxiety, sometimes associated with panic states, nightmares, and flashbacks. Derivatives of the trauma appear in symptoms, dreams, daydreams, in children's play, and in art and literature. In psychoanalysis, trauma is regularly repeated in the transference situation. Long after realizing that some reports of childhood seductions were in actuality fantasies, Freud (1917) stated, "The position can be shown to be that the childhood experiences constructed or remembered in analysis are sometimes indisputably false and sometimes equally certainly correct, and in most cases compounded of truth and falsehood" (p. 367). Actual trauma and internal fantasies could be complementary in the same way that external impressions and influences interacted with internal factors so that both could be codeterminants of vulnerability to trauma and traumatic disorder. The patient who has been exposed to the primal scene may be preoccupied with voyeurism and exhibitionism in analysis and life, as well as defenses against repetition of the trauma. After being traumatized by maternal seduction and nude exposure, the exhibitionist youth and adult may exhibit his genitals to dramatize that he is not castrated and to vindicatively shock the mother surrogate who is held responsible for his own castration shock.

In all these situations, the ego tends to be active where it was formerly passive, and attempts belated mastery of the traumatic situation. This inevitably involves identification with the aggressor but also with the rescuer and comforter and attempts at self-comforting and self-healing in fantasy (Blum, 1986, 1987). The traumatic experience is always elaborated in fantasy and is always assigned unconscious meaning in terms of the patient's prevailing fantasy system at the time of the trauma. The intensity and validation of antecedent unconscious fantasy reciprocally codetermines trauma. Trauma may represent a sadomasochistic gratification or fantasied punishment. For example, the Wolf Man interpreted the primal scene as a sadomasochistic battle with the threat of castration and mutilation. Analogous to physical traumatic injury, the ego is overtaxed and injured; in the recovery phase, the ego attempts to limit and detoxify the trauma as well as to resolve the unconscious conflicts and fantasies associated with the traumatic experience. Unconscious trauma has usually been defensively walled off by the repression which is unstable and incomplete. The instability of the patient's defenses and the threat of return of the repressed are associated with processes aimed at modulation and mastery of trauma; fresh attempts to enact the trauma may serve mastery or provoke repeated and additional traumatic experience. The analyst will closely attend to the weakened traumatized, vulnerable ego—vulnerable to severe regression and traumatic anxiety and to the reactivation of trauma. The traumatized ego is predisposed to fresh and cumulative trauma.

Trauma intensifies preexisting conflicts and validates fantasies such as the patient's fantasies of sadomasochistic violence or fantasies of retribution and punishment. Ultimately, certain defenses such as denial, repression, and isolation of traumatic experience and the persistent interplay of reality and fantasy in cases of parental seduction and child abuse, or severe illness and object loss, will all require careful analytic assessment, interpretation, and reconstruction. One of the greatest difficulties in the opening phase may be the relative weight to be assigned to internal and external factors, the question of what really happened, and whether the patient was actually traumatized or is reporting complex fantasies and family myths rather than real traumatic experiences.

Analysts today are much more aware of actual incidents of incest, and deliberate physical injury of children. However, this awareness does not make the assessment of reality and fantasy any easier. Grains of truth, fragments of experience may lend verisimilitude to situations that are largely based upon childhood impressions and fantasy constructions. On the other hand, many personal myths (Kris, 1956a) are based upon the individual's own attempts at reconstruction of other and earlier traumas. Traumas tend to be telescoped and condensed and may be screened not only by innocuous experience but by other earlier or later traumatic experience. Often, the opening phase can only be understood in the later phases of analysis, and decisions concerning fantasy or real trauma may have to be postponed until there has been extensive analytic data and evidence and further analytic reconstruction. The question of fantasy or reality, of horror story or real trauma may remain unresolved in the opening phase of treatment. In some patients it is very clear that the patient was traumatized, for example, by parent loss in early childhood, by severe infantile illness, or in the aftermath of the Holocaust. In other situations, for example, reports of parental malevolence or of childhood incest may need analytic clarification and analytic conviction about what really happened.

In other situations, such as parental loss or severe illness in childhood, the trauma may be recognized from the outset by both doctor and patient. However, the ramifications of the trauma, its organizing and disorganizing influences in life, and its role in conflict regression, symptom, and character, cannot be deciphered without clinical psychoanalysis. If, for example, there has been a suicide in the family, if the patient reports obsessive reading of obituaries, frequent visits to the cemetery, "discussions with the deceased" at the gravesite, ritual prayer, and silent meditation in the cemetery, if attending funerals and comforting the bereaved relatives and friends is very important, and if the patient then reports fleeting suicidal thoughts, it does not necessarily require years of analysis to infer the patient's traumatization and its specific relation to object loss. If the presenting complaint is depression and insomnia, the analyst may anticipate the grief, guilt, and rage. Separation panic may appear in the later phases of analysis despite a relatively tranquil opening phase. In fact, the opening phase may be characterized by fantasies of rescue and protection and loving reunion with the lost object represented by the analyst.

I have emphasized the importance of defense analysis in the opening phase. This emphasis has to be balanced by respect for the patient's defenses. The opening phase does not call for sudden or disruptive breech of the patient's defenses. In analysis, the aim of the treatment is not immediate reliving of the traumatic experience as in narcosynthesis of the traumatic neuroses of war. Rather, the analytic process and development of the transference neurosis will gradually and piecemeal permit recapitulation of the recent and/or remote traumatic experiences in a modified, miniaturized form that is accessible to both analytic interpretation and further ego modulation.

I do not want to convey the impression that in severely traumatized patients a smooth opening phase or even a typical opening phase is readily expectable. Quite to the contrary, patients with such histories often have tendencies to severe or malignant acting out which can preclude or disrupt analysis from the outset. The patient may not be able to form a stable therapeutic alliance and/or transference neurosis. So much of the neurosis may be involved in the patient's everyday neurotic behavior that such generalized neurotic behavior as well as specific acting out may prevent effective analytic work. Some seriously traumatized patients may require preparatory psychotherapy and others may not be suitable for psychoanalysis at all. In many patients, a very tenuous beginning, whether characterized by periods of remote silence or intense affect storms, may gradually yield to patient-tolerated analytic work and to the progressive unfolding of a real analytic process. Much depends upon the patient's ego strengths and overall personality resources. In the traumatized patient, the capacity to tolerate frustration, to delay action in favor of thoughtful contemplation, to freely verbalize feelings and fantasies with preservation of self-observation and reflection are extremely important. These skills are important for all analytic work, but they are particularly pertinent in the traumatized patient because the original traumatic situation is always speechless. Speech is impossible during acute traumatization, and the frozen cognition, the strangulated affects of silence or screams, and the motor tendencies toward flight, fight, or chaotic thrashing all have to be ultimately replaced by verbalization. The fantasies in which the trauma has been embedded, embellished, elaborated, and validated have to be repeatedly verbalized as a central part of the analytic work. This will begin with the patient's first efforts of free association, even though the fantasies may not be recognized as related to crucial realities. The issue of vulnerability to trauma is pertinent during the opening phase because of the patient's prior sensitization. Patients will attempt to both defend against the trauma as well as to express it and to repeat it for purposes of infantile gratification as well as mature mastery. Analysis will reveal a complex interplay of external and internal determinents and influences; for example, sensitization and vulnerability to trauma, perpetuation and/or repetition of elements of the traumatic situation, enfeebled and successful efforts at mastery of trauma, and long-range effects of the trauma on symptoms, character, and development. Some severely traumatized patients have not suffered so much structural damage that they are unanalyzable, but are nevertheless so well defended that they may appear to be inaccessible. These patients may also be depleted of interest and energy for ordinary activities since so much of their psychic life is concerned with the repression and avoidance of the feared recurrence of the traumatic situation. Analysis may lead to a "de-icing" of numbness and frozen inhibition. In all cases, the return of the repressed is associated with symptom and character disturbance. But in some patients, the analytic process itself may promote excessive regression and revival of trauma in the transference in a form that may not be entirely manageable. These situations try the analyst's skill and patience.

The predictability, reliability, and frequency of the analytic sessions, the analyst's calm, tolerance, and benevolent neutrality, will be helpful long before interpretation can be fully utilized in understanding and mastering the past trauma. Patients with major regressive vulnerabilities to which trauma has contributed may initially use the analytic work for soothing, holding, and organizing regulatory functions. The analyst may be a very important model of identification for calm introspection and communicative verbalization. Analytic clarifications may be used by the patient initially for magical restoration and the feeling that tranquility and reason will prevail over panic and chaos.

The timing, dose, and level of explanation, close attention to defense and resistance, and awareness of traumatic vulnerability and repetition may all be very helpful in the initiation of the analytic process. The child who suffered a fractured skull and ribs as a result of a bicycle accident may regard the analyst as a rescuing and comforting, healing object, but also as a "head shrinker" who might attack his brain. Free association may be a dangerous uncontrolled ride into the abyss. Analysts often have some knowledge of the traumatic situation or can at least grasp traumatic elements which are associated in the patient's mind with the onset of analysis. The link between the traumatic situation and the analytic situation may be superficially clarified for the patient. Connecting the past trauma with the opening of analysis may be a critical factor in sustaining an analytic process. The patient is afraid of being brain damaged or brainwashed, and so wishes to flee from the analytic situation and stop the treatment before it starts. The analysis is unconsciously regarded as a dangerous revival of the trauma. In other cases, or at other times, the patient may seek to repeat the trauma early in the analysis. It is vital that despite the patient's efforts to involve the analyst in avoidance, or in repetition of the trauma, or to inflict the trauma on the analyst, or to invite the analyst to attack or seduce the patient in a fresh repetition of trauma, that the traumatic transference should not be evaded or validated in the analytic situation. I emphasize here not only the transference gratifications and infantile destructiveness on the part of the patient, but the intensification of trauma that comes with repeated reality validation. With mismanagement, vulnerable patients may be traumatized again. For example, patients who have been sexually molested or involved in childhood incest and then seduce and are seduced by their therapist may be severely traumatized anew and become even more refractory to treatment.

A patient's presenting theme or leitmotiv may represent the patient's own attempt at reconstruction of the effective trauma and its impact upon his life. Frequently, this theme is a rationalization and elaboration of a personal or family myth concerning the traumatic experience. For example, the patient's character disorder and disturbance in object relations may be ascribed to an experience of parental psychosis or parent loss. The patient may feel consciously injured by the parent but may not recognize his own guilt related to the unconscious fantasy that the parent was injured by the patient's hostile fantasies. The complaint of feeling traumatized by a particular parent's psychopathology may have more than a grain of truth to it; it may represent important history despite the patient's accusatory account. Analysis reveals that the situation is inevitably far more complicated and that the patient's initial account has left out his own contribution to the difficulties and what he has defended against, adapted to, and synthesized in his own way. Traumas may be activated and dramatized without the patient really recognizing the subtle long-range sequellae of the actual traumatization and his own contributions to both the traumatic situation and miscarried attempt at mastery. Real achievements stemming from mastery of traumatic experience may be overlooked or overstated.

In some traumatized patients, the very nature of the initial consultation and arrangement and timing of analytic exploration may be related to the reenactment of trauma. The timing of the inception of the analysis may actually turn out to be an anniversary response. The anniversary reaction repeats the infantile trauma in a disguised form which, at the same time, maintains major areas of repression intact and temporarily substitutes a reassuring situation for a traumatic one. One such patient arranged to begin analysis on the anniversary of her father's death. The opening phase was a type of analytic honeymoon in which the patient quickly showed great symptomatic relief and the lifting of depression. The analyst represented the lost father with whom she was reunited. Fantasies of rescue and reunion would give way later to fantasies of desertion and betrayal associated with major depression and suicidal ideation. The patient would usually experience transient, mild depression on the anniversary of her father's loss when she was four years of age. But the full dimensions of her complex reactions to this trauma were not understood until she was analyzed. Even her sensitization and vulnerability to separation and loss were not clear in the opening phase which was characterized by friendliness, seductiveness, and propitiation. The deepening of the transference and of the analytic process itself would lead later in the analysis to the patient's preoccupation with death and dying, separation and abandonment, as well as betrayal and murder, rebirth and replacement. In this type of opening phase, sincere desire for attachment and understanding, and what appears to be a beguiling, seductive charm and readiness to engage in analytic work, becomes the prelude to crippling separation, panic, and clinging depression. The task in the opening phase is to recognize the patient's defenses against loss, panic, and depression and particularly the underlying conflicts of ambivalence. The analyst and analysis may be initially idealized as a way of protecting the object from the murderous aggression which is the other side of the patient's ambivalence. Further, the ambivalence has been heightened by the feeling that the object has abandoned the patient, amalgamated with self-hatred for having driven the object away. The calm before the storm may be used to help the patient's awareness of the repressed rage and panic. Traumatized patients are particularly prone to affect storms and acting out with the "return of the repressed." Clarification of initial signs of ambivalence may help the enfeebled ego to deal with the guilt, reproach, and self-reproach associated with the patient's fantasies of murder. Here the groundwork may also be prepared for the patient's confrontation with the fantastic distortions of natural death into mayhem and murder.

One of the major sequelae of traumatic parental loss in childhood may be a lifelong burden of guilt as well as expectation and provocation of punishment. As the patient begins to grasp the transference distortions of the analyst and the confused, irrational nature of the fantasies associated with the childhood trauma, the analytic alliance is strengthened. Insight becomes a burgeoning means of mastering trauma and concomitant unconscious conflicts.

Consider traumatization due to parent loss in childhood. Pioneer analytic attention to the identification with the relationship to the lost parent is balanced by the impact of the surviving parent. The relationship with this parent, with other parent surrogates, and the correlated identifications with surviving surrogates will be repeated in transference. Although there is fixation to trauma and a tendency to developmental arrest at the time of the parent loss (Altschul, 1968), the developmental level represented by the initial transference may vary considerably. The transference to the surviving, sustaining object may be associated with denial of loss and with splitting of the ego and of self and object representations (Blum, 1983). The sequellae are likely to depend upon developmental level and achievements at the time of the traumatic loss, the quality of surviving, sustaining object relations, and subsequent benevolent or detrimental phase reorganization. Object loss syndromes may be more or less prominent from the outset. In my experience, the traumatic situation is apparent in the transference very early, and such transference derivatives may often be matched with the known life history. While experience from parent loss with death is necessarily limited in any analytic practice, experience with parent loss through divorce is now common. The long-range effects of single parenting or of surrogate stepparents, combined with earlier losses, will have enduring influences upon the patient's character, symptoms, and object relations. The analysis may represent life before the loss, and termination may be fixed in advance or at the outset in order to defend against the impact of the fantasied analytic separation and death. Clarification of the patient's fantasy expectations and magical hopes and of the patient's defensive denial, reversal, and undoing of past traumas assist the reality ego and help to confirm that traumatic loss and disappointment will not be inevitably repeated.

The opening phase of a case of parent loss—a male patient who lost his mother when he was fourteen years of age—was particularly instructive.[1] Imprints of the previous loss could be seen in the patient's embittered character as an adult, with marked depressive–pessimistic tendencies. Initially, his bitter, acerbic, sarcastic, and self-denigrating attitudes were hidden behind a veneer of friendliness and ingratiation. He tried to be "Mr. Nice Guy," and at age thirty he was a competent professional, helpful and eager to be liked. He wanted to work hard in the analysis and bring significant associations to the analyst, just as he was always trying to bring packages for other people, do things for others that would win commendation, and avoid accusation or reproach. Yet there were early tendencies toward lateness and acerbic, cutting comments. In contrast to previous psychotherapy, he soon began to react to the end of sessions and weekend separations. He would come late, fighting against dependency upon the "unreliable" analyst who would desert like his mother. At the same time, he was identified with the mother who had cut off time and whose time had been cut so short. He had "killed time" and was a killer; upon leaving sessions he frequently thought of killing someone else or himself. The murderous fantasies in the early period of treatment tended to be rather devoid of affect, although the immense underlying rage and hostility were easily sensed.

His mother had died in an automobile accident, but the patient did not initially connect this with fantasies concerning his own reckless speeding. He spoke of coming to the analytic sessions at 90 mph, having started late and speeding to avoid arriving late. Identifying with his mother in the act of dying, he seemed to almost provoke trauma, acting to invite self-inflicted trauma (as a punishment). He hummed songs like "coming through the wreck" with a reversal of affect. He spoke lightly of other forms of vehicle and bicycle accidents without conscious connection to his traumatic loss. His mother did not survive the wreckage, and his life had then been wrecked. The

[1]I am greatly indebted to Dr. Seth Eichler for this clinical material.

patient could recall, for example, that he thought of sueing the automobile company and of smashing their cars. When cut off by another car he felt like blowing the car up with a bazooka. He was cut off from his mother and yet was responsible for her death. The accident occurred shortly after his mother had left in the car following an argument with her. He was always guilty and always fearful that the sword of Damocles would fall. Some punishment fantasies were overt, including being convicted of an unknown crime in court and brought before a hanging judge.

He had taken his chances on coming into analysis, whether it would result in further loss or restitution, the reward of refinding his mother, and/or punishment for having killed her. The analysis was a great gamble, like a lottery. He always anticipated being a loser, and although he wanted to undo the trauma and be rewarded for nice, kindly, reactive behavior, he expected a negative outcome. Even in the early phase of analysis, analysis was a time machine where he could magically return to life with his mother before she died, leaving him so hurt and guilt-ridden. The analysis might provide for a delay in the death sentence, for a reprieve and clemency, but the analyst could just as easily be the agent of reprisal and retribution rather than rescue. Crime and punishment were also associated with his outside activities and his reading interests. He was interested in murder mysteries and issues of disappearance. The theme of a blip disappearing from the computer screen, representing his mother's death, coincided with deepening of the opening phase of analysis. In addition to chronic lateness, the patient had preset a termination date and seemed determined that eventually he would leave the analyst rather than be left, desert rather than be deserted or rejected. He might disappear from the analytic situation, but actually many issues were being reopened. When his mother died, the file of her accident was closed, and he had been afraid to reopen the file and study the report. As the transference deepened, the analyst represented the lost mother and surviving father as well as the patient's siblings. During periods of repressive revival, of profound separation anxiety, and fears of punitive abandonment, the analyst was tested for reliability and predictability. The analyst, as the surviving parent, could transcend the trauma.

A mourning process was initiated coincident with the analytic process and with the initial lifting of denial and repression. Despite the previous psychotherapy, the patient had not been aware of his "crying on the inside"—his deep internal sadness and longing until the analysis was under way. The opening phase of analytic work had paved the way for the patient to become more aware of his depressive illness and the many subtle ways in which it pervaded his life. The transference attachment to the analyst and the analysis had deepened and the ego had been strengthened by initial clarification and correlation of his conflicts and traumas with his associations and behavior. His curiosity was awakened, and a genuine interest in understanding and insight were linked with his efforts to master trauma. The patient and analyst had inklings of much earlier trauma during the oedipal period when siblings were born and the effect of sibling illness upon his own development. Because of the telescoping of trauma, it was not possible to elucidate the role of his earlier traumatization on his oedipal development and conflicts in the opening phase. Construction of the patient's life was already beginning, and the life history and analytic data were being imbricated toward a meaningful analytic autobiography. The opening phase oriented the analyst toward the major traumas and conflicts, and the significant themes organized in the patient's conscious and unconscious fantasy systems. The opening phase is prologue to an analytic process which gathers momentum and depth as the analysis is under way. The initial resistances engendered by trauma will have been interpreted, but the long-range problems and the organizing influence upon subsequent development will require elucidation in the course of the analysis.

The traumatized patient in contemporary psychoanalysis is hardly the patient who had suffered the single shock trauma in childhood described in the pioneer days of psychoanalysis and dramatized in theater and film. Chronic traumatic states of strain and cumulative trauma have often been punctuated by shock traumas, which in turn are followed by periods of chronic ego stress and strain. The analyst observes attempts at recovery, identification with aggressor and victim, rescuer, and comforter, the revival repetition and reworking of earlier and later traumas, and the linkage to unconscious conflict and fantasy. Trauma often creates considerable distrust, doubt, distortion, and confusion in the patient (Blum, 1987).

Countertransference strains may also be very great, especially in cases in which the patient has been massively traumatized. The analyst may confront his own fantasies of rescue or revenge, his own feelings of pity, guilt, and outrage. The analyst's capacity for empathy, neutrality, and understanding may be severely taxed and strained. The reality of horrible experience rather than fantasy may be more upsetting to the analyst who is closely identified with the patient. Moreover, the analyst must not be misled by historical fact, or denial in fantasy, or by fragmentary, distorted memories. In addition to the avoidance of the shared repetition of trauma in a countertransference enactment with patients, the analyst must also be careful not to minimize or excessively dwell on traumatic elements in the opening phase. Trauma may also serve a defensive screening function. The metapsychology of trauma (Rangell, 1967), its defensive and adaptive functions, are significant considerations as analyst and patient ponder "what happened." How traumatic events have influenced the patient's life and acquired the meaning they had for that particular patient can only be an educated guess in the opening phase.

Patients have a great need to discover their past, their roots, the impact of major alterations of self and family structure and function. The memories and myths of early life which begin to take shape in the opening phase will have to be reconnected and reassembled and affectively reintegrated in developmental context and in a restored continuity of life experience. The weight to be assigned to external and internal forces, to the remote past and the more immediate present, to adult as well as to infantile traumatic experience can only be surmised at the beginning of analysis. The first memories, dreams, and fantasies may contain the traumatic nucleus of the neurosis, more or less disguised. The patient's fear of regression, of loss of control, and of recurrent traumatic states should be gradually, tactfully, and consistently clarified and interpreted. This sets the stage for the uncovering of the intrapsychic experience of trauma in the course of analysis and analytic work on the unconscious fantasies representing the pathogenic conflicts and developmental fixations in which the trauma is always embedded.

Chapter 6

On Beginning an Analysis with a Young Adult

Theodore J. Jacobs, M.D.

Although the principles of beginning an analysis with a young adult do not differ in their essentials from those that guide the initial phase of analytic work with older individuals, there are special considerations related to the psychology of young people that make the launching of treatment in this age group a challenging task.

Standing astride the worlds of adolescent experimentation and adult responsibility, the young person in his late teens and early twenties often oscillates between them. No longer a youth but not yet a mature individual, and trying to make the shift from one to the other, the young person of today often feels adrift in unfamiliar territory. He yearns to go back to the security of his earlier years and yet he feels impelled to go forward. In adolescence much of his behavior resembles that of a customer in a new car showroom who checks out the models and tries out the equipment. Now he must get on the road.

Getting on the road for the young adult means dealing with the here and now. Faced with the age appropriate tasks of choosing a vocation, finding a mate, establishing a home of his own, and bringing long-held ideals and values into better alignment with reality, the young person's energies and interests are focused on the accomplishment of these goals. He wants to deal with the problems and challenges of the moment. He often wants to retreat to the comparative safety of childhood and to turn again to parental figures for nurturance and guidance, but he senses the danger stemming from that desire, and consequently he does not wish to look backwards. Keeping his eye on the tasks of the present and the immediate future, he becomes a living endorsement of Satchel Paige's famous saying: "Don't look back; something might be gaining on you."

Although many young people experience feelings of confusion, anxiety, and depression in the process of getting on the road, and as a consequence, seek professional help, they often do so with much ambivalence. Psychotherapy, and especially analysis, is often experienced as a threat on a number of levels. Attempting still to shed his dependence on parental figures, both in actuality and as internalized parental images, the young adult senses danger in the prospect of becoming reliant on another adult. For that reason he may intuitively wish to limit the frequency of appointments in order to avoid excessive dependency on the therapist. The mobilization in treatment of the old wishes, old fears, and old yearnings of childhood and adolescence also poses a threat. The young person fears the regression that often accompanies therapy. He is afraid, too, to revive memories of earlier traumatic experiences. Particularly where there have been significant losses, disruptions in the family, or a history of serious physical illness or disability, the young adult may resist tenaciously the awakening of such ghosts.

Late adolescence, as Adatto (1980) has pointed out, is the time in which an individual's sexual identity becomes solidified. This is, however, an evolving process and does not necessarily become fixed at any given age. The patient in his early twenties may still be struggling with this and other issues that are often associated with adolescence proper. This includes ongoing efforts to find solutions for both the positive and negative oedipal strivings which are reawakened with intensity in the adolescent years. Psychoanalytic treatment may reactivate old conflicts, in ways that the young person intuitively understands may threaten to upset the balance of forces which he has only recently achieved, and which is vulnerable to disruption under the impact of the transference. The young adult is in the process of establishing new bonds and new relationships both with peers and with potential mates. Many of these relationships, upon close scrutiny, are built upon old sibling and parental ties which form their foundation and which give them shape. The young adult patient has little interest in exploring the sources of these relationships. He needs to blind himself to their roots in order that the displacements and sublimations that are necessary to their development remain undisturbed.

New adjustments are taking place, too, in both the superego and ego ideal of the young adult. As Ritvo (1971) has pointed out, the remodeling of these structures is a necessary development in late adolescence. Here, too, the solutions arrived at, representing newly created compromise formations, may feel tentative to the young adult who, for fear of their being tampered with, resists their exploration in psychoanalytic treatment.

For these and a number of other reasons, young people often avoid analysis. Using as partial rationalizations the difficulties of time, money, and scheduling that often present themselves, the young person wishes to avoid the threats to his hard won stability that he associates with intensive treatment. Moreover many young adults are not yet financially independent and must still rely on their families to help support their treatment. For reasons mentioned above, young people resist such renewed dependency. And even if the patient can accept the idea of analysis, in today's world families are often reluctant to underwrite such treatment. Thus the barriers to psychoanalytic treatment of young adults are formidable. If he is to help patients get into analysis, the analyst must, from the outset, understand the nature of the forces that operate against its acceptance and work patiently and steadfastly to overcome these resistances. In some instances he may also have to see parents whose help is needed to sustain the treatment. In practice this means that young adult patients will often have to be treated in a preparatory face-to-face therapy and that, on occasion, in order to gain their support for analysis, several joint sessions with the parents may have to be scheduled.

If the patient does accept the idea of analysis and the treatment gets under way, the analyst will be faced with launching it in a way that maximizes the possibilities for the unfolding of an analytic process. While, as I have noted, the general principles of beginning an analysis apply equally to the young adult as to the older patient and treatment proceeds from the surface downwards with the interpretation of broad patterns of behavior and warded off affects taking center stage, it is often necessary in beginning work with young adults to emphasize certain aspects of technique and to defer the use of others.

Of great importance in initiating analytic work with the young adult who, for some time, has been sitting up in sessions, is exploration of the meaning to him of the change. While understanding the significance of such a shift is clearly important in all patients who undertake it, in the case of the young adult, progress in the analysis is often dependent on working through the anxieties generated by the use of the couch. For reasons already mentioned, young people are often frightened by the comparative lack of structure and the regression that accompanies lying down. Projecting their own fears and impulses onto the analyst, they fear an assault, sexual or aggressive, on the part of the therapist. This may lead to a paralysis in their ability to free associate and even to communicate in a meaningful way. Even if not obvious, the young person's anxieties may lead him, outside of his awareness, to be wary and self-protective. Thus, although he may seem to be cooperating and saying what comes to mind, in fact, much is unconsciously withheld. The patient is afraid to be touched by the analysis and so wraps himself in a barely visible but tightly woven cocoon. While he is loathe to acknowledge it, the young person has also gained much support from sitting up and being able to see his therapist. There is a feeling of stability associated with the vis-à-vis arrangement that is lost when the shift to the couch occurs. This leads not only to greater anxiety in the patient, but often to considerable resentment over what is experienced as an abandonment. Since this reaction is not rational and the young adult prides himself on his rationality, it often goes underground and is well disguised. It is, however, a response of great importance because it can become the nidus of a concealed, but powerful, negative transference that, undetected, can vitiate much useful work in analysis.

For these and other reasons it is necessary for the analyst, as he begins the analysis of a young adult, to investigate as thoroughly as possible his patient's experience in moving to the couch. If the patient does not bring up the matter, the analyst must do so. He may also have to interpret certain links between using the couch and childhood experiences that have not yet been expressed verbally but have been revealed through posture, gesture, movement, or other nonverbal means. In instances in which a patient has undergone prolonged medical treatments or surgery in childhood or adolescence, it is not unusual for him to experience the analytic procedure in light of these former, and often traumatic, treatments. Thus, a young man who, at age six, developed an acute abdomen and within hours underwent surgery followed by a long, painful recovery, resisted using the couch for many months. When, finally, he did so, he immediately covered his abdominal area with both hands and with his elbows extended attempted to create a barrier to ward off the expected attack by the surgeon–analyst. Another patient who, as a child, developed chronic ear infections which necessitated frequent and painful probing of his auditory canals by his doctor, initially assumed on the couch the identical bodily position that he adopted in the pediatrician's office when his ear was being examined.

It is not only treatments for illness and injuries that may unconsciously be evoked in memory by beginning an analysis. Memories of music, art, and Hebrew lessons or other religious instruction, confession to a priest, and being tutored on a one-to-one basis may be called up and be expressed through bodily movements as well as in dreams and associations. Helping the patient recognize the unconscious connections that he has made between the analytic procedure and these childhood experiences, some of which were felt to be unpleasant and anxiety-provoking, is a task that must be accomplished early on in treatment if the analysis is to be successfully launched.

Also of great importance in working with young people is the question of the analyst's role in the analytic process. While, as with all patients, he must listen carefully, giving the young adult maximum freedom to express himself, in treating this age group the analyst may have to intervene more actively than is the case with the older patient. Fearful of regression, often sensitive to the slightest hint of criticism, the young patient often equates the analyst's silence with disapproval and early on may have limited tolerance for it. Although the titration of silence is an important technical issue in any analysis, in work with young adults it takes on particular importance. The standard technique of listening silently for substantial periods of time may, with young people, have the effect of intensifying resistances. Similar considerations apply with regard to questions of tact and timing. Clearly, the proper timing of interpretations and the tactfulness with which they are phrased are matters of concern in the treatment of patients of any age group. In young people these issues are of critical importance. Poorly timed interpretations or ones that have a negative effect on self-esteem may raise a vulnerable young patient's level of anxiety to an unusually high pitch and increase his fear that the analytic process will be a destructive one. In some instances, the early and direct interpretations of sexual or aggressive material arising in dreams and associations has increased a young person's wariness to such a level that for long periods of time no analytic progress could take place. This situation typically occurs when the analyst has failed to recognize the vulnerability of the young person's self-esteem and the necessity of working slowly, with due respect for this patient's need to maintain defenses for extended periods of time.

Attempting to test himself in the world, trying to establish his competence vocationally, sexually, and in his relations with others, the young adult often feels himself to be woefully inadequate to these tasks. In juding his own shortcomings, he may utilize the standards of an only partially modified, and still unrealistically elevated, ego ideal. This self-criticism is augmented by superego pressures deriving from the need to contain strong sexual urges as well as powerful competitive strivings. The result, often enough, is a self-esteem system that can tolerate precious little in the way of critical comments from others. In this regard the young adult patient still has one foot in adolescence and the analyst's manner of intervening must take this important developmental factor into consideration.

A related technical issue of importance in beginning work with the young adult concerns the dosage and timing of defense and transference interpretations. Typically a young person, absorbed by the problems of everyday living and unable as yet to gain an overview of his contribution to those struggles, spends much time in the opening phase recounting the details of his activities and his interaction with others. The analyst is aware that such communications serve multiple functions. Not only do they express wishes, drives, values, anxieties, and superego pressures, but they are utilized to a significant degree in the service of defense. Not infrequently, especially in individuals with obsessional qualities, the defensive aspect of the communication is its most significant component. In older patients early interpretation of this defense is often useful as it gives the patient beginning insight into the automatic quality of his protective mechanisms and the anxieties that lie behind them. In the young adult patient, such interpretations, given early, may cut off the narrative and the flow of important, though largely defensive, material. The young person initially needs to have a listener who will hear him out, who will pay attention to every exquisite detail of his embattled existence, and who will appreciate the importance of his moment-to-moment struggle. With many such patients the interpretation of defense—or of transference—must wait until this unburdening process has run its course and the young person has had ample opportunity to tell his story.

As he listens, the analyst comments on the action. He does so in several ways; by identifying those affects that are close to the surface and, by naming them, helping them to emerge; by tactfully pointing out repetitive patterns of behavior that are outside the patient's awareness, and by beginning to make connections between the patient's current experiences and aspects of his history. In carrying out these tasks in the opening phase, the analyst not only contributes to building an alliance with his young patient, but, through his interventions, he begins to enlarge his patient's vistas. It is only later in the analysis of young adults, when the alliance is firmer and preparatory work of the kind just mentioned has been accomplished, that interpretations of defense and transference can be expected to produce the kinds of useful insights that we hope will follow from such interventions.

No analyst can follow a set of abstract guidelines, however, and there are instances in the analysis of young people when the active interpretation of defense and of transference resistances must be carried out from the opening bell. In these cases the young person's resistances are such that they have blocked any effective communication. These resistances must then be interpreted in order for the analysis to proceed. In some instances, it is even necessary to offer early interpretations of "deep" drive-oriented material.

Such was the case in my work with a shy, artistic young man of twenty who sought analysis because of multiple inhibitions and phobias. From the outset of the analysis silence was a formidable problem. Try as he might, the patient could not bring himself to speak. For hours he lay on the couch mute and acutely uncomfortable. When he did manage to say a few words, it was only to comment on certain art objects in the room. This communication, sparse as it was, however, was a clue to what was happening. In the course of preparatory therapy, in which silence was not a significant feature, the patient related an incident, occurring at age twelve, in which at the invitation of a junior high school coach he went with him to a ball game. After the game, they returned to the coach's studio apartment where the older man made advances to the youth, lying on a sofa with him and fondling his genitals through his trousers. They boy lay motionless, paralyzed with fear, and to distance himself, looked at all the curios in the room. And while the sexual activity was taking place, the boy asked an occasional question about these objects. Clearly, the patient was experiencing the beginning of his analysis as a frightening and stimulating seduction which paralyzed his ability to communicate. Behind this reaction were active homosexual conflicts which, in fact, contributed in important ways to his symptoms. Although the material was "deep" and quite anxiety-provoking, it had to be interpreted from the outset. A connection was made between the patient's experiences on the couch and memories of the episode with the coach. In addition, his reluctance to speak was interpreted as a fear that if he let down his guard he would discover that he was gay. These interventions were offered in as supportive and nonthreatening a manner as possible and the metacommunication that accompanied them, though not verbalized, conveyed the idea that the patient's fears were ones that could be understood and worked with. This calm and implicitly reassuring tone, together with the acts of giving a name to his terrors and placing them in an understandable historical context, went far in relieving his anxiety. In response to these interventions the patient began to speak, and in his analysis silence was never again a formidable resistance.

To illustrate other aspects of the opening phase of the analysis of a young adult I would like briefly to cite two additional clinical examples.

Ms. R. first consulted me when she was nineteen and a transfer student at a local university. Although she was an attractive, highly intelligent, and most capable young woman, she was rendered almost nonfunctional by multiple phobias which were superimposed on a steady state of diffuse and pervasive anxiety.

Ms. R. spoke and acted like a young adolescent and in her plaintive voice appealed to me for advice and guidance. She wanted me to provide a formula for eliminating her anxiety which she could memorize and apply when needed.

At first impression I thought that Ms. R. might, in fact, be a very fragile person whose impaired ego was not equal to the task of modulating the strong and chaotic impulses that tormented her. I imagined her to be a borderline personality whose defenses, clearly under a state of siege, badly needed shoring up. As I got to know Ms. R. in the course of an extended consultation period, however, I began to have a very different view of her. Beneath the surface presentation of a helpless, overwhelmed child, there was a highly capable and knowledgeable woman who was in retreat from both her sexuality and her competitive strivings. Her childlike facade and the myriad symptoms that she had developed stemmed from the same source: her fear of growing up and becoming a sexual and competent woman who was able to compete for a place in the world. Although Ms. R. begged me for support and I was tempted to meet her needs by supplying the direction, guidance, and reassurance that she craved from a benign parental figure, I soon realized that such an approach would not do justice to her strengths and considerable potential. This was a young woman with a long-standing neurosis. In early and mid-adolescence she had undergone two brief periods of psychotherapy, and while these treatments helped stabilize her, the basic structure of her personality had remained unchanged.

Psychoanalysis was clearly the treatment of choice and this is what I recommended. Initially Ms. R. could not accept the recommendation, and hearing about it, her family was shocked and outraged. Behind Ms. R.'s rejection of analysis lay much fear. She was terrified that analysis would cause her to lose control of her impulses so that she would become wildly sexual and aggressive. She was also afraid that she would revert to being a helpless child. The idea of lying on a couch totally exposed and made vulnerable to attack left her weak with anxiety. Moreover she was wary lest, in the course of analysis, her considerable rage at men and the castrative wishes that accompanied it be exposed. Twice a week therapy was all that Ms. R. and her family could accept and so twice a week therapy was begun. The central goal of this therapy, however, was to explore Ms. R.'s fear of analysis.

Gradually, over a period of several months, Ms. R. was able to discuss these fears, and slowly her anxiety about analysis was reduced. By the end of this introductory phase of treatment, she could not only accept the idea of analysis, but looked forward to beginning the treatment.

Ms. R.'s parents, however, were adamant in their refusal to support an analysis. Since she had no independent means, Ms. R. was totally reliant on their help to finance any treatment that she undertook. Without the parents concurrence there would be no analysis. Faced with this situation, I decided to meet the parents. I realized that such a meeting could lead to later complications, but I thought that whatever difficulties arose might be worked out if analysis could get under way. Ms. R. was given the option of being present at this interview, but she declined.

As it turned out, the parents were more understanding and reasonable than I had supposed. Although both had reservations about the effectiveness of analysis and could not, without sacrifice, bear its expense, when I explained something about their daughter's condition and the reasons for my recommendation, they agreed to support the analysis. They did so, with only minor grumbling, for the next four years.

Beginning the analysis with Ms. R. was no easy task. Although we had discussed her fears and she had some understanding of them, the actual fact of lying on a couch with the analyst out of sight mobilized the most intense anxiety in her. She could barely lie down and every few minutes would turn around and look at me. She needed to see me and to check out what I was doing. During some sessions she lay on her stomach and spoke directly to me. Not only was she frightened by the intensity of her sexual fantasies, but she missed my reassuring presence. In her anxious state she wanted me with her.

Repeatedly I connected her fear of lying down and not seeing me with certain experiences of her childhood involving close and frightening physical proximity to her father. Slowly more memories of these times emerged. As they did, Ms. R. gradually settled down, her anxiety diminished, and she showed evidence of being able to tolerate the analytic process.

In the early months of treatment Ms. R. filled the hours with lengthy recitations about her classes, activities, and roommates. These were described in exhaustive, if novelistic, detail. Although these accounts served primarily defensive purposes, they provided useful information about Ms. R.'s world and her view of it. These recitations were also designed unconsciously to test her analyst. Ms. R. wanted to know if I was truly interested in her and could bear to hear the minutiae of her daily existence or whether, like her parents, I would lose interest and begin to tune out. It was only after I had passed the test by careful and patient listening and by offering ideas about aspects of her behavior that she had not thought about that Ms. R. could trust me sufficiently to hear interpretations aimed at showing her how her narrative style served both to avoid dealing with more frightening issues and to keep me at a safe distance.

Following this initial period of analysis, which lasted about two months, Ms. R.'s behavior shifted to a mode that is not uncommon in the opening phase of treatment with young adults. She began a period of diffuse and uncontrolled acting out which made analytic work all but impossible and which tested in the severest way the analyst's capacity to persevere in the treatment. Ms. R. missed classes, failed to turn in her assignments, took dangerous drugs, and engaged in promiscuous sex. She became pregnant and had an abortion, all the time rationalizing her behavior as necessary experimentation.

While engaged in this behavior, she kept one eye on her analyst. Provocative and challenging, daring me to intervene, she desperately wanted me to do so.

This behavior mirrored a period in Ms. R.'s early adolescence when, under pressure from erupting sexuality, peer influences, inner demands to excel in school, and the need to separate from parents, she acted in provocative and antisocial ways. Falling in with a group of school delinquents, Ms. R. soon became one of them. She drank heavily, smoked marijuana, acted out sexually, and engaged in shoplifting. Although this stormy period came to an end in midadolescence, the conflicts that fueled it had not been resolved. They surfaced again in treatment when strong aggressive and sexual conflicts, mobilized by the transference, once again threatened to overwhelm Ms. R. Desperately, like a teenager, my patient sought to provoke me into controlling her behavior and punishing her for it. Coming early on in the analysis, this period of acting out posed a serious threat to its continuance. Increasingly, Ms. R. got herself into dangerous situations. On several occasions she was mugged while making drug purchases in unsavory neighborhoods and once barely escaped being raped. Often high on drugs, she rarely attended classes, failed to turn in assignments, and was on the verge of flunking out of college.

In the face of such self-destructive behavior I was tempted on more than one occasion to abandon analytic neutrality and to intervene actively. To do so, however, would have been to enact with my patient a scenario in which she played the role of a child who is helplessly out of control and in danger and I the role of the good parent who demonstrates my love for her by saving her from herself. This was Ms. R.'s effort to reverse a script that was written in early adolescence. In those years she felt alone, abandoned by confused and ineffectual parents, but now she was inviting me, as a strong limit-setting father, to come to the rescue. Instead of joining Ms. R. in this complex enactment, however, I made efforts to interpret it. For some time these efforts fell on deaf ears and on several occasions I found myself resorting to the desperate maneuver described by a colleague as interpreting all the way to the door.

Part of Ms. R.'s unconscious motivation in acting out so self-destructively was to disrupt the analysis. Although, rationally, she recognized the importance of continuing in treatment and working through the conflicts that gave rise to her symptoms, on a deeper level the analysis was experienced as a threat to her stability. For that reason she tried to force me to intervene and, in that manner, effectively put an end to the analysis.

While such behavior may occur at various stages in the analysis of young adults, there are two junctures in treatment at which it is most common. The first is in the opening phase when the young person begins to experience the regressive pull of the transference, his defenses come under scrutiny, and dependency needs are mobilized. Feeling threatened and realizing that analysis may entail a good deal more discomfort than he had bargained for, the young adult may feel frightened and trapped. To these feelings he frequently reacts by acting out the mix of impulses, affective states, and defenses that besiege him. The second juncture at which such behavior occurs with some frequency takes place well into the analysis when perverse fantasies threaten to surface. This is another critical period in analysis and, like the opening phase, is a time in which young people are most likely to break off treatment.

It is essential, when acting out occurs, for the analyst to interpret the threatening aspects of the transference as promptly as possible. While older patients experience similar fears of their transference feelings and may also be tempted to flee the analysis, they are less likely to behave impulsively. For young people action is the name of the game and they often act on impulse. It is not uncommon therefore for certain young adults to be analyzed in segments, over a period of time. When in distress they will seek out a therapist, work in treatment for a while, and then when the core of their neurotic conflicts threatens to be exposed, they find a reason to end the treatment. While it is not always possible to prevent such disruptions in treatment, recognition of a young person's need to avoid conflict, to rationalize his behavior, and to use action as a major vehicle for the expression of conflict allows for early and active interpretation of a defensive style that, if not confronted, often brings analysis to a premature close.

My second example will be a brief one. It concerns a young man, Mr. K., who sought help some six months after having seen another analyst in consultation. This former consultation lasted for one session. In the course of it the analyst told the patient that he needed an analysis and recommended that they begin as soon as possible. While the consultant had much reason to make such a recommendation, Mr. K. was not prepared at that time to hear it. Feeling threatened by the prospect of an intense treatment that would expose all of his vulnerabilities and that, in his imagination, was reserved only for severely troubled individuals, he fled from the idea and from the analyst who had proposed it. It took a number of months, during which time Mr. K. felt quite depressed, before he could summon up enough courage to seek another consultation.

It soon became apparent that the first analyst was quite correct in his judgment. Mr. K. was a bright, articulate, psychologically minded young man whose long-standing neurotic conflicts interfered in substantial ways with the productive use of his considerable abilities. Moreover, he had been suffering from a moderately severe depression since graduating from college five months earlier. While clearly, it is important with all patients for a relationship between them and the consultant to be established and an adequate understanding of their history and dynamics obtained before the recommendation for analysis be made, in the case of the young adult it is often necessary to defer this recommendation for several months or until an extended consultation period has been completed. Such an open-ended consultation allows a young person ample time to get acquainted with the therapist and with the process of therapy.

As was true of Ms. R., Mr. K. had a great many fears of analysis and it took three months of twice weekly visits before the idea of analysis could be broached. It then required another month of clarification and discussion before Mr. K. could accept the recommendation.

While he shared with Ms. R. much anxiety over becoming dependent on the analyst, losing control of sexual and aggressive impulses, having his defenses disrupted and, as a consequence, falling into a deep depression, Mr. K. also had a specific reason for fearing analysis. As an adolescent his older sister had been in analysis. In the course of the treatment, she became defiant and antagonistic toward her parents, began to act in hostile and provocative ways, and eventually moved out of the house. Her relationship with the parents since that time was minimal, with much antagonism on both sides. The parents blamed the analysis for causing this painful situation. Although he did not agree with their perspective on what had happened, Mr. K. feared that for him analysis would also lead to alienation from his family.

Other factors, too, played a role in Mr. K.'s anxiety about beginning an analysis and these had to be dealt with from the outset of treatment. The only son in a family of four children, Mr. K. was doted on by the women around him and the amount of attention he received served to stimulate competition with his father. Since, however, the boy could not best his successful and accomplished father either in competition for women or in the sphere of intellectual accomplishment, he withdrew from such competition rather than suffer the feeling of profound humiliation that regularly accompanied his failure to prevail in any contest.

Since Mr. K.'s father was highly invested in the world of ideas, Mr. K. turned away from this arena. He did poorly in school, did not like to read, and avoided abstractions of any kind. Instead he concentrated on things concrete and tangible. He was skilled with his hands and became an expert carpenter and electrician. In high school and college he extended his interests to the visual arts and achieved recognition for his original sculptures.

Mr. K. regarded analysis as falling into the province of his father. It dealt with thoughts, words, and ideas. There was nothing concrete about it. Moreover, his father had been analyzed and often talked of the unique contribution that analysis had made to his life. Mr. K. felt that he could not compete with his father as an analytic patient and was ready early on to drop out of treatment. It was necessary at the beginning of the analysis to work actively with these fears. So strong were they, that for some time they threatened the existence of the therapy. When necessary (but only when necessary) a transference interpretation was made linking the patient's perception of me to memories of his father. The interpretation was made to help Mr. K. understand the strong feelings of despair that overcame him when he compared himself to me. At those times, too, he wanted to leave treatment to avoid competition.

For the most part the early weeks and months of the analysis were given over to clarifying Mr. K.'s fears of the analytic process and their roots. Although many of these matters were discussed while he was sitting up, the experience of using the couch brought them to the surface with an immediacy and vividness that had not been there before.

Some of Mr. K.'s fears of analysis were traceable to painful treatments that he received in adolescence for a chronic medical condition. Unconsciously he linked the analysis to a medical procedure that, for many years, had caused him much pain.

On a deeper level, both Mr. K.'s heterosexual and homosexual impulses caused him much anxiety. He was particularly afraid that homosexual longings would be aroused in treatment with a man and so at the beginning of the analysis he spent much time describing his conquests of women. This material, and the patient's recitation of it, was utilized very largely in the service of defense. Not only was Mr. K. avoiding recognition of homosexual impulses through concentration on the heterosexual but by throwing himself into repeated affairs and recounting these adventures in analysis he was behaving in a counterphobic way. Behind his devil-may-care attitude was a frightened young man who suffered from pervasive castration anxiety and who, as a consequence, feared that he would not be able to perform sexually.

Although the defensive aspect of Mr. K.'s lengthy descriptions of his affairs were apparent from the outset of the analysis, they were not interpreted for some time. It was important in the initial weeks for Mr. K. to tell his story, for him to feel that he was being listened to with careful attentiveness, and for him to begin to build an alliance with someone, who, unlike his father, was not continually showing up his deficits. If his defensive maneuvers had been interpreted early on in the analysis, as is often done in the case of older patients, Mr. K. would not have been able to process the analyst's words correctly or to make use of them. He was too anxious and too ready to hear criticisms from an older parent figure. Mr. K.'s readiness to be self-critical would also have contributed to the inevitable distortion of the analyst's message. It was necessary to wait, to allow Mr. K. to develop trust in the analyst and in the analytic process and to feel that he was a valuable contributor to both.

What I am stressing in the above example is the overriding importance of tact and timing in working with young adults. While these issues exist in every analysis and are of particular significance in the opening phase of treatment, in the analysis of young adults the way in which these issues are handled often spells the difference between an analysis that is successfully launched and one that fails to get off the ground.

An example of the latter situation occurred in the analysis of a bright, obsessional man of twenty-one who, like Mr. K., had much anxiety over his sexual impulses. These he could not speak about in analysis—nor could he talk meaningfully about much else. His hours were filled with ruminations and intellectual speculations. Understanding his defenses against the development of a homosexual transference and against revealing both his deep sense of inferiority and his long-standing wish to be a girl, I tried from the beginning of treatment to acquaint the patient with his resistances to free association and the reasons for them. This effort fell on deaf ears and, in fact, feeling criticized and put down as he had been by his parents and several older siblings, he developed increasingly negative feelings toward me. The analytic process ground to a halt. It was only when, for a period of time, I abandoned my persistent efforts to interpret resistances and listened to the other messages that, along with the defensive maneuvers, were embedded within his communications, that this young man felt sufficiently understood and accepted for him to begin to delve into his deeper fears. Of course it was necessary, later on, to spend much time analyzing the patient's formidable resistances, but this aspect of the work could not be undertaken early in treatment. This situation contrasts sharply with our usual technical approach in working with older patients and it is these variations, not so much in the techniques themselves but in the manner and timing of their application, that characterizes analytic work with the young adult.

In summary, it can be said that the analysis of young adults, while offering rich possibilities for therapeutic benefits at a time of life when in-depth understanding of oneself is uniquely valuable, is a treatment that is underused. This situation is largely due to the fact that the forward thrust of development in young adulthood, combined with fears of regression and of the opening up of old wounds, focuses the young person's interests on the present and immediate future. Many therapists, including analysts, intuitively sense the young person's fear of looking back and of opening up old wounds, and collude with him in avoiding in-depth treatment.

Helping a young adult accept analysis is not an easy task. In most instances, it can be accomplished only slowly, after the ground has been well prepared. In practice this means that the analyst may have to offer a lengthy consultation period or a period of introductory psychotherapy prior to recommending analysis. After the recommendation has been made, it is often necessary for the analyst to work quite extensively with the young person's fears of and resistances to analysis before the recommendation can be implemented.

In beginning the analysis, the analyst must be aware that the usual techniques that he utilizes in initiating treatment with the older patient may have to be modified. While the interpretation of resistance and of transference constitutes the core of analytic work with young adults as it does with patients of any age, the manner and timing of their use requires careful thought.

In beginning the analysis of young people it is of particular importance for the analyst, while listening carefully and holding up a mirror to the patient so that he can view his own behavior, to refrain for some time from interpretations that increase anxiety or conflict with the patient's self-esteem. By working tactfully and deferring such interventions until the young person is ready to hear them, the analyst allows his patient sufficient time and space to develop the feelings of safety and trust in the analytic process that are essential for its further unfolding. For it is only when the young adult, after testing the waters for some time, has assured himself that he can expose his vulnerabilities without fear of criticism, humiliation, or disruption to his emotional stability that the analysis can truly get under way.

Chapter 7

On Beginning a Reanalysis

Milton H. Horowitz, M.D.

The work of reanalysis is a continuing study of both the psychology of disappointment and the inner workings of hope.

It is difficult to attempt any systematic evaluation of reanalyses. Generalizations are difficult and the sufferings of individuals are rarely comparable. The experiences of different analysts are also difficult of comparison. I have loosely assembled some personal impressions gathered over many years. These notes are based upon seventeen reanalyses. In three of the cases I worked with patients I had seen earlier in my career where the analyses had seemed to have terminted in an adequate way. Two more cases were patients seen by me where the work had been interrupted. The other twelve had worked with other analysts, in analysis not in psychotherapy. About half the patients initially viewed the first analysis as successful and the other half considered the earlier work to have failed. In addition, I had the opportunity of comparing notes with three analysts who had reanalyzed patients seen by me in the past, two where my work had been a failure.

Kris (1951) noted that: "no truly experimental conditions can be achieved in which the effects of alternative interpretations can be studied" (p. 21). He then commented that reanalysis provides a possible opportunity for such study. We may now add that reanalysis provides an opportunity for the reevaluation of the entire analytic endeavor: diagnosis, indications for analysis, technique, and the theories of therapeutic results and therapeutic failure. Analysts and analysands may have quite different theories of therapeutic success and failure. Such theories are rooted in the mélange of observations and old fantasy systems that are characteristic of human thought.

These notes will emphasize real clinical experience and only touch upon theoretical considerations. They will not be systematic nor complete but are aimed toward achieving an overall perspective on beginning reanalytic work.

THE INITIAL CONSULTATION

Here is a rare and dramatic interview between the author and a man in his forties, academic in outlook, seeking a third analysis.

> *Analyst:* How may I help you?
> *Patient:* This is like the myth of Sisyphus.
> *Analyst:* The myth of Sisyphus?
> *Patient:* (impatiently) You know the myth of Sisyphus!
> *Analyst:* Yes, but tell me . . .
> *Patient:* (with mild irritation) You know! Sisyphus had to roll a rock back up a hill; it would slip back; that's what all these analyses have been. (Pause) He was punished for treachery to the gods. (Pause) Oh my God! This is too pat! I don't believe it. (Quietly) I don't believe it.

The patient then went on to describe his feeling of responsibility in revealing to his father that his mother was having an affair with a neighbor. The father packed a suitcase and left home. The parents were divorced. These facts had been repeated throughout the two prior analyses. He insisted that he was *"responsible but definitely not guilty."* Until this interchange, despite repeated prior interpretation, he had denied the feeling of guilt. His life history had been replete with self-punishing failures and disastrous relationships with women; it was an unrecognized model of moral masochism. His character structure was obsessional, and isolation of affect was prominent in his presentation of himself. Interpretations of his need to punish himself for the disruption of his parents' marriage had been warded off by saying that he "didn't feel it." When, during the course of the new analysis, we reviewed the first session, he thanked me for what he called my "naiveté" in making him tell the myth of Sisyphus. This unusual event illustrates an overriding principle in consultations, especially with patients seeking reanalysis. Make no assumptions that you know what the patient means, or that you "understand" the patient. The wish and the need to be understood, important as they are for all human beings, may serve as a resistance against being explicit or candid. The "empathic" response may faciliate work with some patients but hinder it with others where an illusion of being understood clouds the patient's exploratory curiosity. This patient's childhood curiosity, exploration, and explicit tattling had all led to disaster and guilt. What a set of choices! But in this interview, guilt momentarily became *conscious* and meaningful change in the structure of conscience could begin.

The initial consultations are to set an analytic atmosphere to establish a connection between patient and analyst which is explanatory and in which issues of transference and resistance make their appearance at the outset. During the consultative process patients often begin, unconsciously, as if the analyst knew a great deal about them. The consultation seems to be a continuation of the prior treatment. The analysand is in the midst of something and the analyst has to begin from scratch.

The initial task is to try to know the total personality and not merely to search out the psychopathology. The suffering patients are likely to present themselves with symptoms uppermost. Their positive capacities and strengths are frequently kept in the shadowy background. The panoramic view of the total personality is the guide for the entire analytic endeavor. The concept of psychoanalytic "diagnosis" is a very broad one, embracing not only the descriptive phenomenology but much else. We want the widest assessment of object relations and the capacity for love and sexuality. We need an understanding of ego functions (memory, thinking, self-observation, identifications, defense, control of regression and affect, adaptiveness, capacity for work, for playful imagination, for humor). Moreover, we want to understand superego functions (guilt, self-criticism, self-punitive trends). Not only is the cross-sectional viewpoint necessary (how do things look at the moment), but the longitudinal viewpoint of history provides a glimpse of indications for analysis as well as some prognostic clues. Not every patient seeking reanalysis should be back in analysis. For about half of the patients I have seen in consultation, other forms of treatment seemed more appropriate. Focusing on symptom complexes alone will obscure the picture; two patients with somewhat similar symptoms may have vastly different underlying psychopathology and vastly different prognoses. Choice of treatment should hinge upon the more wide-ranging attempts at "diagnosis." Ultimately, for some patients diagnosis will depend upon a trial of analysis.

These early interviews have to narrow the gulf between two people engaged in a rather peculiar form of conversation. The patient is also assessing the analyst and the analytic procedure. Prior analysis does not mean that the earlier treatment was appropriate then or now, or that the choice of analysis was or is appropriate. For some patients earlier analysis had been undertaken incautiously. Everything is to be the subject of inquiry.

A lonely man of forty-two had been in an extended, unsuccessful analysis for many years, concluded only by the illness of the analyst. The patient described a pan-neurosis with anxiety, phobias, depression, and obsessional symptoms. He was very successful at his work which required little contact with other people. His only partial therapeutic relief had been in the continuous supportive link with his devoted analyst, which had been accompanied by the patient's fantasies of fusion. An extended consultation helped clarify the contained borderline schizophrenic process. Both the patient and the prior analyst had been clearly aware of the severity of the disturbance. A directly supportive psychotherapy without analytic trappings proved helpful.

FANTASIES OF THERAPEUTIC SUCCESS OR FAILURE

Very soon after beginning the evaluative process, patients tend to present their ideas about why the prior analysis did not succeed or why it did not prevent a return of suffering. With rare exceptions, the "blame" is placed upon the person of the analyst. The analyst is said to have done something noxious or not to have done something loving or caring. As with many human attitudes, there is usually a kernel of truth in the report. But with striking regularity the "theory of therapeutic failure" offered by the patient bears uncanny resemblance to the patient's fantasies of neurosogenesis.

Abend (1979) and Arlow (1981) explored the relationship between unconscious fantasy and theories of cure and of pathogenesis. The authors emphasized that both analyst and analysand might share similar fantasies and that technique and outcome may well be influenced by jointly held unconscious wishes. Each individual has a wholly idiosyncratic unconscious fantasy life which tends to become patterned through a lifetime. The transformations of these fantasies become more complex with maturation and development. New events lead to new conflicts and alterations of function into new editions. Old fantasies can serve new functions. Fantasies *about* pathogenesis, however, tend to be simplified and reductionistic and generally fall into a few categories: traumatic, toxic, and deficit disorder. Arlow described these as related to the "quest for the villain." Patients' fantasies of therapeutic failure usually parallel their ideas of pathogenesis. The "quest for the villain" now falls upon the analyst, and seems to be unrelated to the analyst's school of thought or theoretical predilection. Sometimes the appearance of new symptoms brings a patient back after a successful prior treatment. When the patient tries to explain the earlier success, he often falls back upon fantasies of curative factors whose unconscious roots had been present long before the treatment started. It is one of the tasks of reanalysis to address the relative fixity of old fantasy and psychic structure. In *no* instance did any of the seventeen patients spontaneously connect therapeutic outcome with those resistances to exploration and change which subsequently appeared in the reanalysis. The very nature of these fantasies invites countertransference response. The patients make an appeal to any new analyst's narcissism and competitiveness. They often want the old analyst to be castigated for imperfection of character, bad technique, insufficient empathy, too much empathy, talking too much, talking too little. There are projections of defense: a sexually inhibited man said his analyst would not let him be sexual, a masochistic woman said her analyst would not let her be angry. The new analyst is implored to be the vehicle of delivery of the fantasy of cure. If something did not work in prior analysis, the task is to search out the complexity of contributing factors, not to be in competition with the analyst whose work was not sufficiently fruitful.

TRANSFERENCE RESPONSES AT THE ONSET OF REANALYSIS

Generally my experience has been that the many issues of transference to be explored are clouded at the beginning by a facade of idealization. In the hope that this time analysis might work, the new analyst is imbued with the characteristics of a redeemer. The analyst is asked to make all the old dreams come true. A clinical vignette follows:

A fearful, angry unmarried woman in her forties sought consultation after a failed analysis. A few sessions later, she looked at me with starry-eyed hope. I was supposed by her to have understood her remarkably. I was flabbergasted; I was in fact completely puzzled by her. After the analysis began, she told me that she had heard of a former patient who had married after an analysis; moreover she heard that *all* my patients got married! This feat was to be performed for her and this action would serve as reproach to her younger sister who had declared the patient "unlovable." In the patient's fantasy, this had come to mean "unanalyzable." Her hoped-for success would then reproach the first analyst.

The wish for revenge is a powerful motive for both seeking analysis and defeating it.

A man in his fifties had been in analysis with many analysts since his twenties. It was difficult to know what first brought him to analysis or why he continued to seek it out. His complaints about the various analysts paralleled his reproaches to his parents: lack of concern and coldness. The issue of empathic lack was specially virulent toward someone he styled as a "self psychologist" who was "supposed to be a specialist in empathy." The patient had a fantasy that all his failures in life were reproaches to his parents whose crime was that they had many children. The patient's unconscious crime was in wishing the death of the whole lot. To justify his sadistic fantasies he had to prove his victims dastardly. He was deeply ashamed of his identification with the Nazis, and pitifully apologetic to his Jewish analyst. Careful analysis of the past relationships to the other analysts demonstrated that they were not as originally depicted; instead of being lumped together in a category of defect, they took on individual character. Many of them had, in fact, been helpful.

It is the new analyst's task to faciliate the reevocation of the older therapeutic efforts and to analyze them in the present.

RESISTANCES IN REANALYSIS

When Freud at the end of his career placed the greatest emphasis on the analysis of resistance he was pointing to the necessity of reliving pathogenic conflicts in the analytic situation. It was not an intellectualizing process that was sought but something that touched the heart. Insight is not an intellectual process but an affect-laden triumph of integrating functions (Kris, 1956b). Insight usually follows the crumbling of resistance structures. In a recent paper on insight (1987), I had noted how frequently insights achieved in prior treatment had been reduced to clichés. These précislike statements have a structure similar to screen memories. The reductionistic formulas of pseudo-insight serve as resistances against exploration of what actually happened with other therapists. They were often mocking, as if to say, "What nonsense!" A recent supervisory experience with a colleague conducting a reanalysis alerted me to a related phenomenon: the patient behaved as if only the present experience was meaningful and the past was dross, echoing Henry Ford's dictum that "history was bunk." The recent past and the distant past were hidden behind a sarcastic antihistorical stance.

WHY ANALYSES FAIL

The most frequent clinically demonstrated reason for therapeutic failure is that certain analyses should not have been attempted in the first place. Sometimes this is because of inadequate evaluation and faulty analytic diagnosis. Sometimes it seems related to a mismatch between analyst and analysand. Not every patient is analyzable by every analyst. But there are many instances where failures are only partial. Here my experience seems to point toward two major factors:

1. unanalyzed and perhaps unanalyzable transference reactions, and
2. unanalyzed and perhaps unanalyzable resistances.

These factors had been highlighted in Freud's *Analysis Terminable and Interminable* (1937) in a manner which remains powerfully useful. Freud discussed what he considered limiting factors in the work:

1. The tendency to cling to the mental representation of the early objects and the early modes of gratification.

2. The special tendency toward conflict in certain individuals, a tendency Freud related to aggression. To this we may add constitutionally determined predispositions to anxiety.
3. Conflicts about masculinity and femininity (i.e., fantasies about genital damage and the wish to be of the opposite sex).
4. Resistances determined by the unconscious need for punishment.

These limiting factors do not predict failure; rather they serve to scale down our expectations in some cases and to increase technical alertness in others. Freud's comments provide us with a framework of questions we may ask of the clinical data when starting a reanalysis. In each instance we must try to gauge the contribution to the process made by both participants; the patient and the analyst. Technique has seemed the province of the analyst. Little examined in discussions of technique is the question of how the patient worked at the analysis; in essence, the patient's technique. Analysis is a conjoint effort, not something analysts do to patients. The study of the patient's contribution to the mode of analyzing is critical to understanding clinical failure and clinical success. It is almost instantly directly observable but attention must be drawn to it.

Early dreams tend to alert us to powerful resistances which will appear in more explicit form later in the analysis. I will single out one issue in relation to early dreams: femininity and masculinity.

A woman dreamed after the first consultation (following a partially failed analysis) that she and "an analyst" were on a hiking trip in the Rockies. A rest stop is made and she urinates with a very thick penis. She awakens with the feeling that the consultations are unnecessary. Her associations were of envious memories of her brother who has a close business relationship with their father. Furthermore she envied her first analyst's male patients whom she took to be analytic candidates. "You will ascribe that to penis envy," she says dismissively. When I intervene and point out how lonely she feels, she cries. She hates to cry and thinks only women cry. If she were a boy she wouldn't need analysis. She claims that she didn't dream much during the first analysis.

A man dreams after the second month of the new analysis that he arrives at the waiting room to find a very beautiful woman lounging seductively. He is enraged at the idea that the analyst has given the hour to this woman. She is short and wearing very high-heeled shoes. The patient is short and used to try on his mother's shoes in early adolescence. He had fantasies that women always got what they wanted.

In both examples the dreams had their counterparts in shame-laden masturbatory fantasy. In both patients specific fantasies linked to specific masturbatory practices presented powerful resistances to the analytic work. In effect, both patients desired an abrogation of their biological reality. The pattern of resistance had been heralded in the early dreams, but did not assume full form until considerably later in the course of the work. The connection to masturbatory practices took a very long period of time.

Early dreams often alert us to negative therapeutic reactions and the underlying unconscious need for punishment.

A woman who had a disastrous attempt at analysis with a very imperious, poorly trained woman analyst dreams that she pulls a lever and hits the jackpot at a casino slot machine. Silver dollars pour all over the floor. When she tries to pick them up she sees that her hand is cut and bleeding and she cannot gather up the money. She associates the new analysis to hitting the jackpot but conveys the fantasy that whenever anything good happens something bad follows. She believes that she chose the first analyst thinking that she wasn't a good doctor but she charged small fees.

The dream announced a pattern of suffering and failure following each advance. This daunting resistance makes one very respectful of the power of guilty fantasy. Being alert at the beginning could do nothing to head off the full force of self-punitive ideas, but having a roadmap reduces the surprises of the journey.

THE IMPORTANCE OF FANTASY LIFE IN THE MAINTENANCE OF RESISTANCE

The relative persistence of organized fantasy in the life of individuals who have subjected themselves to analytic scrutiny is quite astonishing. In the realm of unconscious fantasy there tends to be a remarkable sameness, with some small variations, throughout most of a lifetime. The stereotypy of conscious daydreams becomes subject to day to day variations. A phenomenon akin to the use of the day residue in the dream work would seem to account for these variations. New perceptions and new objects of desire are incorporated into old basic patterns giving the illusion of new fantasy. Essentially one sees a new cast of characters playing out an old script.

Daydreams and masturbatory fantasies are directly available to the patient's consciousness. Often, they are kept from the analysis by a barrier of anxiety, shame, or guilt; sometimes the patient will not share the fantasies because they are greatly cherished and there is a fear that the analyst will plunder them or destroy their magic for secret pleasure. Unconscious fantasy is allowed conscious representation by a variety of deletions and other unconscious editorial practices.

In many of the patients I have seen in reanalysis there seems to have been a widespread blockage against the exploration of daydreams. Though in some instances this is a special example of clinging to the early objects and to early modes of gratification, in many patients the early model of fantasy undergoes a change of function. It becomes a template of the ego function of defense.

A clinical example follows:

A young woman who had attempted an unsuccessful analysis in her late adolescence and early adult life had a persistent secret masturbatory fantasy which she withheld. She is lying in bed in a darkened room. A very tall man enters the room, undresses slowly, and reveals a huge penis. She feels almost hypnotized and powerless. The man whispers to her that he will force her to have an orgasm. She silently vows that she will not respond. The painful intercourse seems interminable and against her will she has an explosive orgasm. After months of analysis, she reveals with shame that she has masturbated with some variations of this fantasy every day since she began to menstruate. The revelation follows an interpretation that she behaves as if she is being forced to be in analysis. The fantasy had become the model for resistance in the analytic work.

Conscious fantasy may provide important data in understanding the form of resistance. The shape of inner life determines the shape of behavior.

Conscious fantasy *about the analysis itself* can be sequestered and thus can hide other fantasies critical to the understanding of the total neurosis.

A man had been in an analysis which had failed to relieve his symptoms or his characterological difficulties. He was very angry with his older, illustrious analyst who had disappointed him. Throughout the first analysis the patient who had the session following his had been a very pretty woman. He had the conscious fantasy that he was an irritant to his analyst who preferred her. He imagined that he and the analyst had to endure the frustrations of "fruitless" analysis while the woman patient and the analyst carried out an illicit romance. None of this was revealed to the first analyst on the basis of its being "foolish." Hidden in the fantasy was the patient's wish to be a woman, to be pregnant ("fruitful"), and to enthrall his father. His hypochondriacal mother seemed to have captured his father's attention through the means of endless complaints.

The reanalytic experience puts into high relief the necessity of exploring every available avenue of fantasy. I often ask patients if there is anything they *didn't* tell the first analyst. The answers have sometimes been quite astonishing. The experience has alerted me to the likelihood of repetition in the new analysis and should warn us about the importance of conscious withholding in any analysis.

REANALYSIS OF TRANSFERENCES TO THE PREVIOUS ANALYST

It is a frequent analytic experience that after a very brief period filled with anamnestic data, it is as if the patient lost sight of his or her own life story and focuses all attention upon the analyst's person, the analyst's functions, the setting of the analytic procedure, the other patients, and so on. The transference phenomena, many of which were latent, now become manifest; the past has kaleidoscoped into the present. In fact, resistance appears to be an exploration of the past, recollection and memory having been replaced by the need to repeat the past in transference action. In reanalysis, there is a tendency for the earlier analytic work to be effaced. The relatively recent past of the other analysis follows the infantile past into an oblivion, only to resurface in transference repetition. One of the major tasks of the new analysis, from its onset, is the exploration of the earlier transference situation. This task is resisted with the entire force of transference resistances, and after the initial idealizing honeymoon, resistances are relived with the new analyst. What is of significance is the question: "What actually happened?" with all its initial "Rashomon" implications.

A male patient had a persistent fantasy about his first analyst that she had a "countertransference" problem with him. He depicted her as "unempathic," irritated, and bored by his temper outbursts during his sessions. She had declared him "unanalyzable" and attempted to do some supportive psychotherapy. He abandoned the effort. Later, he resumed analysis with me, but soon began a repetition of temper outbursts in the new analysis. These experiences interested me because occasionally he held his breath, turned bright red, clenched his fists, and altogether resembled a small child in a tantrum. Surprised that I was interested in the similarity to childhood experiences and not at all critical of him, he developed some heightened curiosity. He had been an "impossible" child and his parents had "given up" on him. They seemed to have been "good enough" for the other siblings. Gradually, he became aware that many experiences in the first analysis belied his conviction that the analyst had been bored. In fact there were many examples of her being in tune with him. His aroused curiosity caused him to speak to his mother about his infancy and childhood. He had been a colicky, unsatisfiable baby, severely hyperactive and aggressive, different from his siblings, and requiring her constant attention. His fantasy of being unloved had to be revised to include his early physiological disturbances and the need to externalize blame. The transference fantasies about the woman analyst could be seen as repetitions of earlier fantasies of maternal badness. He began to feel a love for his mother never before experienced; his anger with the first analyst gave way to sadness about the many missed opportunities in his life, especially with women. Here the emphasis is upon repetition in the transference of a mélange of early experience and resultant fantasy. What had been unanalyable with someone who directly represented mother could be analyzed in the slightly more neutral atmosphere presented by a male analyst. Much of this work took place within the first year of the new analysis. It is not usually so easy. Though the patient was left with a greater than usual volatility, his temper tantrums disappeared; he had developed a capacity for control that he had thought impossible. His reexamination of the prior analysis became a regular part of the analytic work, usually initiated by him. Here we see that the exploration of transferences in the reanalysis hinged upon the development of heightened ego capacities of self-observation, curiosity, and insight. The mere reliving of certain crucial affect-laden experiences had been insufficient to effect change. Even the "good-enough" mother can be discouraged by her inability to comfort a distressed infant, and even the "good-enough" ("empathic-enough") analyst may have difficulties with some patients.

All technique has to be attuned to the real needs of each patient. There cannot be a Procrustean couch. Life is not dreary repetition. It is ever new. Analysis should be no less.

Chapter 8

On Beginning with Candidates

Adrienne Applegarth, M.D.

The question of whether the beginning of the analysis is different when one is treating candidates is really part of the larger issue of whether and in what ways the analyses of candidates differ overall from the analyses of patients who come into treatment for therapeutic reasons alone. Therefore I will review the work bearing on the general question and will turn later to consider further some of the features of the training analysis which might have a special impact in the beginning phase.

The training analysis took form and evolved relatively slowly. In reviewing the development of the training system as a whole, Balint (1954) describes five stages. In the first, the stage of pure instruction, students mainly learned from published work without having the experience of analysis themselves. It was rapidly recognized that some analysis was desirable, and the second period, that of demonstration, was ushered in. At that time, the period of analysis was very short, and served to impart some conviction and experience of unconscious processes. This was described by Freud in *Analysis Terminable and Interminable* (1937):

> For practical reasons this analysis can only be short and incomplete. Its main object is to enable his teacher to make a judgement as to whether the candidate can be accepted for further training. It has accomplished its purpose if it gives the learner a firm conviction of the existence of the unconscious, if it enables him, when repressed material emerges, to perceive in himself things which would otherwise be incredible to him, and if it shows him

> a first sample of the technique which has proved to be the only effective one in analytic work. This alone would not suffice for his instruction; but we reckon on the stimuli that he has received in his own analysis not ceasing when it ends and on the process of remodelling the ego continuing spontaneously in the analyzed subject and making use of all subsequent experiences in this newly-acquired sense. This does in fact happen, and in so far as it happens it makes the analyzed subject qualified to be an analyst himself [p. 249].

However, dissatisfaction with this limited aim rapidly arose, as it was felt that an analyst should at least be as well analyzed as his patients, and thus, in the third stage, the training analysis was conceptualized as being of the same extent and depth as a therapeutic analysis. In the fourth stage, the goals became more ambitious. The training analysis should go further and deeper than therapeutic analysis and should constitute a sort of supertherapy. Under the impact of this goal, training analyses became ever longer, often extending well after graduation. Out of skepticism about the actual effectiveness of such supertherapy, it began to be conceptualized as research, which Balint describes as the fifth stage.

From this brief description, it is possible to see what might be considered to be some important differences between the training and therapeutic analysis. In particular, the goals seemed to be different, at one time the training analysis being limited to an introduction to the psychoanalytic process, whereas later on, the training analysis was to be far more ambitious in its goals. Over the years, discussions have focused in addition on other differences; for example, the different conditions under which candidate analyses are conducted, ways in which candidates themselves differ from ordinary patients, differences observed in the analytic process, and lastly, various technical and administrative mechanisms which have been proposed to minimize these differences.

As early as 1926, Eitingon (1926), in a conference on training held under the auspices of the International Psycho-analytical Association, discussed the training analysis briefly. He regarded the main difference from therapeutic analysis as lying in the aim and not in the technique, as he stated that: "there is only one psycho-analytic technique, namely, the correct one" (p. 132).

In 1938, Anna Freud posed the problem succinctly, as she outlined what would be considered gross errors in analytic technique and pointed out that these all characterized the training analysis as it was carried out at that time.

> We do not hesitate to brand it as technically wrong if for the purposes of therapy an analyst selects his patients from his circle of acquaintances; if he shares his interests with them or discusses his opinions either with them or in their presence; if he forgets himself far enough to judge their behavior, to disclose his criticism to other people, and to permit it to affect decisions; if he actively manipulates the patient, offers himself to him as a pattern, and ends analysis by permitting the patient to identify with him personally and professionally. Nevertheless, we commit every single one of these deviations from the classical technique when we analyze candidates. Further we do not inquire frequently enough how far these deviations complicate the candidate's transference and obscure its interpretation [pp. 420–421].

In her discussion, she went on to point out evidence that the results of the training analysis seemed often to be unsatisfactory as judged by the prevalence of unresolved transference fixations to the analyst which produced problems in the analysand's clinical and scientific work.

Since that time, a number of authors have turned their attention to the various problems which seem to be inherent in the training analysis (Sachs, 1947; Gitelson, 1948, 1954; Balint, 1954; Heimann, 1954; Bibring, 1954; Lampl-de Groot, 1954; Grotjahn, 1954; Nielson, 1954; Nacht, 1954; Bernfeld, 1962; Kairys, 1964; Tartakoff, 1966; Benedek, 1969; McLaughlin, 1973; Calef and Weinshel, 1973; Flemming, 1973, 1978). The literature prior to 1964 has been well reviewed in the article by Kairys.

The differences noted between training and therapeutic analysis seem to have fallen into several categories:

DIFFERENT REALITY CIRCUMSTANCES UNDER WHICH THE ANALYSIS IS CONDUCTED

Much Fuller Social and Professional Contact Between Analyst and Patient

In the earlier days of psychoanalysis this was most pronounced. However, as institutes have become larger, the possibilities of avoiding extensive contacts have improved, but it still remains as a difference. The lack of incognito for the analyst was considered by most authors to contaminate the transference and to increase resistance somewhat. However, a number of authors regarded this problem as less important for the candidate than for the analyst himself and one which can be handled by the usual technique (Bibring, 1954; Heimann, 1954; Lampl-de Groot, 1954; and Beredek, 1969).

The Analyst Acts as a Judge of the Candidate's Suitability for Training and also Plays a Role in his Progression

This factor has received a great deal of attention from all authors, inasmuch as it is clear that under these conditions a reality exists that matches various aspects of the infantile fantasies that are developing in any case. There is wide agreement that there is a tendency for this to make it more difficult for the patient to recognize the role of infantile fantasies in his reactions to the analyst and to the situation. However, a rather wide divergence of opinion has been expressed concerning the degree to which this is an important obstacle. Benedek (1969) has taken the position that the analytic and the evaluative function are separate mental functions which need not interfere with one another. Flemming (1978) goes further, stating that the training analyst has important observations to contribute concerning the analysand's ability to undertake analysis and that an essential function is avoided if the analyst does not report on these. Bibring (1954) also acknowledges the problems of having the analyst act to some extent as judge but, like Flemming, holds the view that this is nevertheless an important function of the training analyst.

On the other hand there have been a number of papers making the case for a total separation between the training analysis and the process of making administrative decisions concerning the candidate. Kairys (1964) suggested this answer to the problem of the transference contaminations which occur, and, more recently, McLaughlin (1973) has contributed experiences and observations from his Institute, where a nonreporting stance is adhered to. He is careful to make his nonreporting position clear both at the start of the analysis and later on. It is his opinion that this procedure makes it possible to deal dynamically with all issues including those of progression. However, he does note that, occasionally, severe problems in the analysis of certain candidates have forced him and his colleagues to communicate certain judgments either to the Education Committee or to the candidate or both. He notes some measure of conflict between the educational and the analytic responsibility of the analyst, but takes the position that the nonreporting pact can be adhered to except in extreme cases. On the other hand, Calef and Weinshel (1973) take issue with this position on a number of grounds. In their opinion, it is a mistake automatically to equate reporting with violation of confidentiality, and that, while personal material must be guarded, it is possible to communicate certain types of material. They feel that it is an oversimplification to state that reporting is a reality and thus not analyzable, pointing out that in analysis we deal always with mixtures of fact and reality, and that in addition we deal with a number of other realities established in the analytic situation and that significant analytic work is done around these. Moreover, they doubt if an analysis can be successful if the candidate is not able to work on the intrapsychic aspects of all these realities. As they point out, the assessments reported are not moral ones but rather concern the development of essential abilities of the candidate to do analysis. In their view, making a pact not to report may represent a collusion with resistances.

INTRINSIC DIFFERENCES BETWEEN CANDIDATES AND PATIENTS IN THERAPEUTIC ANALYSIS

Differences in Motivation

Many authors have called attention to the fact that candidates more frequently enter analysis with the conscious motivation of professional advancement. This is in contrast to the wish of the neurotic patient to be relieved of his distress. However, both A. Freud (1938, 1976) and Sachs (1947) point out the relative universality of neurotic problems and describe, from their experience, the promptness with which a variety of unconscious motivations come to the fore, so that the differences between the two groups of patients are, in this respect, more apparent than real.

Differences in the Personality Structure

Here a number of authors have commented in considerable detail about what seem to be some important differences between the two groups.

Sachs (1947) mentions that although neurotic traits are universal, the candidate is more apt initially to present himself as normal. He finds that the technical problems may be more difficult, especially with the group which is especially well adapted to reality and has strong narcissistic defenses and resultant rigidity, making it difficult to reach unconscious processes,

Gitelson (1954) has discussed extensively the problems presented by the "normal" candidate. It may be quite important for such a candidate to maintain the sense of normality, and he may use his prior knowledge of psychoanalytic ideas to assist in denial of symptoms. He may show paranoid or manic defenses when challenged. The candidate has been able to assimilate his libidinal and aggressive impulses and the defenses against them into the ego with the assistance of highly satisfactory work adaptations, which allows freedom from anxiety and many gratifications from the environment. The very utility of these defenses may make analysis more difficult. Gitelson presents some of the problems he has encountered in work with such character types. He notes in particular that there may be more resistance to the development of the transference neurosis, because the analytic process carries the threat of disturbing the hard-won reality base of the ego which is helping preserve hidden oral gratifications. He stresses the necessity of meticulous analysis of these defenses, especially the factors involved in the candidate's choice of analysis as a career. Gitelson mentions but differs with the proposals which some have made to introduce special active measures in such analyses, pointing out that these would too closely duplicate the sorts of parental manipulations which led to this type of "normal" character in the first place.

Tartakoff (1966) also has considered the problems of "normal" candidates in detail. They tend to present themselves for analysis either for reasons of professional advancement or because of dissatisfactions with their personal lives. Often this takes the form of some problems with competition, or with the quality of object relations, or the feeling of not having fulfilled the promise which they felt they showed. They may present with anxiety, depression, or psychoneurotic symptoms. They seem to have the feature in common that they believe that their virtues and talents will be rewarded if they work toward their selected goals and their mental harmony seems to depend on accomplishment of these goals. Their defenses are quite adaptive, especially the energy with which active mastery is pursued. Complying with the rules of the game is expected to produce acclaim for achievement, which is a different focus from the pursuit of libidinal aims and the associated fears of castration seen in the usual neurotic. The analyst may be seen as a highly idealized figure who will endow the patient with these qualities if suitably appealed to. This personality constellation is not unique to candidates, but, as Tartakoff points out, certain factors in training exacerbate the problems which it may produce. The support to the narcissistic defenses and gratifications afforded by the fact of selection for training may make it quite difficult to get to the infantile roots. Also, the action orientation may interfere with the psychoanalytic process, as it acts against self-observation. In passing, Tartakoff mentions another factor which may affect the analysis of candidates, namely the possibility of divided attention between fields; for example, the neurosciences, which may offer rewarding areas of work with much acclaim which can be used against the analytic process as well.

Lampl-de Groot (1954) has described the special difficulties presented by analysands with uncorrected fantasies of omnipotence and grandeur which cover feelings of inferiority. Such a person feels abused if he feels slighted and reacts with hostility and aggression.

Anna Freud (1976) has also called attention to the problems presented by the healthy candidate with many achievements and ego syntonic defenses supported by them. Since the defenses are stronger, uncovering of unconscious material, including the unconscious aspects of the resistances, takes longer than it does in the neurotic analysand. On the other hand, neurotic patients may show firm attachments to neurotic substitute gratifications (i.e., resistances from the id), and so may show change more slowly than the healthier candidate. Thus, in the training analysis, more work may be spent on the resistances noted above, while in therapeutic analysis, more may be spent on the slow working through of the neurotic attachments. She also notes certain differences in the development of transference. The healthier analysand takes longer to show transference, as his emotional life is more attached to real present objects. The task in these analyses is to produce the readiness to transfer, while in the neurotic this is already present. She also describes some differences in emphasis in the transference in candidates, with more weight on sibling jealousies and on conflicts over infantile curiosities which emerge in the form of curiosity about what senior analysts do with each other and with their patients. Also, while conflicts over submission and revolt are ubiquitous, they may appear in the training analysis as vacillations between theoretical positions.

All the authors cited seem to agree in general that differences in the reality circumstances of the training analysis exist, and that candidates may present somewhat different personality structures as compared to other analysands. However, there is some range of opinion as to how much effect these factors have on the progress of the analysis itself. Those authors who have commented most specifically on outcome (Sachs, 1947; Calef and Weinshel, 1973; A. Freud, 1976) seem to feel that in the long run the outcomes are quite similar. Generally speaking, the articles all focus almost entirely on the apparent disadvantages confronting the training analysis and it seems interesting that almost no one has paid attention to what might seem to be some inherent advantages. It is a common experience for us to note that our patients who are not candidates or in the mental health field often do not have the same interest and curiosity about the function of the mind. Rather they are more motivated by relief of suffering, and when their lives are better they may stop prematurely. To be sure, the candidate also is to some degree captive, in that a successful analysis is required for his training. Lacking the same interest in the mind, the nonprofessional patients also may fail to experience some of the pleasure in the analytic process that often may leaven the painful times in the training analysis. An additional stimulating feature for the training analyst may also be his opportunity to relate closely his analytic observations with what he hears about the work function in the field he knows so well.

With this material as background, we can now turn to the basic issue of this paper, namely, what features characterize the beginning of the analysis in the candidate and to what degree there are important differences from a therapeutic analysis in this early phase.

It will assist in this discussion to define in general terms what I would refer to as the beginning phase of analysis. One could go about this in several ways. A good case could be made for defining the limits of this period by means of certain dynamic changes (e.g., in resistance structures), which would allow one to feel some confidence that the patient was truly engaged in the analytic process. However, it is undesirable to define the period under observation in terms of the phenomena to be observed and compared. Also, it is sometimes rather difficult to be sure about the timing of the engagement in the analytic process oneself or to demonstrate it to others, so that I will use the first six months as defining the beginning, which should allow the observations to be compared more simply. This roughly corresponds to the minimum length of time which many institutes require their candidates to be in analysis before the rest of their training can begin, although some require more.

It seems to be more common for candidates to present themselves for training analysis having had prior analysis or analytic psychotherapy. Certain complications may be intensified when the therapy or analysis has had to be interrupted in an unfinished state so that the training analysis may be started. This may be especially common in institutes where either the training analyst is assigned or where a change of analyst is required in any case even though the original analysis has been conducted by a training analyst of that institute. In any of these situations, the beginning phase is colored by the necessity for the change. A variety of reactions may be seen. At times, an analysand may have had difficulty extracting himself from a treatment which he regards as unfruitful and may have applied for training in part to effect the interruption. He may or may not be aware of his relief at the change that has enabled him to avoid his conflict about his wish to leave. Or the requirement for the change may fit all too well into the infantile fantasies of being deprived of a beloved object by stern outside authorities as a punishment. The candidate may react with rage and the wish to make the new analyst pay, sometimes by abusing him, sometimes by attempting to defeat the analysis. Or he may begin to become attached to the new analyst and experience a conflict in loyalties and a sense that he is betraying the old therapist or analyst and also that he is losing him by virtue of the new attachment. For those reasons the candidate may struggle to remain unaware of the new attachment or of any criticisms or disappointments in the old one. In these situations it is common for the criticisms of the old therapist to be externalized onto the training analyst, and the analysand then is vigilant against expected criticisms of the former therapist on the part of the training analyst. However, none of these situations is unique to the training analysis. Noncandidate patients may also have had prior treatments, and may have had to change for reasons of illness or death of the prior therapist or analyst or because they wish to change from psychotherapy to analysis. These circumstances will inevitably color the early phases somewhat as the training analyst turns his attention to the resistances involved.

Inasmuch as candidates in recent years have tended to come from programs where much analytic theory has been taught and clinical work has centered around psychoanalytic psychotherapy, they may present at the outset more tendency to defend themselves by intellectualizations and by watchfulness of the analyst, rationalized by the fact of their being in training. Apparent freedom to entertain ideas consciously may protect against recognition of the existence of these same ideas unconsciously and the force which they exert. These factors are not absent in other patients. As an example, I recall a patient, a young woman, not in the mental health field, who was in analysis for several years with less than an optimal outcome. She broke off the analysis and told me for the first time, almost as she was going out the door, that she had learned about the Oedipus complex as a seven-year-old child and made a resolve that one day she would be in analysis and prove it was not so.

All of the issues mentioned earlier, which have been fully described by many authors, appear and color the beginning of the analysis. Issues are raised around confidentiality, being judged, about the analyst having a voice in the candidate's future, and so on. The candidate naturally tends to focus on these as realities and needs help in being able to see the various other meanings which are present as well. These factors represent a significant difference and a real problem only if the analyst also views them too much in their realistic aspect and thus may join in their use in resistance. The fact that these realities are present to use as resistance lends a different flavor to the analysis of a candidate, particularly in the beginning, but as Anna Freud has noted, once the process gets under way, the force of it tends to submerge the surface realities. Factors arising out of the personality structures of candidates may affect the opening phase more, as Anna Freud has described. In particular, the adequacy and adaptive advantages of certain defenses in candidates make the early ego analysis somewhat more difficult and prolonged but highly necessary. Another factor which she mentioned would affect the early work, namely that the normal candidate tends to develop transferences less readily and that more analysis needs to be done in the beginning phases on the resistance to the awareness of the transference. However, in my opinion, the overlap between candidates and other patients is quite extensive in this regard.

The conclusion which emerges then from this discussion is that various differences have been described between the personalities of candidates and neurotic patients who present themselves for analysis and also between the conditions under which each group undertakes this work. However, there seems to me to be a persuasive body of opinion which holds that, although these conditions exist and their effects can be seen, perhaps more readily in the early phases of analysis, nevertheless the analytic process as it gathers momentum is really very similar in both and that the analytic results obtained may be very similar also, in spite of a certain amount of pessimism expressed about this over the years. It would follow from this that the technical guidelines for proceeding in the training analysis can and should be the same as with any other throughout all phases including the beginning. In general, there is agreement that perhaps the most important learning about how to do analysis occurs in the training analysis, and it would be most regrettable if the analytic careers of candidates needed to begin with the lesson that the standard technique is not expected to be effective.

Chapter 9

Externalization: A Resistance in the Beginning Phase of Adolescent Analysis

Judith Fingert Chused, M.D.

The beginning of an analysis is like the beginning of a courtship. As each participant attempts to define himself to the other, he is eager for acceptance as well as for understanding and authentication. The analyst knows that soon his persona will be viewed through transference-filled eyes, and in these first sessions he wants to present himself and the task of analysis in a way that encourages participation in the work and tolerance (or at least, an intellectual understanding) of the lack of immediate gratification.

The patient also hopes to be understood and accepted; however, the more his difficulties arouse embarrassment and shame, the more understanding and acceptance seem like irreconcilable desires. The adolescent patient, in particular, is in conflict over the presentation of his persona, in large part because as he struggles to reconcile ideal and reality, he constantly falls short of what he wishes to be.

The beginning of analysis has many functions. It is the time when patient and analyst assess each other to see how they will do together; it is an educative period when the patient learns what analysis will be; it is the phase during which the patient reveals his character structure, his developmental concerns, and his pathological compromise solutions before they have entered the transference and ensnared the analyst; and it is when the patient and analyst develop a baseline of collaboration. The collaboration will be threatened each time transference resistance arises. But by then, ideally, interpretation and clarification of the transference will have meaning.

In the beginning phase of an analysis, the goal of engaging the patient in a collaborative process of self-exploration is the same regardless of the age of the patient. The techniques by which one achieves this goal may vary, reflecting the analyst's perception of the patient's psychic structure, his level of functioning, and the form and severity of his pathology. In addition, during adolescence the approach to beginning analysis will also depend on the patient's age and his individual response to the ongoing developmental process. With an early adolescent the task of engagement is not easy. Many young adolescents are wary of adults; the regressive pull to dependency is often so strong (and abhorrent) that analytic understanding is experienced as seductive and threatening to autonomy. With these adolescents, it can be useful, in the very first session, to address their reluctance to enter therapy, their discomfort in seeing the analyst as anything other than an agent of the parents, and to work with them on the mistaken notion that being strong means having no need of help. For many years analysts have spoken of "the need to make rapid contact with the adolescent" (Spiegel, 1951, p. 390). Even with an early adolescent who is desperately unhappy or cripplingly symptomatic (with obsessions, phobias, or hypochondriacal preoccupations), the analyst must make the recommendation for analysis tactfully, in words the adolescent can understand, with an emphasis on the strength that is required to seek and accept help. For when such an adolescent has recovered from the intensity of his symptoms, he too often pulls back from the therapeutic relationship because of its similarity, in his eyes, to the one with the parents.

With a midphase adolescent in active turmoil over the upsurge of libidinal and aggressive impulses and frightened by the emerging awareness that growth (i.e., becoming an adult) is an inexorable process, one can often address rather directly the adolescent's confusion and discomfort with his inner sensations. In addition, to the extent he is conscious of his difficulty in reconciling his new, less idealized, and more ambivalent perceptions of his parents with the wish to still depend on them for nurturance, one can help the adolescent articulate his distress in feeling so young and inadequate to the tasks ahead. In this phase, the adolescent is often less fearful of the regressive pull than the progressive one. For him, an early understanding and articulation of conflictual affect is helpful.

By late adolescence, the decision for treatment cannot be made by the parents; unless the adolescent is a willing participant, analysis is not possible. Although I believe the analyst should meet with the parents to hear their concerns, elicit their support, and to explain the reasons for recommending analysis, with a late adolescent the contract needs to made with him. This may require a longer evaluative period than with the younger adolescent, where the final decision for analysis is often made by the analyst and parents. In explaining the need for analysis to a late adolescent, one should speak as directly as possible, detailing the concerns that he has expressed, not contradicting his rationalizations and projections, but emphasizing that given the situation he has to deal with, effective functioning is hindered by internal conflicts not under his conscious control.

Though age-related variations in the technical approach to adolescents are important, throughout adolescence there is one characteristic of the beginning phase of analysis which consistently stands out and must be addressed. This is a distinct increase in the *resistance to the development of transference,* an increase directly related to the phase-specific tasks of physical separation, psychic individuation, and identity formation. This resistance is manifested in multiple ways, most prominently by the extensive use of externalization.

Externalization is the process of projection into the external world of attributes of one's personality, of one's inner world; of conflicts, fantasies, affects, ego and superego attitudes, of instinctual impulses, perceptions, ambitions, or ideals. Externalization may be seen in combination with displacement, another process common to adolescence, in which reactions to one object are experienced in relationship to another. For example, attributes may first be externalized onto a parent and then displaced onto the analyst. Externalization has multiple functions for the adolescent. Used defensively, to disown anxiety-producing ideas and impulses, it protects the adolescent from the painful awareness of internal conflict. Used developmentally, in the process of identity formation, it allows for differentiation and individuation from parental introjects. In the same individual externalization can be both part of normal adolescent development and a pathological defense, used so rigidly and extensively that it interferes with adaptive behavior.

When thirteen-year-old Susan said she'd rather die than see a shrink, her parents threatened and cajoled until she reluctantly agreed to "see the bitch." Similarly, when five-year-old Steve refused to go to a "feelings doctor," his father picked him up and took him there.

Susan was coerced into entering my office, but she adamantly opposed treatment. For Susan, I was an agent of her parents, and though she acknowledged that life was not as she wished, she felt no one "employed by the opposition" was trustworthy. That she was confused and miserable, totally unaware of what was troubling her, only made matters worse. She spoke as if acknowledging that she needed or wanted help would give credence to her fear that she was going crazy; being angry was more comfortable than being scared. When she finally did begin to talk, her resentment over being coerced continued for many months, for she held tightly onto the claim, "my parents think I'm sick," to keep her own anxiety at bay.

Steve was also resistant to treatment. He sat mute throughout the first session and attempted to destroy my office the second. Yet, in contrast to Susan, within several weeks Steve was engaged and fully participant in the analysis. In spite of his initial resistance, his hunger for new object relationships (a function of his age) made him responsive to my interest and enabled us to begin a dialogue.

The differene between Susan's and Steve's behavior during the initial therapeutic contact exemplifies a major issue in many adolescent analyses—how to engage and begin treatment with someone who has trouble acknowledging any interest in, need of, or use for either the work or the person of the therapist. A vehement rejection of help, such as Susan's, is not uncommon. Although these adolescents may eventually be very productive participants in a useful analysis, in the beginning the complete lack of cooperation can be daunting. Frightened by fantasies of "going crazy" or "being queer," locked in an uneasy struggle to separate from parental figures, scared they may yield to the temptation of dependency, they are disturbed by even the idea of therapy.

Some adolescents, once they have met and spoken with the therapist, are more accepting of help. But there are others who cannot give up the battle with the external world. In a struggle to contend with internal conflicts, both conscious and unconscious, they may rely on defensive externalization so extensively that it renders everyone in the adult world suspect. Paradoxically, even when these "externalizing" adolescents complain about adult authorities, they may not avoid them; in fact, often the opposite is true. Some seek out confrontation and end up in a psychiatrist's office "as a last resort," prior to school suspension, incarceration, or hospitalization. It is often the adolescent who wishes to believe that his problems are caused by the "authorities" who will exert enormous effort provoking these same "authorities."

Of the less angry and less action-prone adolescents, there are many who are not overtly resistant, who may even ask for the initial consultation. Within this group a significant number talk relatively freely about their problems, their symptoms, or fears. Some adolescents even become enthusiastic about exploring the impact of past events on current interactions, particularly if the cognitive activity of analysis can be used for defensive intellectualization. Similarly, the hardship of the time and energy commitment required by analysis may provide relief for the more masochistic, guilt-ridden adolescent, and they too may not be overtly resistant to the treatment. And finally, the lonely adolescent who is struggling to free himself from parents, but is still uncomfortable with peers, may embrace a relationship with the analyst, particularly if he sees the analyst as a mentor.

But even adolescents who are eager for a therapeutic experience, an intellectual adventure, or an idealized mentor, find it difficult to maintain a belief in the potential benefit of analysis and stay with the work that is required, once a regressive transference begins to develop. Resistance to an awareness of transference and to the deepening of the transference, as manifested in the extensive use of externalization, is a serious problem in adolescent analysis. It is a rare adolescent, filled with ambivalence toward his primary objects, and beset by conflict, who seeks resolution of his distress within himself. This resistance to an awareness of transference can also be a major problem in the analysis of adults, particularly those who are impulsive and tend to involve the external world in enactments of internal fantasies and conflicts.

During adolescence the intense resistance to the development of transference is related to developmental phenomena. These include an increased instinctual pressure with concerns about sexuality and sexual performance (along with the wish not to expose these concerns), a push to separate from parents and parent surrogates, a need to complete individuation and to stabilize internal self and object representations, a wish to be independent and functionally autonomous, and a fear of exposure (particularly to oneself) of inadequacies. Any one of these issues would make participation in a regressive transference experience difficult; considered all together they suggest that engaging the adolescent in any analytic process might be impossible.

Analysis during adolescense *is* possible, but with some distinct differences from the process of adult analysis. These differences are evident at the very beginning of treatment in how the adolescent responds to the analyst as an object for transference and as an object for the externalization of current developmental conflicts. More specifically, the task of separation–individuation, of identity formation with stabilization of self and object representations, will have a profound impact on the analytic relationship (as they do on all intimate relationships during this phase).

Completing the "second individuation phase" (Blos, 1967a) requires a decreased investment in the parents and parent surrogates with changes in both their internal representations and the ego and superego structures built on an identification with these objects. This is accomplished, in part, through projection of conflictual aspects of the self back onto the external objects (or their representatives in the transference), which decreases both the appeal of the objects and the identification with them.

Conflicts with the primary objects obviously do not emerge "de novo" in adolescence. They are shaped by earlier experiences during the initial separation–individuation phase and the oedipal phase, and by the success and failures, the achievements and relationships, of later childhood. However, during adolescence conflicts with the primary objects often have a desperate quality.

In beginning an analysis, the analyst tries to establish a relationship in which regressive transference elements (and, ideally, the transference neurosis) can flourish. This requires an investment in the analyst modeled on important object relationships from childhood. But as positive and negative reactions to the analyst intensify (based on both displacement of feelings for the parents of the present and early transference manifestations reflective of past relationships) with a regression to more primitive conflictual impulses and modes of cognition, the developmentally determined struggle to individuate from the parents increases resistance and may lead to a flight from treatment before the transference has consolidated into a recognizable, interpretable pattern. As Anna Freud (1965) said, "the adolescent needs to move away from his childhood objects, while analysis promotes the revival of the infantile relationships in the transference.

This is felt as a special threat by the patient and frequently causes the abrupt ending of treatment" (p. 35). The adolescent does not distinguish between the parents of the past and the parents of the present. Externalizing onto the analyst attributes of parental introjects, responding to him as to these primary objects (past and present), determined to differentiate himself and equating differentiation with physical separation, the adolescent all too often ends treatment prematurely.

I think of two aggressive, angry, and impulsive young men, aged four and fourteen years, whom I treated analytically. Both were fixed in sadomasochistic relationships with their parents.

Donald at four years was uncontrollable in most situations. During the first three weeks of treatment, he unwrapped the fingers and beat on the knuckles of other children on the jungle gym (and caused one child to break an arm when she fell), bit and kicked children and adults alike when crossed, and wreaked havoc with my office and my tolerance for child analysis.

By six, after eighteen months of analysis, he was able to maintain control over his impulses in most situations, including those with considerable stress. He still became rageful whenever he lost a game, had difficulty learning a new skill, or felt unwanted (i.e., at every separation, including the end of sessions). Each experience of stress was associated with narcissistic injury which he tried to master through aggression and controlling masochistic provocation. However, by six he had learned to contain his angry impulses, *except* in the presence of his parents. With them, and only with them, he continued to provoke and attack until he was severely punished.

Donald had learned to adapt to the disparate situations he found himself in and could even begin to understand that the fights with his parents were to a large extent at his behest. The objects he was fighting with were the parents of his more primitive past—that he was able to achieve a mode of relatedness with his parents of the present that echoed the past was due to their susceptibility to participation in his enactments. These external objects were behaving as his fantasized internal objects, though, to be sure, the same psychology facilitated their participation in past and present situations. However, with all other current objects, even before his conflicts had been worked through, he was symptom free.

Eddie was fourteen when I first saw him. I was the third therapist called to treat this delinquent, truant, suicidally depressed, drug dealing and abusing young man. Eddie, like Donald, repeatedly engaged everyone in his environment in sadomasochistic interactions. But there were major differences: Donald weighed fifty pounds; Eddie one hundred and sixty five. Donald could be physically restrained by all adults; Eddie was able to severely injure most adults (and was terrified by this ability). Donald, in the process of developing his internal object representations and ego structure, was learning to distinguish which behavior would be tolerated by which adult and child. Eddie, in the process of reorganizing his ego structure, was externalizing all over the place, and though not psychotic, was unable to differentiate the response of one object from another—all bore the projection of his hostility.

After the first month of therapy, Donald responded to me as an object different from his parents. My limited tolerance of his rage reactions was clear to him and he began to limit the destructive part of his acting out. He still was easily injured by frustration, and still reacted with anger to limits, whether internally determined (as when he could not print his name correctly) or externally (when he was not allowed to cut up a doll), but his fury no longer escalated out of control. As our work together continued, he often became provocative. However, with the now self-imposed limit on actions, the provocation, the stimulus, and what it was designed to elicit were more understandable within the transference aspects of our relationship. Not so with Eddie. He began treatment with the same problem with behavioral controls as Donald—but I had little ability to modify Eddie's behavior. (The same relative impotence—reflective of Eddie's fear of impotence—was experienced by Eddie's parents. Both had had much therapy and parent guidance for themselves before Eddie even began the analysis and, for the most part, their behavior with him was consistent and appropriate. However, his perception of them as of me was distorted by multiple externalizations.)

Eddie did form an attachment to me and eventually got some important analytic work done, but there were many weeks that were lost because he was too "stoned" to come to more than one or two sessions. My persistent, nondirective interest was of value but was not nearly as immediately useful to him as it was to Donald. Donald used the experience in our sessions to differentiate between me and his parental introjects in a way Eddie could not. Even when Eddie was present and free of drugs, he was hyperalert to imagined directives.

The difference between Eddie's and Donald's initial ability to use the analyst reflects the difference between a child who is receptive to new objects and an adolescent who is trying to free himself from old ones. Neither is an organized transference response—that comes later—but both affect the beginning of treatment.

Prior to adolescence, the child is dependent on the adult. The child knows his tools for dealing with the world are inadequate and he uses the adult both for external care and as an model for how to cope, adapt, and behave. The analytic relationship with a child will be affected by his use of the analyst for identification (in the process of structure building) as well as for elucidation of information received via the transference. This can lead to problems if the child analyst bypasses conflict resolution to direct the development of compensatory structures and modes of interacting or uses the readiness of the child for introjection and identification as the primary therapeutic tool (Chused, 1988).

There are different problems, and, correspondingly, different temptations with adolescent patients. Adolescence is truly the "second time around," providing an opportunity for the individual to rework structures based on the relationships and identifications of childhood. In the process of reworking structures, the adolescent goes through a period of rejecting previous modes of relating. As genital primacy and a push for greater independence develop, relationships with parental figures often feel dangerous (the danger increasing as the instinctual impulses and the capacity to act on these impulses increase). Decathexis of the internal representation of these previously all-important objects and a change in the psychic structures based on introjection and identification with these objects follows. This does many things: It leaves the adolescent hungry for new objects; it creates tremendous uncertainty and confusion within him regarding his identity and his capacity to function independently; and it leads to a vulnerability to and fear of internal conflict, with a push to externalization. Objects alternatively become the recipients of externalizations of psychic attitudes and the models for internalization and imitation. In pain over internal conflicts, the adolescent will externalize conflictual impulses or ego or superego attributes onto a hated object one minute, only to ally himself (and identify) with the same (or another) object the next. Just as affects fluctuate rapidly, reflecting the internal dynamics of the moment, so do the trial identifications, selected in the service of identity formation.

Internalization and externalization serve a variety of vital functions throughout life. Both aid in the separation from and tolerance of loss of the primary objects. However, when used extensively, both can interfere with the development of a utilizable transference. Identification with the analyst, particularly if the analyst alters his behavior in an effort to facilitate this identification, can interfere with the use of the analytic process for exposure of past conflicts. And externalization, by too quickly generating a distorted perception of the analyst and analytic process, may interfere with the acceptance and use of the analyst for productive work.

In the very first therapeutic contact, externalization of developmental conflicts may be evident in the adolescent's responding to the analyst's words as if they were directive or critical. Many adolescents who are apprehensive about independence and "self-reliance" try to convince themselves that the wish to be independent is unconflicted and that they have no desire for passive receptivity and dependency. Their externalization helps maintain the fiction that the analyst, like parents, wants to take over, and permits them to claim an unambivalent desire for independence, expressed as a wish "to be left alone."

There *are* adolescents who seem truly unconflicted over the issue of independence, who are "pseudo-mature" or "counterphobically autonomous" or who seem content to be passive, having retreated to a regressed, dependent position because of fear of failure or of losing control over instinctual impulses.

There are also adolescents who present with prominent neurotic symptoms, with little evidence that they are actively engaged in developmental struggles. Some retreat before they begin; they may look more like obsessional, ritualistic "little old men" or inhibited, constricted, compliant latency children than like vital adolescents. Still other adolescents make a stab at autonomy and fail, beginning treatment with depression as the major symptom.

But however the adolescent presents in the opening phase of the analysis, when the transference begins to intensify, the struggle for autonomous functioning becomes part of the process. At some point in the analysis, each adolescent I have seen (no matter how eager he was for relief from his symptoms) has fought to be free of me when developmental forces once again asserted themselves. No matter the type or degree of discomfort that brought him to my office, as soon as the adolescent freed up energy from his maladaptive symptoms and began the work of analysis, he began to struggle against his attachment to me. I am not talking about negative transference, though that enters the analysis of an adolescent as it does every analysis. Instead it is that soon after there is energy available for analysis, there is also energy available, once more, for development—which includes separation from parental object representations.

As the wish for separation is not unconflicted, so the wish to leave analysis is not unconflicted. Instead, distress leads the adolescent to externalize the conflict, and, if in analysis, he may claim that the cause of the distress is the analyst, that the desired goal (friends, grades, college, a job, therapeutic benefit) is the analyst's, and that all the analyst wants is to control him and not let him be free to make his own decisions. On the surface his behavior may resemble that of the passive–aggressive character disorder, but both the fixity/variability of the behavior and the intent of it differs. In the adult with fixed character pathology, the perception of the analyst as controlling and directive contains within it gratification of regressed libidinal impulses, defense against projected aggression, as well as symbolic expression of other conflicts. Though these same determinants may be operative in the adolescent, this is not always true. The perception of the analyst as controlling, though containing derivatives of the original separation–individuation phase, may be primarily an expression of the reworking of this phase in adolescence, and need not bespeak of anal fixations nor projected aggressive impulses. This is not just a theoretical distinction. Technically, when a distorted perception of the analyst reflects an "almost conscious" externalization of current conflicts, it can be addressed early. On the other hand, in treating a patient with a passive–aggressive character disorder, focus on the misperceptions and resultant behavior often should wait until the transference has consolidated and the determinants of the misperceptions are clearer.

I do not mean to suggest that all adolescents seek to flee from directives or from therapists they perceive to be authoritarian. Some depressed or anxious patients find relief in their belief that the analyst's words are directive rather than exploratory. They may even idealize the analyst and see him as benevolent and omniscient. But those who start by seeking a magic cure may also want to end prematurely, frightened of the seductive "magician," or disappointed when the magic doesn't work.

For example, when fourteen-year-old Sally came to analysis after a suicide attempt, she was eager to have someone "to talk to." And she talked, readily sharing her concern about the confusion inside her head. Her father had been correct when he called the attempt "a cry for help," when he said it was prompted by anxiety rather than depression. But Sally quickly got over her fear she was going crazy, and within days this very loquacious adolescent became scared she had said too much, too soon. As she sat, silent, I asked, somewhat rhetorically, what she feared I might be thinking about her. She remained silent, then blurted out that I seemed different, somehow not so nice. It was clear to both of us that her perception of me had shifted. As an awareness of this shift was now all we shared, we talked about it, about how people seemed so different sometimes. This was the opening wedge in our work together; eventually it led to an exploration of the fantasies her self-criticism (projected onto me) reflected.

At first, when I had commented that Sally now seemed scared to talk to me, she had heard me as directing her to talk. That I would arouse her concern about control was not surprising; it was to become one of many repetitions within the analytic situation of current and past, real and fantasized, events in her life, which eventually made the experience of the analytic process vital and productive. However, before a repetition can have therapeutic value, the patient, as well as the analyst, must recognize that perceptions can originate in a psychic reality that is different from external reality. At the beginning of treatment, this was not yet true for Sally.

The distinction between psychic and external reality cannot be learned through cognition alone; experience plus analysis is required, such as occurs when, for example, the analyst does not retaliate or criticize as anticipated, then clarifies the difference between what he did and what the patient expected, and explores the fantasies behind the patient's expectations. Unfortunately, after an unpleasant experience, the adolescent often does not want to stick around long enough to permit any analysis of the experience, hence the need to articulate resistances to treatment early. I suspect it would have proved useful when Sally "spilled" at the beginning of the analysis to anticipate that shame or guilt over what she was saying could lead later to a fear of criticism.

The earlier, and more persistently, resistances to treatment are articulated, the less they will interfere with the later understanding of transference resistances and that they will ultimately defeat the analysis. More than thirty years ago, Fraiberg (1955) noted, "In my own experience a case is more likely to be lost in the early stages of treatment, that is in the initiation to treatment, than any other time. If we can overcome these initial resistances and establish a therapeutic attitude we find many factors in the pubertal situation which go to work for us" (pp. 285–286). It *is* important, however, to avoid prematurely interpreting these resistances as transference resistances. Adolescents are extremely sensitive to "being understood" before they understand, and are quick to be as judgmental of the analyst as they fear he is of them. It can be quite destructive to future collaboration when the analyst and his words fail to connect with the adolescent's experience.

It may seem ludicrous to talk about establishing a collaborative analytic process with an adolescent, particularly if one imagines that the collaboration might continue for any length of time. By definition, adolescence is a time of progression, not regression, of integration and synthesis, not dissection and retrospection, of separation from primary objects, not reunion with those objects as represented in the transference. But in spite of the developmental push away from the type of interaction that characterizes the analytic process, it is feasible to treat adolescents analytically. In fact the intensity of their drive activity and the acuity of their intellectual skills enable them to make as full a use of analysis—*once engaged in the process*—as patients of any age group. Once engaged, many adolescents will continue the work of analysis to completion, particularly if the analyst sticks with the task of analysis and does not get derailed into enactments over control and self-responsibility. But that phrase, *once engaged in the process,* is the sticking point. As already mentioned, the adolescent's feelings for his primary objects can be so intense that they color his perception of the analyst before the latter has even spoken. These feelings and the associated misperceptions are often not interpretable, they are displacements rather than transference, but they enter through the door with the adolescent and exert a powerful influence on his participation in the process. How they are addressed is an issue, for often the adolescent's accusation or stated fear that the analyst will respond to him as his parents did or do lead the analyst to protest that he is different and will listen objectively. But no sooner has he spoken these words (no matter how subtly stated, the implication being that he, unlike the parents, is disinterested and can be trusted), than the analyst has laid a trap for himself. The adolescent will pick up first that the analyst wants to be trusted and therefore is not as disinterested as he claims, and second, that he is not unsusceptible to rivalry with the parents. In fact, the very act of being reassuring informs the adolescent that the analyst can be manipulated (to reassure). Every word, tone, movement of the analyst is noted—and that this is done secretly without comment (in the manner of the best spies in novels) should not fool the analyst into thinking himself unobserved.

This hypervigilance has definitely influenced my approach to beginning adolescent analyses. It has lead me to try to be as open and explicit about my therapeutic intent as I can, essentially providing the adolescent with the verbal equivalent of extending empty hands. I hope to demonstrate by this that I am uninterested in warring but am aware of the potential for warfare in our relationship. At the same time, I begin "an analysis" of our interchange almost immediately. I do not try to cajole a belligerent or sullen adolescent to talk to me and I try to steer clear of addressing what the adolescent might be feeling. As indicated earlier, analysis primarily from a position of "empathic knowledge" often leads to disaster. Instead, I try to demonstrate the analytic method through examples of "analyzing the analyst." Thus when a teenager comes in and responds to my initial greeting with a malevolent gaze and a snarled "There's no point in talking to you," I might say, "Yes, I got that idea from the way you were looking at me." Then I might fall silent, perhaps do a bit of knitting, and then say, "It seems kind of silly just sitting here. I could ask you about school or friends, or how do you think the Redskins will do this year, but that will just be making conversation. It's hard for me to think of anything to say that won't make it seems like I'm trying to trick you into talking." I think the specific words are unimportant—it's the music in the message that counts. I want to convey that I don't want to fight and I know I can't win a fight, but I'm not turned off by his attitude and would like to find a way to engage other than by coercion, seduction, or authority. My intent is to get the adolescent's attention; only then can I address his apprehension about the therapeutic process and begin to relate it to other concerns. I try to present in understandable language that although independent growth and collaborative therapy may have different agendas, they can coexist and ultimately prove to have the same goals. To name the battle yet not participate goes a long way to preventing it from becoming an insurmountable resistance to treatment.

Nonetheless, the enormous difference that seems to exist between the process of analysis and that of adolescent development leads even those adolescents who begin analysis infatuated with the analyst and the concept of unconscious conflict to become, all too soon, unenthusiastic about a process that requires them to look within themselves for the origin of their distress and which, by not supporting externalization, is experienced as challenging it. It is not just the angry, confrontational, acting out, impulsive adolescent who finds the task of beginning analysis an anathema.

For the adolescent is both desirous and fearful of outside influence, and a supportive ally can quickly become an enemy. On occasion an analyst, seeking to be abstinent, will not respond when his support is sought for a particular position. The adolescent, hearing this as disagreement, will suddenly decide, after several weeks of collaborative work, that analysis is "no good." Inevitably he will find a rationalization for this judgment.

Cynthia, an intelligent, impulsive sixteen-year-old whose readiness to break rules was matched by her readiness to confess her transgressions, be punished, and forgiven, was referred for analysis after she was suspended from school for intoxication. She had been caught once before and was worried that she would continue her behavior at her new school. Cynthia was depressed and suicidal, and even before the analysis began, she "knew" that her drinking and thoughts of suicide were related.

During her first session as Cynthia began to tell me her "secrets," she got up to check the door, stating that she did not want her mother to hear her or "she'll kill me." I assured her that the door was closed and that I would not reveal any of what she said.

Several months later, as Cynthia was criticizing her mother for her failure to discipline, she complained about the ease with which she could lie to her mother undetected, in spite of the mother's insistence that she always knew what Cynthia was thinking. When I asked what made the mother easy to fool, Cynthia immediately became indignant, quick to defend her mother against my attack. She reminded me of the initial session and my "insistence" that only I and not the mother could be trusted with her secrets. Cynthia was so adamant that this exchange had occurred that I felt any reminder that it was she who was concerned with being overheard by mother would lead to a struggle over who said what, with no good outcome. At this point I realized it would have been more fruitful, in that first session, to explore what made it essential for the mother not to hear, not to know the truth of Cynthia's activities, than to reassure Cynthia about confidentiality. That might have begun the exposure of the harshness of her superego, which initially had been projected onto the mother and now was perceived as within the analyst. Instead my reassurance played into her defensive externalization.

This type of mistake is probably familiar to most therapists of adolescents. Trying to reassure or ally oneself with the patient (as different from parents and teachers) in the hope that by so doing the patient will be more accepting of the process, less resistant to communicating verbally, and more trusting of the analyst, is understandable; nonetheless, it almost always leads to difficulties. Sometimes adolescents trust (without question) and idealize out of desperation to have someone fill the void left by separation from the parents (hence the best friend and mentor relationships). However, intimate relationships with peers or mentors easily become contaminated by incestuous fantasies and conflicts. An adolescent infatuation, no matter how all-consuming, can vanish instantaneously as soon as it is reciprocated or demands are made. An idealized mentor can fall rapidly from his exalted status as soon as his principles appear compromised by self-interest. And nothing falls more rapidly than a therapist's stock when he becomes a target for the patient's externalizations.

There is no analytic behavior that provides a guarantee of the future. Not only must the analyst be prepared for the probability that he will be narcissistically injured in the process of treating an adolescent (his competence, sensitivity, appearance, intelligence, and moral values all seriously challenged), he should also accept that even his most neutral behavior will be used by the patient for externalization of a self-condemning attitude, and that attempts at clarification or interpretation may be heard as the defense of the guilty.

It is easy to remind oneself that analytic tools serve one well at all stages of the analysis, in the beginning as well as in the middle. It is hard to remain analytic when, before the transference has even begun to consolidate, a heretofore agreeable, accepting adolescent suddenly decides that he hates you (or you hate him) and that there is no way he can work with you.

Thirteen-year-old Alice was brought to analysis by parents who were being driven frantic by her intensely ambivalent feelings for her mother. She was extremely negative at home, rejecting all overtures from her mother or father, while at school she sought out exclusive relationships with one girl friend after another. These friendships were all short lived, however, primarily because of Alice's possessiveness. Repeatedly she would be infatuated with a new friend, only to become whiny and despondent, abandoning the relationship after several weeks when the friend was "disloyal" or expressed interest in being part of a larger group.

Alice was quite suspicious during the early weeks of treatment and questioned every one of my comments. Nonetheless, I tried to avoid being defensive and instead worked hard to understand how she misheard me. This pleased her, and she soon spoke of how I, unlike other grown-ups, was willing to listen without prejudgment. She responded to my interest, and the intensity of her fights with mother and friends gradually diminished. Then, almost overnight, I became the recipient of Alice's contempt. We quickly established that her irritation with me was related temporally to seeing another female adolescent in the waiting room, but Alice completely denied any causal connection between the event and her anger. My attempts to pursue it were met with resistance and accusation of coercion and "brainwashing," and her positive infatuation was replaced by disgust.

It did not develop into an irretrievable situation; fortunately she was able to explore with me my motivation for "brainwashing," and the exposure of her fantasies (that I was frightened of losing both her and my "reputation") together with my nondefensive and nonretaliative stance, permitted her to achieve some understanding of the displacement that had taken place from her relationship with her friends to her relationship with me (only much later were the determinants in her relationship with her mother and the projection of her conflictual homoerotic impulses explored). However, for a while it was unclear whether she would continue to work, and I, for one, would have preferred more time together before such ferment developed. For just as one task in beginning an adolescent analysis is to establish a relationship in which transference elements can develop, another is enabling the adolescent to tolerate the transference.

Difficulty tolerating the transference because of the intensity of the impulses stimulated is only one of the potential problems in analysis that becomes exaggerated during adolescence. Analysis, with its focus on unconscious wishes and intrapsychic activity, more than any other therapy increases the patient's awareness of being responsible for his actions. Given that the adolescent is already anxious about being "held accountable," the analytic process becomes increasingly uncomfortable, for it undermines the use of externalization and highlights the developmental conflict over autonomous functioning. The realization that one is responsible for one's own actions (and thoughts) is an issue for all adolescents; however, this realization develops sooner in analysis, where denial and projection are so scrutinized.

Twelve-year-old Matt began analysis after swallowing forty-six aspirin in a suicide attempt. Although he avoided talking directly about himself, he did talk about his collection of Superman comic books and his ideas for a perfect world. The aestheticism of this land, where humanoids lived by photosynthesis and reproduction was the result of carefully planned hybridization in controlled nurseries, was not lost on me and I proceeded most gingerly in my exploration of this land and its creator. However, the patient was sensitive to my tentativeness as well as quick to project the harsh superego which had contributed to his suicide attempt. Matt accused me of being afraid to speak directly to him, saying it was clear I thought both he and this imaginary world were "weird," but was afraid of hurting him by saying so. After a short pause, I asked, "should I be?" Matt, who was expecting a heated denial, blurted out, "yes"; and for a moment this very withdrawn boy's wish to be accepted and fear of his "craziness" was exposed. I was careful not to indicate either that I accepted Matt (too much intimacy in that) or that I didn't think the world was weird (I wouldn't have been believed), only that Matt's concern had been heard. I went on to say, "I thought you were worried I might be critical of your ideas." This statement, which focused on Matt's concern without defensively attacking his externalization, gave us an opening to explore the externalization. It also gave Matt several important messages: first, that his perceptions would not be discounted; second, that the analyst would not cover over pain with false reassurances; and third, that he and I could talk to each other. This is not to say that in the heat of the transference the trust that had developed between us didn't disappear, for indeed it did. But by then the analysis had truly begun.

Self-destructive behaviors, such as Matt's ingestion, unfortunately are not uncommon presenting symptoms during adolescence when the combination of a decrease in environmental constraints and breakdown in ego controls and superego structure leads to a high incidence of overtly pathological activity. Although pregnancy, delinquency, psychosis, and suicide have always been serious problems in adolescence, the existence in the past of a more rigidly enforced code of behavior led to a compliance with authority in many adolescents, which if not growth-promoting, at least provided external structure and support during this period of increased inner turmoil. Currently, the external milieu of adolescents, like the analytic milieu, tends to be less authoritarian. This does affect the process of analysis, though not necessarily negatively.

Adolescents both desire and fear passive dependency, and though they may find relief in yielding to the authority of the analyst, it can increase their concern about being crazy or perverse (particularly if the relationship is eroticized). Fear of passivity, of sexuality, and specifically of sexual perversions, is a common theme in adolescence, although patients are usually reluctant to expose these fears, even to themselves. Nonetheless, most adolescents eventually have to deal with a number of disquieting self-observations; first, that they have the wherewithal to do what they imagined only other people did; second, that they are limited in what they can do by gender even while beset by the desire to do things which are "disgusting"; and finally, that they have feelings toward their parents which feel dangerous and "wrong."

Laufler and Laufler (1984) have discussed the severe pathology, the transient breaks with realilty that may occur while the adolescent struggles with the responsibility for his sexual preference and performance—the instances when he wants to believe that his behavior is controlled. Although their patients sound more disturbed than the patients I treat analytically, many of the issues are the same. For even my "healthier" adolescent patients have less complete repression of their instinctual fantasies than do adults with comparable pathology.

But in spite of incomplete repression, adolescents are usually not fully conscious of the fantasies associated with their "perverse instincts." Instead, they are sexually aroused, have erections, sudden temper outbursts, or unpredictable, frightening autochthonous thoughts, which lead to a whole series of "secondary" fantasies about what their behavior represents. Controlling impulses is hard, and a boy may try on mother's clothes, stand in front of the mirror with his penis hidden, shave his legs, worry he is gay, but be unable to inhibit himself. When this adolescent comes to analysis, even after asking his parents to get him someone to talk with, he may be completely unable to articulate what is troubling him. Tears, terror of doing something impulsive or dangerous, an intolerance of being alone, an inability to concentrate, fear of death and of suicide—this he talks of, in vague "you know" terms. What appears initially to be a reluctance to speak, either because of embarrassment, fear of narcissistic injury, or a wish to be pursued with questions (as an enactment of some passive fantasy or past experience) may be partly due to the wishes and fantasies still being unformed. Blos (1972) may have drawn his conclusion that the infantile neurosis and transference neurosis does not take form until the end of adolescence from observations of this kind of unorganized adolescent behavior. Fantasies that are symbolically operative and fully recoverable in the ten- to eleven-year-old who has been in analysis for several years are often not available if that child is seen for the first time at twelve to sixteen.

However, as the analyst becomes a participant in the patient's explorations, transference fantasies do take form. Although the fantasies may not be articulated directly, they will emerge in his mode of interaction, and even, in the less mature adolescents, be expressed in stories, drawings, or Lego constructions. But unless the adolescent is obsessional, with the affective distance that provides, the words and ideas are often not yet there at the beginning of the analysis. This puts a burden on the analyst: *not to provide the words.*

There are two temptations to avoid in beginning analysis with adolescents. The first is the temptation to tell the adolescent that his struggle is not unique. This form of reassurance is of minimal value; it encourages dependency, sounds patronizing, and may make the adolescent feel that the analyst has no appreciation for the specific pain of *his* struggle. The second temptation to avoid is that of trying to articulate the conflictual impulses and fantasies *for* the adolescent. Even the suggestion that the analyst knows what is troubling can be frightening to an adolescent who does not know himself. Better to begin by addressing the discomforting affect, asking the adolescent to describe it in physical as well as psychic terms, and to explore with him his understanding of his feelings.

We analysts all wish to be accepted by our patients, and it is particularly tempting to try to be acceptable to those patients who have found all other adults dumb or insensitive. Most of us, by dint of our training and the life experiences that led us to become analysts, are sensitive to affective experiences and are accustomed to using this sensitivity as a therapeutic tool. Sensitivity can be useful with adolescents, but it can also feel frightening and intrusive, particularly at the beginning of the work, when the world of therapy is still unknown and the therapist may seem omnipotent. The "dumb" therapist who asks rather than tells can often be more effective. And although the parents may also want the analyst to be an omniscient authority, their rivalry and envy tend to make them more supportive of a therapist who asks for information, rather than acts as if he can handle everything by himself.

Before beginning an adolescent analysis, it is often useful to establish a working relationship with the parents, particularly if the adolescent still lives at home. Unlike adults, for whom parents exert their influences primarily as internal object representations and structural precipitates, the parents of adolescents continue to be active in both the internal and external world. Though the analysis of an adult's character defenses and deformations based on pathological identifications can be difficult, at least the internal objects under scrutiny don't act on their own. Not so the parents of the adolescent and child. Parents are responsive to the behavior of their children and are often drawn into participating in their difficulties. There are some parents who can support an analysis (both financially and emotionally) with minimal involvement in the process. But many need to be prepared for their adolescent's reaction to the treatment and his tendency to externalize conflicts (neurotic, developmental, and analytic).

At the beginning of treatment, the adolescent is often critical of his parents. The parents, in turn, may accept this criticism because of their guilt, thus participating in their child's use of externalization. Later, as he struggles with separation and individuation, the adolescent may split the good and bad, depriving and gratifying, images of the parent between parent and analyst. He may ally himself with the parents, hinting (sometimes not so subtly) that the analyst has been saying negative things about them.

There are also moments when the analytic process with an adolescent is flooded with diffuse, rapidly fluctuating derivatives of psychic reality, in which past conflicts are so interwoven with displacement of current developmental concerns that it is difficult to tease out the transference. This plus the tendency in the adolescent to consolidate his self representation (self-perceived identity) through action (i.e., his tendency to define himself by what he does) can lead to alarming acting out or persistent demands for termination. At these times parents can be enormously helpful to the analytic process, redirecting the adolescent back to the analysis and leaving the decision to quit or continue to the patient and analyst. But without a positive relationship with the analyst and some understanding of the process, parents may give up and withdraw their support of the treatment.

Parental support can be essential for the viability of treatment, but it does not develop without work. In the beginning of treatment, when the adolescent experiences the analyst's noncompliance with his demands as judgmental rather than analytic, the problem may be, in part, a lack of understanding of the analytic method. Similarly when a parent participates in an adolescent's defense processes, it may be lack of understanding rather than *difficulty letting go* (a common pejorative term for "uncooperative" parents). Cooperation and understanding are not givens; like the development of tolerance for transference misperceptions, they are a goal of the beginning phase of treatment, goals to be worked toward with both adolescent and parents. Although most of the analytic work is with the adolescent patient (as with all patients in analysis), the importance of parental support should never be underestimated. Anyone can be susceptible to manipulation by their adolescent children, even colleagues.

Of course, there are some adolescent patients who do not want the treating analyst to meet with their parents at all; when this is the case, I feel the request should be honored (as well as analyzed). In addition, if the parents need treatment or extensive parent guidance, I regularly refer them elsewhere, for to continue with them myself gives the adolescent a confused message about the intent of our work. However, in general, even with the parents who move on to their own treatment or parent work with another therapist, I believe it is essential to try to establish a positive alliance with them, beginning during the evaluation. Not only will this provide the support for the analysis that is needed at moments of severe regression, symptom formation, or acting out, but in addition it will *convey to the patient* the fact of parental support. Almost all the parents I have met, including those with psychopathology so severe that it significantly impaired their functioning (including their parenting), have a strong wish to provide for their children. And though the adolescent child may be aware of a parental ambivalence that matches his own, and even have some inkling of the not-so-benevolent unconscious fantasies of the parents, he still turns to his parents for approval and support. The adolescent wants the analyst and parent to like (or at least respect) each other and even when he promotes it, he is not comfortable with parent–therapist antagonism. Adolescents long for ideal parents (accepting the parents' limitations is part of the analytic work), and it is not comfortable for the adolescent to proceed with a therapy that is covertly opposed by the parents. In the same vein, though it is not for the therapist to act as the parents' advocate, he should not join voice with the patient in attacking the parents; here too abstinence and neutrality are valuable tools.

I believe the main contraindication to contact with the parents is that it may interfere with the analyst's capacity to maintain an abstinent stance regarding the patient's behavior outside the office. The patient's concern about confidentiality, if not extreme, can be handled by maintaining confidentiality (in both directions).

Establishing a baseline of collaboration is hard with an adolescent; fearful of intimacy because his heightened impulsivity and biological maturity makes the possibility of incestuous activity a genuine threat, quick to externalize (thus rendering the world and the analyst uncertain and dangerous), he is caught in a developmental struggle, alternatively demanding and rejecting of that which was demanded. A therapist who tries to provide what the patient wants or seems to need has a tough time with adolescents; neutrality, regardless of the therapeutic modality, is important in this developmental stage. Though an adolescent may be filled with hunger for paternal nurturance (Blos, 1963), the last thing he may be able to tolerate is a nurturant attitude. Abstinence and respect for the other's space are important ingredients in the treatment.

Adolescent analyses do tend to end prematurely. Some are stopped like child analyses by parents who are satisfied (or horrified) by their adolescent's symptomatic changes, or who do not have a real understanding of the process. However, most of the prematurely terminating adolescent analyses that I am aware of from the literature (Adatto, 1966; Blos, 1972) and from my own and my colleagues' practices were stopped at the patient's behest. Although there are many reasons cited for this, my sense is that a common problem is the analyst's attempt to actualize the patient's fantasy of the good parent by being an understanding, accepting therapist, and his failure to address, from the earliest hours, the externalization that is so common in adolescence. It is true, as Blos (1980) has pointed out, that interpreting the patient's resistance in response to the threat of premature termination can be perceived as seductive and coercive, and may only heighten the adolescent's determination to leave. However, focusing on the patient's externalization, his wish to have the analyst be adamant about the need for treatment (which allows the adolescent to oppose it) may lead to a recognition of the internal conflict and a decision to continue the work (Chused, 1990).

In summary, the goals for the adolescent in beginning an analysis are: (1) the understanding that perceptions have multiple determinants (i.e., accepting that psychic reality and external reality may be different); (2) the recognition that a goal of treatment is autonomy from internal conflicts, not from external objects and demands; (3) the acceptance that treatment does not provide gratification but helps with the development of the capacity to achieve gratification; and (4) the development of the ability to tolerate the experience of an impulse without acting on it. The achievement of these goals is an ideal; nonetheless, they do define the direction of our early work. When the adolescent can acknowledge the existence of internal conflict, he has taken the first step of analysis and the first step toward achieving a measure of genuine independence.

PART III
ON BEGINNING WITH MODIFICATIONS

Chapter 10

On Beginning with a Reluctant Patient

Arnold Rothstein, M.D.

It is a common experience that prospective analysands object to one or another aspect of the anticipated analytic situation: they desire lower fees, different and/or less frequent hours, and they may object to the supine position. In this chapter analytic data will be presented from two attempts at analysis in which the patients were reluctant about attempting the minimum four times per week frequency of the analytic situation.

Many colleagues consider the four times per week frequency and the use of the couch essential aspects of the analytic situation. They would view any patient who was unable to begin in this usual manner as not suitable for analysis at this time. They might recommend that the patient be seen less frequently, and sitting up in a treatment that they would regard as preparatory psychotherapy rather than psychoanalysis. They might also suggest that when a patient completes this preparatory phase that he be referred to another colleague to begin an analysis.

In this chapter I am proposing advantages to conceptualizing these less frequent beginning efforts as modified introductory phases of psychoanalysis. I am emphasizing that, particularly in the introductory phase, it is the analyst's attitude toward the patient and his behavior and verbal associations rather than the frequency and/or the use of the couch that is the essential characteristic of the analytic method. However, I do consider a patient's ability ultimately to accept and experience the four or five times per week frequency and the use of the couch as important characteristics of a successfully *completed* psychoanalysis.

In this chapter I will discuss a group of potentially successful analysands who at the beginning of their analyses were unable to accept aspects of the routine parameters of the analytic situation. These patients' initial objections are conceptualized as *enactment resistances.* It is a premise of this chapter that a particular analytic attitude toward their objections facilitates some patients beginning an analysis. The prospective analysand's objections are viewed as enactments that are analogous to symptoms. These symptomatic enactments often have a transference significance and derive from unconcious fantasies that are best understood as compromise formations. The analyst has to be able to accept that the patient must do it his way first before the enactment can be understood. Stated another way, the analyst has to be able to accept being frustrated by the patient while the patient is gratified. An analytic attitude that accepts the patient's imperative desire for gratification as an aspect of a symptomatic enactment may engender a collaboration with the analysand so that his objections to accepting the analyst's recommendation can be understood as resistances. When these defensive aspects of the enactments are sufficiently understood as resistances, the analysand, if analyzable with the particular analyst, should be able to proceed with the analysis at the recommended frequency. In a sense my attitude toward the patient's enactment is similar to my attitude toward a child in play therapy. The prospective analysand's enactments are conceived of as analogous to his playing in the transference. The "play" must first be a shared experience before it can be understood and discussed. A sense of humor is helpful.

I inform the patient that I am willing to begin his analysis with him sitting up and at the frequency he suggests with the agreement that we will attempt to understand why he is unable to accept the recommended frequency. I frequently refer to the recommended frequency as the minimal frequency for the optimal treatment, and I often suggest that he seems afraid to allow himself to have an analysis or be in analysis.

I suggest two distinct reasons for considering these beginnings modified analyses rather than preparatory psychotherapies. First, the analyst and analysand have agreed to consider these less intense beginnings as resistances and to work toward the goal of establishing a usual analytic situation by understanding which fantasies concerning the analyst and analysis are interfering with his accepting the analyst's recommendation. Second, because many colleagues, including this author, prefer doing analysis to psychotherapy, the analyst, thinking of himself doing analysis, feels better about himself and his patient and is more likely to be successful in working with the types of resistances being considered in this chapter.

It is beyond the scope of this chapter to discuss in detail questions of indications for analysis and analyzability. However, I am emphasizing that definitive assessments of analyzabililty can only be made after an analysis is completed. All that is required initially is a judgment regarding patient suitability for a trial of analysis. Integral to this judgment is the question of who might be irreparably hurt by such a trial.

At this point I will present brief descriptions of "trials" of analysis with two patients with whom significant modifications were employed during the introductory phases of their analyses.

Mr. S., a very angry thirty-eight-year-old engineer, sought couples therapy for himself and his current lady friend. Mr. S. had two previous experiences with twice weekly individual psychotherapy with analysts because of his difficulties getting along with people. These therapies "dried up" after six to eight months. Mr. S. never worked in the transference in these endeavors. After a consultation that consisted of a joint session with the couple and a number of individual sessions with Mr. S. and his friend, the analyst recommended analysis to both parties. Mr. S. was outraged and insisted on working with the analyst once a week. He seemed impressed with the fact that two previous therapies had failed. This time he would succeed. The analyst agreed to work with him with the understanding that we would attempt to explore his reasons for resisting an analysis. After two months the analyst felt Mr. S. was wasting his time in a once a week therapy and told him so. Mr. S. expressed his feeling that he had to try it "his way" until he was forty. If he didn't solve his problems "his way" by that time he would start an analysis. Mr. S. did it "his way" and slowly increased his "modified" analysis to three times per week over a six-month period. In analyzing his rage at the cost of his treatment, the analysis of a silent moment revealed that Mr. S. was angrily ruminating about the cost of a four times per week analysis. In response to these associations the analyst offered Mr. S. a fourth hour. He responded, "Four times per week is your religious belief. You don't know it's any better than three times per week. It's a ritual." He added angrily, "Anyway, the time is impossible; it's bad enough I have the frustrations of coming here and paying. At least the time should be convenient. . . . I'll just wait until another time becomes available. . . . A patient will leave or die."

After nine months Mr. S. was able to accept the prescribed analytic situation. Although Mr. S.'s analysis has been long and characterized by a series of acting out resistances it has been productive. It is worth emphasizing that at consultation I experienced Mr. S. as a very "difficult" patient. In fact, there was something about Mr. S.'s anger that frightened me in a manner I experienced as "different." These feelings and fantasies influenced my view of Mr. S.'s prognosis as guarded. I learned subsequently that some of my apprehension was related to countertransference. These data emphasize that at the beginning of an analysis only a judgment of the suitability for a trial of analysis is possible.

Mr. F. was forty, an only child, in his second marriage, and the father of two children. In response to complaints from his wife, he sought a consultation. He reported that although his wife was quite dissatisfied with their marriage, in spite of certain symptoms, he was quite satisfied with his life and their life together. In addition, he reported he had had three experiences with therapy in response to a variety of life crises. These therapies were brief and helpful. In the first session, the analyst shared with Mr. F. the analyst's tentative impression that analysis was the optimal treatment for his lifelong difficulties. Mr. F. stated emphatically that he had no interest in analysis, he was too busy, it took too long, he knew too many dissatisfied patients and he didn't believe in it. However, he added that he liked the analyst's style and what the analyst had to say and he would think about seeing the analyst for further consultation.

Mr. F. called seven weeks later and made another appointment which he subsequently canceled. He arrived at his second session a week later dressed in an obviously expensive suit, silk shirt, and tie. He reiterated his appreciation of the analyst's comments and his disinterest in analysis. Analysis was not for him. In striking contrast to his costume, clubs, and hobbies, all of which were for the privileged wealthy few, Mr. F. expressed his feeling that an important determinant of his aversion to analysis was that it was pretentious. The analyst asked Mr. F. what that meant and listened to what the analyst considered rationalization as Mr. F. spoke of it being only for the rich. The analyst told Mr. F. that the analyst did not understand his objections to analysis as pretentious when so much in Mr. F.'s life centered on the enjoyment of expensive possessions and hobbies. Mr. F. proceeded to inform the analyst that he would like to see the analyst once or twice a week. The analyst suggested that if he really wanted a less intense psychotherapy he should seek it with a therapist who believed it was the optimal treatment for him. In response to his objections the analyst added that if he was intent on working with the analyst, the analyst would collaborate with Mr. F. twice weekly with the understanding that we would work to understand better what the analyst understood as Mr. F.'s fear of analysis. Mr. F. then found it impossible to accept any of the hours the analyst offered him. Sensing that his character resistances were threatened by the ordinary parameters of the analytic situation the analyst offered a second modification: we could make weekly appointments on a "catch as catch can" basis. Mr. F. liked the idea.

Mr. F. began the next hour by telling the analyst that he liked the flexible arrangement in regard to hours. He added, "It would kill me to pay for a missed hour." Inquiringly the analyst repeated the word *kill.* In response to his rationalizations the analyst suggested that even though he knows better it felt like it would kill him. The analyst added that this was his way of saying he was very frightened. Mr. F. stated, "I would feel like I was in jail if there were fixed times and I had to be here four times a week. I want to do what I want to do when I want to do it. Control is a big issue for me." Mr. F. paused and then associated to a friend's analyst who was indicted for sexually abusing his patients. Mr. F. added, "I also like to know everything that's happening here." The analyst interrupted, "In analysis you're afraid that I'd know more than you." Mr. F. concurred and associated that his father always had to have his own way. It was as if the father was only satisfied if he was king. Then Mr. F. commented on my fee being on the upper end of the spectrum of analysts' fees and on his being a multimillionaire.

He began the next session talking about people using him. He spent the entire session telling me of a passionately important business relationship in which he saw his friend and colleague every day for ten years only to be abandoned when he was no longer of use. The analyst interpreted his fear of a similar experience with the analyst.

In the next session he spoke about his fear of analysis and intense involvement with the analyst. He associated to his father who, he felt, swallowed him up if he allowed himself to get too close to him. He added, "I cease to exist."

In the ensuing month Mr. F. worked on his rage when his sense of entitlement to ideal hours was frustrated. In the eleventh session he reported his first dream. "I had a dream last night I don't understand. I dreamt I was in a church or maybe it was a bombed out city. I'm who I am only I'm a bit younger. There was a young child going out of control biting and eating everything in sight. I was frantically trying to control him." Mr. F. conjectured, "I guess maybe both people are me." Then Mr. F. described being at his father's birthday party the previous day. Mr. F. stated, "Everybody I love and hate was there." The analyst interpreted, "You're afraid of losing control with your family and with me when you're frustrated. You speak of wanting to control people and situations when you're afraid of losing control of yourself." In response to the interpretation Mr. F. associated to a fantasy of throwing his wife out of the window of their brownstone and of an urge to open his fly and exhibit his penis at a party. The analyst interpreted his fear of experiencing similar murderous and sexual feelings with the analyst.

Mr. F. began the next session by telling the analyst that he began seeing him with the fantasy that talking to the analyst would magically cure all his problems. He felt anxious in response to his awareness that analysis was hard work that didn't yield ideal results.

Some weeks later Mr. F. began the session before the analyst was scheduled to leave him for three weeks by requesting two scheduled hours. He associated to his rage at his father. The analyst interpreted the displacement and interpreted that he was similarly enraged at the analyst for leaving him and for not giving him ideal hours. The analyst added that Mr. F. had a fantasy of being treated "special," which meant never being disappointed. Mr. F. confirmed the interpretation by adding that the pursuit of that fantasy was why he didn't enjoy his children and was at the root of some of his other problems. He stated, "I want to be a special child and be taken care of."

During the fourth month of Mr. F.'s modified introductory phase, Mr. F. began a session by telling the analyst how meaningful treatment was becoming for him. He stated, "I'm beginning to ask questions about why I do things." The next day Mr. F. came to the analyst's office for an imagined additional third session that was not scheduled. The analyst interpreted this acting in the transference as reflective of a frightening wish to be closer to and more involved with the analyst.

At the beginning of the fifth month the analyst identified that Mr. F. never raised the issue of his fear of a four or five times per week endeavor. The analyst added, "You wait for me to raise the issue in relation to one of your thoughts. You treat the issue as if it were my concern." Mr. F. responded, "Yes. It's like with my wife. If she says something is good for me I have to prove she's wrong and my way is correct. You say four or five times a week and I say I'll show you once or twice a week is as good." The analyst interpreted, "So the substance of the recommendation drifts into the background and it becomes an issue of self-esteem. You feel you defiantly want to prove that you're right and I'm wrong."

During the ensuing month, Mr. F. deepened his appreciation of the defiant meaning of his modified treatment plan and its narcissistic gratifications. He felt "special" and victorious doing it his way. This analysis of the transference was associated with an increase in trust in the analyst and a decrease in anxiety. After six months Mr. F. was able to accept a five times per week endeavor.

DISCUSSION

In a letter written on January 4th, 1928, Freud commented on his papers on technique and the tendency of his followers to ritualize his suggestions. He wrote, "My recommendations on technique . . . were essentially negative. I thought it most important to stress what one should not do, to point out the temptations that run counter to analysis. Almost everything one should do . . . I left to . . . tact. What I achieved thereby was that the Obedient submitted to these admonitions as if they were taboos and did not notice their elasticity. They would have to be revised someday, but without setting aside the obligations" (Freud, cited by Grubrich-Simitis, 1986, p. 271).

In this chapter I have presented analytic data that emphasizes the elasticity of the parameters of the analytic situation in its opening phase. I have presented data from the introductory phases of two trials of analysis in which the prospective analysands were unable to accept the minimum four times per week frequency of the analytic situation. The basic premise of this chapter is that the analyst should begin the analysis in any way the patient is able to, so that they can begin to understand the defensive aspects of the analysand's objections as resistance. In addition, I am suggesting that at the beginning of a trial of analysis a great deal of attention to questions of diagnosis and analyzability is not required and may be counterproductive. I am not suggesting that evaluation is unnecessary. Clearly every analyst would maintain some counterindications to a trial of analysis. However, I am emphasizing that an analyst's excessive interest in doing an evaluation of ultimate analyzability and making a specific diagnosis may contribute to creating an analytic situation that may hinder a trial of analysis.

In this chapter I have emphasized that an analyst's attitude toward questions of indications and contraindications for an analysis, and the related question of the relationship of diagnoses to considerations of analyzability, influence his attitude toward prospective analysands, and the resulting outcome of consultations and attempts to recommend and begin an analysis.

Although a trial of analysis is not indicated for all patients, I consider a trial analysis indicated for most patients I see in consultation. My attitude in consultation is that a trial analysis is the treatment of choice for the vast majority of patients who present with anxiety, depressive affect, inhibition, and/or feelings of dissatisfaction with their lives. In addition, I am stressing it is very difficult to know with any certainty in a consultation who cannot profit from a trial of analysis. In a related vein, I have noted that, "Analysts are left with the awareness that among a large group of subjects considered 'typical' narcissistic personality disorders, some will have optimal analytic experiences while others will accomplish much less. Paradoxically, it is worth emphasizing that an individual with an unanalyzable narcissistic personality disorder may experience significant therapeutic gain from an incomplete analytic endeavor" (Rothstein, 1984, p. 140).

I am emphasizing that in doing a consultation with "difficult," "disturbed," and/or disturbing patients, it is helpful to pay particular attention to a prospective analysand's sensitivity rather than to considerations of diagnosis. It is often helpful at the beginning of a modified trial of analysis to pay particular attention to an analysand's sensitivity to the analyst's style, his office, and the parameters of the analytic situation and to explore the meanings of the sensitivity.

In the process of developing the point of view presented in this chapter I have found that when I have not recommended a trial of analysis, a *countertransference,* in the broader sense of the term, was operative. Analysis of that countertransference has frequently facilitated the development of an analytic collaboration.

It is important to emphasize that at the beginning of these trials of analysis an analyst cannot know the meaning of a patient's objections to the recommendation of an analysis. In addition, it is important to emphasize that I am not suggesting that the analyst gratify the analysand. Rather I am emphasizing that the analyst accept and tolerate the gratifications that the patient experiences in his initial resistances. I am suggesting that the analyst consider the analysand's objections as analogous to symptoms and not insist that the analysand immediately be able to relinquish his symptoms and accept the frustrations of the analytic situation. This is analogous to the treatment of the phobic patient who is compelled to bring a companion to the analyst's office.[1] The analyst would not insist that the phobic patient relinquish his companion. The analyst would accept the phobic analysand's gratifications and attempt to understand the defensive functions and superego contributions to the overdetermined enactment.

The data presented is intended to support the premise that at the beginning of analysis only a judgment of suitability for a trial of analysis is possible. Once such a judgment is made, significant modification of the analytic situation is sometimes indicated in order to create an ambiance in which analysands' resistances can be experienced and understood. A modified introductory phase of approximately six to twenty-four months may be required before a less modified analytic situation can be created.

I am explicitly employing the term *modification,* as does Stone (1954) in his classic paper on the "widening scope," rather than the term *parameter* employed by Eissler (1953). I do so because I suggest Eissler's term was derived from an idealized conception of analysis while Stone's term suggests a more realistic and relativistic conception of what occurs and can be accomplished in an analysis. Eissler began his cases with the phobic patients he described, in the traditional manner, and introduced a parameter only after interpretation during the midphase of the analyses failed to bring desired results. In addition, Eissler required that the meanings of the parameter be successfully analyzed prior to termination for the analysis to be considered successful. Stone modified the analytic situation, in the spirit I am

[1]I am indebted to Dr. Charles Brenner for this analogy.

stressing in this chapter, to accommodate the character resistances of his patients.

Ideally we would like all analyses to begin without modifications and we are keenly interested in the influence of such modifications on subsequent process. However, many patients are lost as potential analysands if the analyst insists that the patient begin in a particular manner. Flexibility in the introductory phase that allows for modifications to accommodate character resistances may facilitate some patients' induction into an analytic experience.

Chapter 11

On Beginning with Borderline Patients

Michael S. Porder, M.D.

The question of how to begin treatment with a borderline patient is a problematical one, since I do not consider *borderline* to be a specific diagnostic category. Instead, I believe that the term describes a group of diverse patients whose psychopathology lies somewhere between psychosis, on the more seriously disturbed end of the spectrum, and neurosis and neurotic character on the healthier end. As a result, I seriously question whether there is a specific treatment approach to such a heterogeneous group. There is a large range of psychopathology within the borderline group itself, and many borderline patients seen in an outpatient analytic practice are less disturbed than those patients seen by analysts in the context of an inpatient psychiatric hospital. However, I disagree with the conclusion of Meissner (1988) and others, who believe that there are two distinct types of borderline patients; a sicker group who display different dynamic conflicts and who use more primitive defense mechanisms; and a healthier group of borderline patients, such as those described in the monograph *Borderline Patients: Psychoanalytic Perspectives* (1983), written by Drs. Abend, Willick, and myself.

What I will present in this chapter is a description of the beginning of treatment with those sicker patients who consult and are treated in an office practice of psychoanalysis and psychoanalytically oriented psychotherapy. I will continue to use the term *borderline* to refer to the entire group of sicker patients even though, as I have mentioned, the degrees of pathology observed in these patients may be quite diverse. As compared to other patients seen in an office practice, it is quite clear that most of these patients are severely ill. They act out, are self-destructive, often present as severe suicide risks, are seriously narcissistic and paranoid, and usually demonstrate a disturbed "relation to reality" (Frosch, 1964, 1970) or a distorted "socialized reality" (Hartmann, 1956), as well as presenting significant failures of reality testing. Their lives are severely chaotic and often brief or supportive psychotherapy has failed them. In some there is a history of drug or alcohol abuse, anorexia or bulimia, and significant depressive episodes. Their object relations are usually narcissistic, infantile and dependent, or schizoid, and are quite unstable. Their sexual adjustment ranges from normal to dysfunctional to seriously perverse.

Although I do not do a formal diagnostic assessment or a "structural interview" such as Kernberg (1975, 1976) describes, I do take a complete history and make a thorough assessment of the patient's ego functioning. Therefore, it is usually quite clear after a few interviews that the patient is severely disturbed. I then propose an essentially analytic contract to the patient. By this I mean that I explain to the patient the rule of free association and the relative inactivity and neutrality of the analyst. I will return to this point later when I discuss my modifications of the traditional analytic position which many of these patients require. I recommend that we meet for sessions four to five times per week, and explain that I recommend this frequency because of the chronicity and the fixity of their emotional problems. I realize that this means that there is a significant self-selection among my patients, since those who are too frightened by my recommendation and who wish to be seen less frequently will not continue with me. However, I have not had many patients stop at this juncture because most of these patients wish to have an intense psychotherapeutic and personal involvement despite their fears of intimacy and the various meanings such an involvement may represent. I am also aware that many analysts and analytic psychotherapists see such patients much less frequently. In my opinion the latter arrangement puts both the therapist and the patient at a disadvantage, because I believe that therapeutic regression and psychic restructuring is the best treatment for these patients, as compared to an entirely or primarily supportive approach. In order to conduct an analysis or analytic psychotherapy, the frequency of the sessions and the continuity of the material are essential.

I tell those patients who are most disturbed that there are certain limits to what I will offer in the treatment. If hospitalization is a serious possibility, I let them know that I cannot follow them in the hospital, but that, if it is mutually agreeable and practically possible, the treatment may be resumed after the hospitalization. I also tell them that if a trial of medication is indicated, I will refer them to a psychopharmacologist, who will be in charge of the management of the drug or drugs. If suicide gestures or suicide attempts have been a significant part of the clinical picture, I acknowledge their seriousness and let the patients know that I will try to help them to understand their need for self-destruction, but that I can offer them no guarantees. I am aware that all of these statements, when made at the beginning of a treatment, may possibly affect the transference in an analysis or an analytic psychotherapy, but I believe that these issues must be presented clearly to these fragile and chaotic patients, in order to enlist whatever healthy ego may exist in the service of the therapeutic process. Furthermore, as I shall make clearer, I have not found it possible to conduct an unmodified analysis with most of these patients.

Another modification that I make at the outset is that I leave the patient an option as to whether or not they wish to use the couch. Of course, I try to explore their feelings on this subject. For many patients the fear of isolation and the lack of cues from the analyst's face and gestures leave them more at the mercy of their paranoid fears, their fear of sexual and aggressive instinctual upsurge, and the possibility of further regression to a more schizoid and isolated state. If they choose to remain sitting up or even to require other more unusual arrangements, I comply with these wishes after an attempt to analyze and modify them has been made.

Once a therapeutic contract has been agreed upon, my own way of proceeding is different from that of many other analysts. To highlight some of these differences, I will arbitrarily divide the varied approaches to therapy with these patients into two categories:

1. The first group derives from the British object relations school and is currently represented by Kernberg (1967, 1975, 1976). He believes that confrontation of aggressive conflicts as they appear in the negative transference and the interpretation of splitting mechanisms should be given priority over other interpretations at the beginning of the treatment. Kernberg works primarily with split-off self and object representations which are projected onto the analyst. He also focuses on the idealization and envy of the analyst, or the deg-

radation of the analyst, accompanied by omnipotent and grandiose or devalued images of the self. Because he believes that profound anxiety is engendered in the patient by any attempt to bring all-good and all-bad images together, he recommends that interpretative efforts at the beginning of treatment should be focused on these issues in order to confront the defense of splitting and the distortions of the transference which are the result of this and other "primitive" defense mechanisms. According to him, dealing with extratransferential conflicts, extending supportive efforts, and/or attempting to make genetic interpretations will only distract from this central focus and will be either nonproductive or counterproductive.

2. The second group believes that the primary task for the analyst during the initial phase of treatment is to create a secure "holding environment" (Winnicott, 1953, 1960); or to develop a "therapeutic alliance" (Greenson, 1965); or to act as a "container" for projected intolerable affects (Bion, 1959, 1967); or to help develop "self-soothing introjects" (Adler, 1985, 1989), so that the patient will become more trusting toward the analyst. This group, which also includes Modell (1968) and Buie (1982–1983, 1985), sees this step as necessary, believing that the patient has failed to progress satisfactorily through one or another of the early development stages. They invoke different aspects of failures of early mothering to explain how these patients lack trust, lack the ability to modulate internal tensions, and lack the ability to withstand separations without the eruption of extreme regressive psychopathology. The consequences of such failures of development are often referred to as "ego defects." The work of Mahler (Mahler, Pine, and Bergman, 1975) on separation and individuation or the analytic theories of Winnicott (1953, 1960) and Kohut (1971) are used to support their theses. Within a neutral analytic framework, these analysts may be quite supportive to their patients, and will allow a focus on reality issues dealt with outside the framework of the transference, in order to help the patient gradually begin to trust the analyst. This group also believes that genetic interpretations during the early phases of treatment will be either unhelpful or disorganizing, on the grounds that such interpretations may promote a paranoid regression, which runs counter to the attempt to develop a more trusting relationship with the analyst.

Aside from the obvious fact that the recommendations of these two groups appear to be so mutually exclusive, neither approach fits in with my own experience in the treatment of borderline patients.

Because the borderline group is so heterogeneous, any such preplanned, exclusive approach to these patients, derived in part from questionable speculations about excessive aggressive drive endowment, the presence of so-called primitive defenses, and/or the presence of "ego defects," seems quite limiting and inflexible. Furthermore, my own view of treatment for all patients, including those we call borderline, follows Freud's ideas about how analysis proceeds:

> The analyst is certainly able to do a great deal, but he cannot determine beforehand exactly what results he will effect. He sets in motion a process, that of the resolving of existing repressions. He can supervise this process, further it, remove obstacles in its way, and he can undoubtedly vitiate much of it. But on the whole, once begun, it goes its own way and does not allow either the direction it takes or the order in which it picks up its points to be prescribed for it [1913, p. 130].

Therefore, I believe that it is incorrect to devise a sequential formula for the treatment of these patients.

Nonetheless, despite the heterogeneity of this group of patients, I do believe that there are some common features that one can observe at the beginning of the treatment. Unlike most neurotic patients, the transference, both negative and positive, tends to be intense from the beginning. (The exception is the "frozen" patients, whom I will discuss later.) Most patients begin as Stone (1954) described:

> [I]nsatiable demands may appear; or the need to control or tyrannize over the therapist; or, failing that, the polar alternative—to be completely submissive, passive, obedient, to be told what to do; . . . or the transference may be literally narcissistic, i.e. the therapist is confused with the self or is like the self in all respects; or . . . the therapist must be omnipotent, omniscient, God-like . . .[pp. 584–585].

The combination of extreme demandingness and dependency, massive separation anxiety, coupled with the paranoid anxieties about closeness, and the usually withheld sadomasochistic coloring of any erotic transference feelings, makes the beginning of the treatment intense, chaotic, and confusing.

I try to deal with these massive transference feelings in the following ways. I actively interpret the projections which occur and suggest to the patient that he is uncomfortable accepting these projected feelings as his own. My point of view is substantially different from Bion's (1959, 1967) recommendations that the analyst should accept and "contain" the patient's projections until a later time in the treatment, when they can be reintrojected in a healthier form. In addition to interpreting projection, I suggest to the patient that much of what he is experiencing with me can be understood as aspects of relationships with images of significant people from his past, as aspects of himself which he believes to be in me, or that he may act toward me as he perceived figures from the past had acted toward him. Often I indicate to him that he is trying to tell me, albeit in a disorganized and confused form, what he felt like as a child. If the evidence is convincing enough, for example, that an important caretaker was alcoholic, severely depressed, chronically ill, or purportedly narcissistic and withdrawn, I will make comments addressing the possible relationship between these external events and their potential impact on a child. In presenting these ideas to the patient, I do not make "wild" genetic interpretations or reconstructions, but I make it clear that much of the transference, which is manifest from the beginning of the treatment, can be connected to these various mental representations from his past life. Unlike other analysts who believe that such interpretations are either unhelpful, disorganizing, or potentially fostering of intellectualization, my experience has been that these patients are in such a chaotic state, that they are often relieved to consider that some of their confusion may be understandable and modifiable. I explain cautiously and tentatively that their need for grandiosity, wishes for fusion, extreme guilt over sexual and sadomasochistic or aggressive impulses, and their need to idealize or devalue me or themselves, all have dynamic meaning. If it is at all clear, I always try to point out the central dynamic conflict which is active at that moment. However, because of their chaotic organization, these patients' dynamic conflicts may shift quickly within a session, or between sessions, in a way which is unlike that of most healthier patients. Therefore, it is often impossible to focus on a particular area of conflict with any consistency during the early phases of treatment.

In approaching the patient in the way I suggest, I am not proposing that one can accomplish a thorough reworking of either preoedipal or oedipal conflicts at this early stage of treatment. What I do believe is that libidinal and aggressive conflicts from all psychosexual stages can be addressed at this early time by working both within and outside of the transference. Any and all defenses can be interpreted along with the dynamic reasons for their utilization. I have not observed that such an approach leads to an unmanageable regression. In fact, it has been my experience that these patients will regress from the beginning of their treatment no matter what approach the analyst takes, even if it is a purely supportive one. However, my approach is different from others, in that I attempt to make use of genetic connections from the outset, in order to help the patient understand his psychic confusion and disorganization.

Another objection I have to the recommendation of a limited and prepatterned approach to the beginning of treatment is that I do not believe that one can work with these patients in a truly systematic way. I have already stressed the shifting nature of the transference and of the variability of the dynamic conflicts. In addition, there is the undeniable observation that these patients may seem to be unresponsive to any interpretation for significant periods of time because of their profound transference resistances. These patients are often so frightened that they deliberately withhold significant dreams, accounts of their life activities, affective responses, memories, and transference thoughts and feelings, to a much greater extent than is likely with most healthier patients. Because of the intensity of their transference feelings and because they both evoke and provoke such strong countertransference responses in the analyst from the beginning of the treatment, one cannot easily proceed with one's usual analytic attitude. By this I do not mean that one cannot be neutral and nonjudgmental. What I do mean to emphasize is that because of the confused and preedited material, coupled with the intensity of the transference and countertransference which is evoked in the sessions, it is likely that the analyst will find it difficult to maintain the same measure and quality of freely hovering attention that one has during the analysis of a healthier patient. As I have stated elsewhere (1987), these patients do not simply speak, they are constantly enacting something within the treatment. As a result, the analyst is bombarded with affectively charged, chaotic material directed at him, and inevitably he must have intense affective responses of his own. Such strong emotions in the analyst, coupled with the patients' disorganization and withholding, make it impossible to be as sure of the central conflicts which may exist in these patients at any given moment, as compared to what usually takes place in the treatment of healthier patients.

In the face of these difficulties, I often modify my technique in various ways. However, I hope to be able to interpret these modifications more fully later in the treatment. One early modification which may be necessary involves the interpretation of projection. These patients believe their projections so completely that there is a significant failure of reality testing around the image of the analyst. As a result it may be necessary for the analyst to specifically deny the affect or the meaning of interpretations or comments which the patient attributes to him. Thus, one may have to say, "I was not feeling enraged at what you said; perhaps you were feeling that toward me." Such a specific denial of what the analyst is feeling is never necessary in the treatment of less disturbed patients.

Another similar step may be necessary when the patient is in a paranoid, narcissistically withdrawn, masochistic stance in which every comment from the analyst is experienced as an attack and an attempt by the analyst to degrade and twist all that he is saying. At first I repeatedly point out to him that his suspicions of the analyst are transferences from a past object or objects, and a projection of his own wishes to control and regulate the analyst. I may also interpret how the lack of trust and the danger of intimacy are the result of past disappointments with significant objects, so that he cannot communicate with the analyst and can only trust himself. I may then propose an "agenda," one in which the patient may tell how he views what is transpiring in the treatment without interruption; to be followed by his allowing the analyst a similar opportunity to tell the patient without interruption what the analyst has been able to observe. The aim is both to interpret the transference distortion as one would with a neurotic patient, and to allow the patient to express his fantasies and fears at the same time. Over a period of time, using this modification, both analyst and patient may learn a great deal. This is not to overlook or to deny the fact that such a modification must have unconscious significance to the patient, who is caught up in the enactment of various fantasies; for instance, his need to control, to triumph over, and to reverse the relationships from the past, by distorting the analytic situation. However, such a modification of treatment may be necessary for the treatment to proceed. I think of this as an example of the concept of "optimal frustration" which Loewenstein has recommended for treatment. That is to say, one may allow certain acting in to occur in the transference, in order to prevent overwhelming affects from developing in the patient, which would interfere with the analytic process and with the patient's ability to gain greater understanding of himself.

Despite the distortions of reality testing which may exist, particularly around the perception of the analyst, it is often possible for such a patient to gain significant insight early in the treatment, despite the severity of his psychopathology. Although such a patient may be too close to certain of his unconscious fears to be able to tolerate some interpretive sequences directed toward the transference, it is often also true that his awareness of unconscious factors may allow him to appreciate and express some aspects of unconscious conflict earlier in the treatment than may be the case with a healthier patient, who might have more difficulty accepting and understanding the milder regressive reactions which occur early in the treatment. The borderline patient may have much more insight than the analyst is aware of, even earlier in the treatment, and may be communicating more about himself, albeit in a disguised form, than the analyst can comprehend. However, let me emphasize again that whatever insight may be gained during this early time, it requires years of patient work for it to be assimilated, often even longer in such a patient than might be required in a healthier one.

In the face of the typically confusing presentation by such a patient, and of his demands for relief from his painful affects, I often have to make some educative and semiclarifying remarks or even reassuring or supportive ones during the early phases of treatment, in order to allow him to continue to explore his associations in a productive way. I always try to couple these relatively superficial or supportive remarks with fuller interpretations. For example, when the patient angrily complains that I am insensitive and unhelpful and expresses his desire to discontinue treatment, I will tell him that I do not think it is a good idea to discontinue at this time and that it is likely that he is running away, either from a conflict which I can point out to him or from an unknown conflict. I may also couple my encouragement for his continuing with an interpretation about his fear of transference closeness, his sexual or aggressive transference feelings, or his feelings of anxiety, shame, or guilt in relation to the analyst. Whatever the appropriate dynamic interpretation may be, such a patient often needs a specific encouraging response from the analyst as well. This approach is not necessary in most healthier patients.

Another modification of technique which I use with such a patient is to anticipate affective responses which he is likely to deny or withhold, as well as to attempt to put together for him troublesome life situations which he would prefer to avoid mentioning. Such avoidances may be simply not discussing or ignoring physical illnesses, major employment or interpersonal issues, or transference associations which have strong affects associated with them. He may deny the importance of my absence or the hurt which he may feel from a remark I have made, or he will forget that a bill has been given and will focus on a trivial comment instead. Prominent amongst such avoidances are the denial of intense sexual feelings during the hour. I will return to this subject later. Consistent with what I have already mentioned, I always try to show him how such avoidance and denial are the result of some dynamic conflict which is operative at that moment and has a painful affect associated with it.

My purpose in making all of these modifications is to attempt to prevent the disruption of treatment, by which I mean not only flight or termination, but also the possibility of a further withdrawal into the narcissistic, solipsistic world which the patient has created for himself and is reluctant to have me intrude upon.

It is almost always true that extreme reactions to separations and loss make narcissistic regression and withdrawal a common occurrence. In this regressed state, such a patient will either become desperately clingy and demanding or will act out by withdrawal, in order to deny the pain of loss. As a result, in addition to interpretation, I often indicate to the patient that I will be available to him to discuss his anxieties should the need arise between sessions. I make it clear that my offer is based on my awareness of the painful, anxiety ridden responses to separation which he has presented to me. However, I do not make this offer as simply a supportive gesture, nor do I conclude that such a need represents a specific defect from early infantile development. Adler (1985, 1989) hypothesizes that this need represents specific failures in the capacity to develop both "evocative recall" and "self-soothing introjects." According to Adler, these do not develop properly because of maternal failures in early infancy. I believe instead that the patient's sensitivity to separation issues is the result of a number of dynamic forces which may influence how he reponds to separation. Such forces include actual separation and loss during childhood; depressed and narcissistically withdrawn parents; conflicts over aggression and guilt, guilt over libidinal wishes, particularly incestuous ones; the need for an omnipotent protector in a paranoid world; and a masochistic need for rejection, to name but some of the more frequently encountered dynamic issues. The important technical approach to issues of separation is to keep the concept of multiple determinants in mind, and to focus on clarifying the central dynamic conflicts which may be operative at any given moment. This is in contrast to those other approaches which assume that the central dynamic issues must necessarily derive from separation conflicts in the first two years of life.

I would like to emphasize in this context the particular technical difficulty which ensues because the relative neutrality and/or silence of the analyst reproduces in the patient the experience which he may have had with a depressed or narcissistically unavailable parent. This experience is most likely one which is continuous during the patient's childhood and not limited to his infancy. I believe that this issue must be addressed directly early in the treatment in order to help the patient to talk and not simply to withdraw or to cling. An acknowledgment of the patient's experience with a parent or parents does not undermine the importance of the fantasy distortion which may have taken place, but instead may allow the patient to talk more openly about forbidden topics. This is not unlike the problems one faces in the treatment of a molested or otherwise traumatized child.

In the end, except for the modifications I have indicated and my availability and my encouragement to continue the work, I try to convey the neutral, accepting, and investigative attitude that I consider to be basic to analytic work. Some may wish to call this a "holding environment" or a recapitulation of the mother–infant dyad. However, I do not conceptualize it in that way. I think that it is a relatively unique human situation that does not include within it the full caretaking of the mother–infant dyad, nor is it representative of the truly protective environment that one ideally makes for a child. It is most accurately described as the open, nonjudgmental attempt to listen to and understand another human being. A mother may attempt to do that and she does much more in other ways. However, no mother makes the explanations, clarification, and interpretations that, I believe, are of great help to the patient in the early stages of treatment. Furthermore, I believe that it is incorrect to view the analyst as merely a new object, who is able to correct a psychological defect in these sicker patients. I view the analyst more as a new object who is also an interpreter of important and crucial dynamic conflicts.

Let me now turn to another issue which colors many discussions of the treatment of borderline patients. Sometimes when I read authors who write about these patients from an object relations point of view, I have the impression that they think that ego psychologically oriented psychoanalysts follow only the oedipal associations and the seductive libidinal and sexual transference from the beginning of treatment, to the exclusion of all other material. They imply that all our interpretive efforts focus on oedipal triangulation and castration anxiety, and that we interpret all of these fantasies directly to the patient whatever the alternative views of the conflict might be. Even early in this century, Freud cautioned analysts about such a limited approach to the clinical material, and generations of classical analysts since that time have documented their understanding that preoedipal conflicts must be worked with intensively in all patients and not only in sicker ones. Nonetheless, many analysts, who take an object relations theoretical approach, write as if most "classical" ego psychological analysts interpret to their patients in this limited way and ignore preoedipal and aggressive and dyadic conflicts as well as narcissistic ones. Nothing could be further from my own point of view and that of almost all of my colleagues. The interpretation of all the dangers of childhood, including loss of the mother, loss of the mother's love, the power struggles of the anal phase, the problems of separation and individuation, and the narcissistic and self-esteem issues, must all be analyzed beginning early in the treatment of all patients whether healthier or sicker. These issues, which are mainly but not exclusively preoedipal, are a major part of all analyses.

On the other hand, unlike many object relations analysts, I would not shy away from telling a borderline patient early in treatment that they had sexual anxieties and sexual guilt, both in the transference relationship to me and in their past and present experiences with members of both sexes including their parents and siblings. I would make such interpretations if there was evidence of these conflicts in the material, just as readily as I would interpret anxiety and guilt about aggression, separation, and dependency issues, narcissism, and other partially preoedipal conflicts. In fact, I wonder, when reading analysts who write primarily from an object relations or developmental point of view, whether they may not inhibit the emergence of sexual and oedipal fantasies, both positive and negative, by their exclusive focus on preoedipal and infantile conflicts. In my experience, the oedipal, sexual, erotic, and romantic transferences may often be conscious from early in the treatment, but they are withheld because of excessive shame and guilt and anxiety in these sicker patients. Of course, it is also true that they may be repressed as in neurotic patients, so that one often cannot be sure which mechanism of defense is involved. In either case the regressive expression in preoedipal terms of all of these conflicts often allows these patients to avoid a more intense sense of shame, embarrassment, or guilt than they might experience if they were to speak directly about their oedipal fantasies. In this sense these patients, like healthier ones, usually leave the fullest expression of oedipal conflicts to the later stages of treatment, although the derivatives of these conflicts may be observed and interpreted from the beginning of treatment. I am aware that at one time in the history of analysis, too much emphasis may have been given to the sexual and erotic presentation in patients who masked preoedipal issues behind this clinical picture, but it has been a long time since analysts regarded such a presentation as evidence of only an oedipal conflict.

In contrast to my point of view, Klein (1946) and Kernberg (1975, 1976), in particular, believe that the early presence of oedipal material in these patients is the result of the predominance of preoedipal aggression which permeates all of their conflicts. Thus, even though positive and negative oedipal conflicts may be observed from the beginning of treatment, both Klein and Kernberg believe that these conflicts are mainly fueled by preoedipal issues. They support their position by postulating that these patients have "prematurely" entered the oedipal phase at a time when the predominance of preoedipal aggression will doom any normal oedipal resolution in both male and female patients, because of the intensity of preoedipally loaded castration anxiety. In contrast, I do not think that we can conclude with any assurance that any developmental conflict is dominant over another, whether one is speaking of healthier or less healthy patients. In addition, I believe that we cannot reconstruct the first few years of life with sufficient accuracy to permit certainty about dating the sequence of these developmental phenomena. What one can observe, is that there are strong preoedipal, sadomasochistic, narcissistic, oral dependent, and fusion elements observed early in the treatment of these patients, and that these conflicts may appear to be quantifiably greater than those found in many healthier patients. However, one cannot conclude with any certainty from analytic data that these elements are present because of excessive aggressive drive, because of developmental failures or "defects," because of regressive phenomena, or whether they are the result of the subtle interplay of dynamic forces which are the end product of complex unconscious fantasies. Most theories minimize this latter consideration, although I believe it offers the most accurate and useful way of accounting for what we can observe clinically.

Another important aspect of the beginning of treatment with these patients is the special attention which one must give to the *countertransference.* I will use the term in the larger sense to mean not just the interfering, disadvantageous, and conflictual affective responses in the analyst, influenced mainly by the analyst's intrapsychic conflicts, but will include as well those affects and responses in the analyst which are in the main determined by aspects of the patient's behavior. Because of the continual enactments which take place in the treatment hour and outside, these patients continuously bombard the analyst and stir up affective responses in him. This is quite dissimilar in intensity from what transpires with most healthier patients, who are more likely to talk and associate rather than enact. As I have described elsewhere (1988), much of the patient's behavior may represent a double-tiered transference–countertransference interaction. The surface transference reaction has the patient experience the analyst as the transference image of the dominant pathological parent, while the patient feels like a helpless, suffering child. Unconsciously, at the same time, the patient is acting like the replica of the pathological parent, and creates feelings in the analyst which the patient had experienced as a child. This is what I believe others have been describing as *projective identification;* although I am aware that many Kleinian authors use the term more extensively to describe all transference interactions in treatment, which are under the influence of projection and introjection. Since clarifying my own views on this problem, I have begun interpreting this transference reversal or "identification with the aggressor" to the patient, early in the treatment. This creates a painful awareness in the patient of his identification with the image of the pathological parent or parents. Such awareness may often add to his sense of depression and may be yet another source for his sense of being criticized and misunderstood by the analyst. Nonetheless, I have been surprised that this material may be close to consciousness in these patients from early in the treatment. At this time, I cannot offer a final judgment as to how often this interpretation can modify disruptive behavior within the treatment, but it has done so in a few of my cases, where there has been a marked diminution of projection and/or a greater acceptance of the possibility that what they may be experiencing in the transference may involve this role reversal.

Throughout this chapter, I have studiously avoided the terminology of object relations theory, while describing the beginning of treatment with these sicker patients. There is no doubt in my mind that self and object images may be "split" during the treatment of these more disturbed patients, such as object relations theorists describe, but I believe that this clinical picture is the result of ambivalence, displacement, and projective and introjective mechanisms, which are ubiquitously present throughout the borderline spectrum and in healthier patients as well. I question the value of the term *splitting* as a specific primitive defense mechanism as defined by Klein and Kernberg. Kernberg believes that "splitting" originally derives from the psychological immaturity of the infant's psychic apparatus and persists pathologically into the second year of life because of excessive aggression or faulty mothering or failures in separation and individuation. These are interesting hypotheses, but I prefer to use *splitting* as only a descriptive term, because I believe that such extremes of ambivalence exist in both sicker or healthier patients and may be the result of conflict from both preoedipal and oedipal stages of development. For the same reason I have refrained from referring to the other so-called primitive defenses, including projective identification, which I have already discussed.

No chapter on the sicker patient should fail to include a comment on the "frozen" patient. This subgroup, usually male, often perverse, displays elements of the schizoid–paranoid group, coupled with extremely narcissistic and obsessional features, as well as a severe affective constriction. Nowadays, they might be called schizotypal or narcissistic characters, and in past years, we would have called them schizoid characters. This group presents quite differently from the others described. They agree easily to the therapeutic contract, come to their sessions regularly, and either talk with blunted affect or find it hard to talk. They do not act out or act in in the usual dramatic way of the other sicker patients. If they are occasionally late or miss a session, they are unaware of any affective or fantasy life which may have had an influence on their action. Instead they are extremely concrete and explain their behavior by rationalizations. Similarly, if they report dreams, they have meager and concrete associations. They are willing to consider transference implications, but they cannot feel any of the connections. They may or may not complain about the constriction in their affective life, but they are able to see that it may affect those around them including the analyst. Some may enjoy coming to the treatment and being listened to, while the majority complain that nothing is happening in the treatment, although not with a great deal of affect. The wall between them and their affective life and between them and others is extreme. Their sexual fantasy life is usually constricted or withheld, so that the underlying perverse material may not come into the treatment for years. This particular group of patients, of whom I have treated only three, although I have also consulted on and supervised the treatment of several others, has been particularly disappointing in terms of outcome. I have found that years of treatment are required for even modest gains. In my experience, neither analysis, analytic psychotherapy, or supportive psychotherapy or medication has been significantly helpful to them, so I do not have any technical recommendations for the treatment of this highly resistive subgroup.

Other than this subgroup, I believe that the majority of sicker patients will benefit from analysis or intensive analytic psychotherapy. For many who begin in analytic psychotherapy, the latter part of the treatment may well be changed to a more traditional, unmodified analysis. During this latter phase there may well be an opportunity to analyze the various unconscious meanings of the modifications of treatment which took place during the earliest phase of analytic psychotherapy or modified analysis. During the beginning phases, however, one must be willing to endure the regressive conflict which begins immediately and may persist unchanged for long periods of time, while the eventual outcome remains seriously in doubt. Despite the fact that the early years of the treatment of these patients are very difficult and very different from a usual analysis, the rewards of successful work are very great for both patient and analyst.

Chapter 12

Acting Out: Special Considerations of Diagnosis and Technique

Martin H. Stein, M.D.

It is generally recognized that the symptom known as *acting out* offers a therapeutic challenge, and that its presence is a sign of a "difficult case." The fact that the term is all too often loosely defined, to include any kind of irrational or merely mischievous behavior, introduces an element of uncertainty which makes the task even more difficult. It is therefore necessary first to agree upon a more precise working definition.

The Diagnostic and Statistical Manual of Mental Disorders (DSM-III [1980]) offers only limited help. It does list a category, "301.50. Histrionic Personality Disorder," which contains some of the descriptive criteria we observe in this group of analytic patients; for example, A(1) "self-dramatization" and A(3) "craving for activity and excitement," also B(1) "superficially warm and charming." But the description fails to include the repetitive pattern of behavior and other characteristics essential to our psychoanalytic concept of acting out. And since it avoids dynamic statements, there is no mention of the unconscious structure regularly underlying this distressing condition. The manual also states that it is diagnosed far more often in females than in males. Whether it *occurs* more often in women is another matter. In my experience (limited, necessarily to an analytic practice) the condition is as likely to occur in men as in women; there is no clear evidence of a sexual preference for recurrent and circumscribed fantasy-driven behavior. My two brief examples are derived from the analyses of women, only because they happen to be more suitable for clinical presentation.

Freud's original statement in "Remembering, Repeating and Working-Through" (1914) was dynamic rather than descriptive: "we may say that the patient does not *remember* anything of what he has forgotten and repressed, but *acts* it out. He reproduces it not as a memory, but as an action; he *repeats,* without, of course, knowing that he is repeating it" (p. 150). Freud's formulation is dynamically precise, but its relevance can be established only after analysis has proceeded for some time. It cannot, therefore, at the beginning constitute a rigorous description for our purposes.

In an attempt to establish a definition which would be useful clinically, and still avoid the careless use of the term which had become ubiquitous in discussion. Anna Freud and others limited *acting out* to certain types of behavior which occurred *only* in the context of the analytic transference, thus: "Unlike the neurotic, the delinquent, the addict and the psychotic act out habitually, i.e. also without the releasing benefits of the analytic technique" (1968, p. 168). However, this formulation introduces problems of its own. In the course of analyzing neurotic individuals, we have found that their acting out behavior had been evident long before they began analysis, although it may have taken the analysis to identify it as such. As we become familiar with the patient's history, we discover that his acting out in the transference is in fact a repetition of a pattern which has been manifest earlier, often since early childhood. The observation of a lifelong pattern is therefore not confined to "the delinquent, the addict and the psychotic." In the neurotic patient, the pattern may fail to be recognized for what it is until he has been in analysis long enough to have his past behavior understood in psychoanalytic terms. It would be more useful therefore to consider that acting out *occurs* as a neurotic phenomenon before, as well as during, analysis; but it may not be recognized as such and be *understood* until it has been subjected to analytic scrutiny.

This requires a definition of *acting out* which is more inclusive than Anna Freud's, and yet avoids the loose use of the term which led her to define it so narrowly. Acting out is a symptom marked by a special type of behavior, lying somewhere on the continuum between normal and psychotic. It may be conceived of as a complex phenomenon, consisting of action at variance with the individual's usual modes of conduct and occurring in discrete episodes. These events have a driven or compelled quality and are typically marked by serious lapses of judgment. The individual feels that he cannot prevent himself from taking action, even if he is aware that he should check himself in his own best interests: often he will not allow himself to become aware of these interests until later. While essentially irrational, these actions are goal-directed, not chaotic. The symptom is neurotic in structure and is generally accompanied by anxiety, phobic reactions, and depression, but is not associated with major psychotic features, such as delusions or paranoid systems. Our patient, when he is not acting out, may appear to be a thoroughly reasonable person, who thinks clearly and functions well in his environment. It is this last feature which distinguishes him from the borderline, psychotic, and sociopathic individual.

Further exploration has revealed that he enacts not a simple memory of a traumatic scene, as Sigmund Freud's 1914 statement might be taken to imply, but rather something more elaborate, a series of interconnected memories which have been responsible for the formation and persistence of a highly organized and elaborated unconscious fantasy. It is rather as if he were living out a myth, the origins of which have been buried in history, yet which still exerts its power, rather like the Homeric myths which influenced the attitudes and behavior of ancient Athens (Stein, 1973).

The fantasy which lies behind acting out has its sources in childhood and has been present in some form since then, at least during the early oedipal phases, and perhaps even earlier. In its reenactments, reality testing is temporarily suspended, but is not grossly impaired over long periods, as in the case of the psychotic and the sociopath. As a consequence, the individual's awareness of conflict recurs again and again, usually *after* each episode, although he may have recognized in advance that he was about to do something which, if not against his will, defied his better judgment. He recognizes that he has been engaged in some piece of irrational action and sooner or later is ready to admit or at least question it. The psychotic individual, on the other hand, may fail to do so, or if he does, his retrospective judgment remains highly impaired. The sociopath is inclined to justify his actions by self-serving rationalization.

The character structure of patients with tendencies to acting out is marked by certain prominent features, which are pretty much invariable (Stein, 1973). The term *acting out* in itself implies a predilection for action as opposed to thought, particularly verbalized, secondary process thought. This feature is in fact a necessary ingredient, but it may not at first be easy to detect without a thorough understanding of the individual's patterns of behavior. Many of the most severely afflicted may be highly verbal, fluent, and articulate. But words are used, not so much for the communication of ideas or the achievement of self-understanding as for rationalization, for charming others and oneself, and for magical purposes. "Intellectual," or more correctly, verbal insight is common, but it is of very limited value in achieving control of destructive behavior, a fact which must be taken into account in evaluating technique and making prognostic judgments. Greenacre (1950, 1963, 1968) was led therefore to suggest that the origins of the predisposition to acting out were to be found in the early phases of language development. This is a plausible hypothesis, which may explain a good deal. It is not easy to demonstrate in practice, since it is rare that preverbal experience is recalled in a convincing form during the course of an analysis. It may be that children who grow up prone to acting out may also be liable to some type of disturbance in early language development. Only a well-controlled long-term study of young children could give the answer.

The sense of drama is especially highly developed, to the extent that the patient becomes writer, director, producer, and star in a personal drama, a tragedy rather than a comedy, based on an unconscious fantasy, which he acts again and again throughout life. He is always hopeful that the ending can be changed, to yield success and happiness instead of a repetition of past failures. But the ending is preordained, for the success which he seeks is the gratification of an essentially incestuous and grandiose wish. In the typical case, he enters into some action, hardly knowing that he is doing so, but behaving as if he were possessed of some assurance that it would work out *this* time. (In this respect he has something in common with the compulsive gambler.)

Some individuals prone to acting out are characterized by the psychology of the "exception," the demand and expectation that they will be treated differently, protected more effectively, and forgiven more promptly. This is likely to be a significant complication in those with a history of severe childhood illness, accompanied by the lavishing of concern and attention, along with feelings of powerlessness and humiliation, and the spur to narcissistic preoccupation, the latter especially facilitating acting out. This characteristic may be counted upon to complicate the transference, and to create countertransference problems as well.

To perform these repeated and futile actions requires that reality testing be suspended for some limited period of time. It is striking that at other times, and with respect to other matters which are not engaged in the fantasy structure, the sense of reality may be very acute and judgment unimpaired. Ego functions are intact in most respects, but severely affected in others—most often with respect to urgent instinctual gratification. We have all observed the sad fate of talented and well-organized individuals in political, corporate, and professional life, who destroy their careers through their inability to resist the acting out of personal dramas, the meaning or even the existence of which remains a mystery to them.

This ego regression is only intermittently evident; it consists of a preference for action over thought, impairment of judgment, inability to delay, self-centered attitudes with disregard for another person's feelings, lack of ability to gauge the future results of contemplated actions. This takes place in individuals who are most of the time in reasonably good control of all these functions. In some cases the patient experiences dreamlike sensations and a tendency to fuzziness of recollection—something like sleepwalking. Not infrequently, patients refer to themselves as "having been in a daze."

A feature common to all these cases is a recurrent need for excitement, leading to behavior which satisfies that need, often accompanied by sensations of danger ("thrill seeking"), which, on some level, is erotically charged. Often this occurs in conjunction with a masochistic character disorder, vividly portrayed in the popular novel, *Looking for Mr. Goodbar*. Very often, a rising sense of anxiety and frustration, which may be verbalized as a sense of "boredom," is a preliminary to a serious episode.

When we recommend analytic treatment, we imply that the patient is capable of using the transference situation and insight with ultimate benefit. When the clinical picture is *dominated* by psychotic episodes, sociopathic behavior, or driven self-propelled sexuality, we are much more cautious in suggesting analysis, although we do so now and then when these symptoms appear to be counterbalanced by favorable factors; for example, long periods of well-controlled behavior, areas of intact reality testing and useful insight based on earlier treatment or introspection—manifestations of what is sometimes referred to as ego strength.

To employ Brenner's terminology (1982), it may be appropriate to view acting out and its underlying fantasy structure as derived from a complex of compromise formations. Analysis reveals the multiple drive derivatives, defenses, and the roles of superego and the environment that contribute to the establishment of such a complicated and stubborn symptom. It is also of value to apply Waelder's principle of multiple function (1930), in understanding the functioning of the various psychic structures. The underlying fantasy, which plays such a central role, can be taken as a focus, a synthetic expression of multiple factors, a phenomenon intermediate between the less highly organized forces, including drive derivatives and defenses, and the manifest symptom, the pattern of overt action. From the point of view of technique, these complexities are explored in detail during later phases of the analysis, the process of "working through," which, in these cases, is likely to take a good deal of time.

The definition of such a complex category makes it necessary to decide what ought *not* to be considered acting out. There are certain actions that are compelled and repetitive, are of great psychological interest, but have no pathological significance in themselves; for example, creating works of art on repetitive themes, like the later works of Picasso and Degas. Whatever the roles of memory, fantasy, repression, and repetition in determining behavior (in this case artistic creation), we gain nothing by classifying that behavior as acting out, and by implication, pathological (although the dynamics may be similar!). The fact that the artist may also be inclined to act out fantasies in his personal life to the extent that we may consider them to be of symptomatic significance does not entitle us to categorize his *creative* work as acting out, no matter how many connections between the two we may postulate. It is evident in such instances that sublimation and symptomatic behavior, acting out, may operate in parallel.

The lives of certain individuals are dominated by ambitious fantasies which seem grandiose at the time; they do not necessarily result in acting out of any significant degree. Our most familiar example is that of Sigmund Freud, who was obsessed with the idea of writing a book on dreams and making discoveries that would have a lasting impact on the world. This fantasy was repeatedly represented in his own dreams; for example, that of "The Botanical Monograph" (1900). It would be absurd to classify his devotion to this task, as acting out, although the dynamics bear some similarity. While behavior may be strongly influenced by fantasies based on infantile experience, this does not in itself justify the diagnosis. The criteria we use are the extent of the intactness of the reality function, the control of impulsivity, the capacity for careful planning, and the steadiness of determination. Even though, in a given case, we may pick out specific incidents of failed judgment and lapses of reality testing, to which not even the healthiest is immune, we need to establish a major pattern of discordant behavior to establish the diagnosis. It is only those ambitious fantasies which are lived out to the point of recurrent failure that are more likely to represent acting out, since these failures are most often determined by periodic lapses of judgment and impulsive decisions. We are inclined to apply the label "dreamer" (in a pejorative sense) to such individuals, while they are likely to regard themselves as victims of bad luck.

Neither is it worth while to classify as acting out certain brief and occasional symptomatic acts, parapraxes, that do have some pathological significance, generally slight, while their underlying dynamic structures are usually relatively simple. Forgetting one's car keys, a common enough lapse, should not be included under the same rubric as, for example, a repetitive pattern of disastrous sexual infatuations or financial disasters, nor does it constitute by itself an indication for analytic treatment. The concept should not be trivialized: actions should be categorized as acting out only when they are of major significance, occur in a discernable pattern, and can be traced ultimately to an organized unconscious fantasy.

It is also important to avoid stigmatizing rebellious or merely unconventional behavior as acting out. If the behavior is of major significance, our judgment will depend on the results of subsequent analytic study. Active opposition to current social and political systems may represent the activation of unconscious fantasy and take a pathological form; it may also be a manifestation of deeply held convictions, connected perhaps with old fantasies of rescue and adventure, but nevertheless be supported by coherent, morally consistent, and rational judgment. Whether we or the rest of society approve is not the point. We judge by the presence of impulsiveness, lapses of judgment, periodicity, and above all whether we can trace a clear connection, or detect a discordance, between conscious thoughts and actions. These features give us at least some idea whether we are dealing with serious, purposeful, and rationally based patterns of behavior, which may be in conflict with the more conventional attitudes of society, but are not necessarily of clinical significance, or rather with neurotic acting out, which is.

Actions which are violent and accompanied by serious thought disturbances are sometimes called acting out, rather than impulsive, psychotic, or simply crazy. The same is true in describing actions which can better be denoted sociopathic or criminal. This may be permissible for lawyers pleading for lighter sentences for their clients, but it makes no sense clinically to classify Jack the Ripper as neurotic.

The same objection obtains in the consideration of substance abuse; the chronic alcoholic or drug addict may be fighting his memories, but he is employing a mode of action which is not readily accommodated under the heading of neurotic acting out; it is far more archaic in its mechanisms and dominated by access to ready relief by a mind-altering substance, rather than by a complex, fantasy-driven, piece of action. He is not so much *acting out* his fantasies as attempting to deny them. In the case of impulsive behavior, for example, that of the prototypical barroom brawler, the fantasy, if any, is likely to be crudely paranoid and affected by alcohol. Although these conditions share certain features, it is not useful for our purposes to classify them as acting out.

Above all, acting out should be judged by its incongruity in the context of the individual's habitual and characteristic behavior. The career criminal who steals is performing an act totally in accord with his character and subculture; his stealing is in no way aberrant in this sense, no matter how it looks to society at large. When he disobeys the rules of his group, repetitively and with lack of judgment, he may indeed be acting out. Unless we are given the opportunity for analytic study, which is unlikely, the diagnosis must remain no more than a guess.

Some degree of acting out is universal, to be detected in adolescents in whom it might be considered, within limits, as a quasi-pathological feature of normal development (Blos, 1963). With luck, the adolescent outgrows this tendency. A kind of acting out is also to be looked for in the terminal phase of even the most satisfactory analyses of "good" patients, those not notably prone to it under ordinary conditions, and whose previous life revealed little tendency to major acting out. Here it is so directly linked to the transference neurosis, that it becomes an integral part of the resolution of that phenomenon. If it does not appear in at least some minor form during this phase (when it can be brought into the analytic situation), I am inclined to be concerned that it may flare up later, a concern parallel to that which we may experience over a too persistently well-behaved adolescent, "who never gave his parents a moment's worry" (Stein, 1981).

To summarize, I have emphasized the distinction between the broader concept of action, in the sense of enactment, and a more narrowly and specifically defined conception of acting out. All complex actions are in a sense enactments, representing in some sense unconscious fantasies which may be thought of as compromise formations; only some of them are symptoms, and only some of the latter should be classified as acting out. The definition I employ here, of acting out, restricts it to compelling, impulsive, organized and repetitive enactment, associated with temporarily impaired judgment, in individuals who are otherwise generally rational and responsible, in other words, neurotic. Acting out may be thought of as occupying a place on the continuum between minor symptomatic acts (parapraxes) at one end and disorganized psychotic behavior at the other.

The initial consultation may furnish some clues to the presence of significant tendencies to act out; or we may reach such an impression only after some period of analysis. These signs would include, for example, a history of a series of self-destructive sexual experiences, frequent difficulty at work, with changes of job, more than an expectable number of serious vehicular and other accidents, and a pattern of what seem to have been irrational decisions, "stupid" actions by an otherwise intelligent person which, these days, may include a certain amount of substance abuse. Such patients often seek danger to avoid boredom or depression, and their activities are likely to be marked by a series of cliff-hangers. These features may represent neurotic acting out and be considered as such until enough evidence is accumulated to confirm or contradict the diagnosis, a process that may take some months of analysis. It will require yet more time to expose the structure of the neurosis and that of the underlying fantasy or fantasies.

We may still not be certain, after a series of consultations, that we are dealing with an essentially psychoneurotic individual, who has a good chance of benefit from analysis, or someone much more seriously ill, whose prognosis is poorer. At first sight it might seem wise to take a systematic history, but even this procedure, so well advised in practically every other therapeutic situation, from brief psychotherapy to the practice of internal medicine, carries with it certain disadvantages in beginning an analysis. For one thing, a prospective patient may omit important information for fear of embarrassment, or merely because he doesn't realize that it is important; or he may not think of it at all. He wants the analyst to recognize that he needs help, but at the same time, wishes to create a favorable impression. Another may try to give a complete and frank history, the "facts" of which, having been verbalized, are treated as if they never have to be mentioned again. The patient has used the opportunity to tell his story for its dramatic value, and perhaps as a way of getting a reaction from the analyst—to evoke interest, perhaps shock. Often it takes months or years to bring this material into the analysis, when it can be put into context and evaluated more accurately. Many of these patients are adept at self-deception—and in the deception of others, including consultants. This is not necessarily the result of a conscious attempt, a feature which makes it even trickier to evaluate; it is part of the drama.

Another disadvantage of making an organized search of the patient's history is that we may inadvertently introduce questions which become for him a series of premature confrontations or even interpretations. This may be enough to stop the process in its tracks. For the most part, we are forced to proceed with impressions based on an incomplete and often inaccurate history, supplemented by what we can glean from direct observation over a few hours of unstructured consultation, which may proceed into something like free association. In order to decide whether to advise analysis, we must rely on intuition tempered by experience. Once we have decided that our prospective patient is probably not predominantly psychotic, sociopathic, or subject to overwhelming and uncontrollable anxiety or serious addiction, we make some judgment about his capacity for useful transference and insight. We find ourselves therefore making use of subtle and elusive clues to support the decision to recommend analysis, as opposed to some less demanding procedure.

In general, beginning the analysis of such a patient requires the application of the same principles we use in any other analysis, but in a slightly different order. We listen carefully and encourage openness, maintaining so far as possible an attitude free of moral judgment. We try to facilitate free association and intervene at first only to aid that process. When we observe resistances, we interpret them (to the extent that we understand them); the same for transference, when it becomes a significant resistance. (For the discussion that follows, I am especially indebted to Greenacre [1941, 1950, 1963, 1968].)

The special needs of these patients do require some modification of the usual procedure. First, it is necessary to place the history of acting out behavior in a verbal context, describe it, point out its periodicity, its compelled quality, its dramatic features, and its correlation with lapses in reality testing and judgment. The patient must be helped to understand that he has been behaving in a particular way, a *peculiar* way, in a sense, over which he has the most limited control. Only after the symptom has been described and outlined, is it advisable to proceed with what is generally thought of as analysis proper, the interpretation of transference, the description of the underlying fantasy, and the reconstruction of significant infantile events.

I can best illustrate this by an experience with a young woman whose acting out in adult life turned out to be significant, if limited in severity. During the initial consultation, she had the greatest difficulty in explaining why she wanted help. Her husband had urged her to be analyzed, she wasn't sure why. She seemed to have no well-defined symptoms at all, impressing me at first as being emotionally blunted and not very intelligent. She looked attractive enough, but colorless and bland. Her responses too were bland and monotonous and her complaints (e.g., not being happy, being bored, uncertain of herself) could only be described as banal. She appeared neither guilty nor depressed in mood, and it was difficult to detect any active conflict or anxiety. I wondered what could make analysis possible or desirable for someone so lacking in curiosity and motivation. I did not anticipate that she would be prone to acting out; in fact I didn't know what to expect.

I was struck, however, by a notable incongruity: this apparently unintelligent, constricted young woman had received a degree with honors from one of the most intellectually demanding universities in the United States. Something else came to my attention at the same time. In talking with her I noticed a fleeting expression which belied her dull affect; it was a smile, subtle and mysterious in quality, at variance with everything which made up my initial impression of shallowness and banality. It suggested that there was much more to her inner life than she was willing or able to reveal at the time. These clues aroused my curiosity and contributed to my decision to advise analysis.

It took only a day or two to discover that she was indeed very intelligent, consumed by anxiety, and suffering from many neurotic symptoms, including somatic disturbances not even hinted at in the initial interview. She proved to be willing and able to work at the analysis for reasons of her own. But, how was I to know that these apparent discordances were evidences of an analyzable neurosis and not some less promising condition? For one thing, she presented no evidence of grossly destructive behavior as part of her history. Although her marriage was a bit unusual for one of her background, it was not bizarre, and her treatment of her children, while far from perfect, did not suggest severe pathology. Her judgment in most matters was good, on a level with her intellectual ability. She demonstrated all the characteristics of an "A student" and a "good patient," who kept her appointments, associated well, and was in manifest respects cooperative. I had no reason at first to suspect that acting out had played an important role in her life and would continue to do so in her analysis.

She had been reared by highly respectable "good" parents who were members of a Christian sect which, while liberal in philosophy, made severe moral demands on its members, both explicit and implicit. She had always been well behaved and law abiding, sexually restrained if not totally abstinent as an adolescent. Shortly after graduation from college she married a professional man, a member of a close Jewish family. Her own family she had regarded as cold, distant, and subtly but powerfully moralistic; she hoped that by entering a Jewish family she would find warm family life, deeper understanding, and a less moralistic atmosphere. She was to find only the last.

Acting out took the form, for the most part, of tricks with money, both with me and others, and a degree of petty dishonesty (a little minor shoplifting), clearly representing her protest against her rigidly moralistic Christian background. These episodes were marked by gross lapses of judgment. For example, she paid me in unreported cash which had been skimmed off her husband's family business. She never considered that my fees would be eligible for substantial income tax deductions (more generous in those halcyon days), and that it would have made much better sense to use reported income. She fantasied that like her husband, I wouldn't report the cash I received; I would become a fellow-criminal. She paid their rent and their housekeeper in the same fashion, in cash, inviting disaster at the first tax audit. It sounds stupid; such behavior was certainly strange in one of her high intelligence, general truthfulness, and capacity for law-abiding and ethical behavior. It was hard for her at first to recognize how irrational her actions were and how much at variance with other aspects of her personality.

It took some years to learn the secret of her acting out and even longer to understand the origins of her mysterious smile and the highly charged fantasies behind it. Interestingly, she became aware of their nature in a doctor's office while waiting for her child to be examined by a pediatrician; it was an indirect way of bringing her fantasy life into the context of the transference. She enjoyed a rich imaginative life, consisting of highly exciting erotic fantasies, which only rarely reached consciousness, but were betrayed by her facial expression. What she had acted out for years, not very flagrantly, it is true, was the role of a sensual, money-grubbing Jewish prostitute, daughter of a prototypical Jewish mother. Her acting out, which was never mentioned initially, was an attempt to enact these fantasies.

She was impelled to reject her own heritage, as the child of a highly respectable, moralistic, austere Christian family; she never felt sufficiently loved by them, an impression gained, I believe, more out of their emotional restraint, than true neglect. She had achieved a revenge on her parents by rejecting, through her behavior, the moral standards they stood for and which she had found so oppressive. Her wish to be free of her parents' standards was in some sense expressed in her marriage. But her husband turned out to be not especially warm in his responses and her mother-in-law, rather than being truly affectionate, was intrusive and interfering. She did find the corruption, her desire for which was entirely unconscious. Her wishes for a different, "closer" kind of family life were gratified, but in the manner of the wishes granted by a wicked fairy; her fantasy and its consequences became a caricature both absurd and tragicomic. As acting out goes, hers was mild, and required no measures aside from appropriate interpretation.

I have chosen an "easy" rather than a typical case to demonstrate how difficult it is to know what we have to deal with, until it is revealed by the analytic procedure. In her case, this required no more than the usual demands for understanding and tact inherent in any analysis. I was not faced with the temptation to interpret the underlying erotic fantasy prematurely; in any case, I had no idea at the time what it was about. Fortunately, her acting out episodes did not seriously threaten the structure of her life or the continuation of the treatment. The nature of her symptoms became clear within a few weeks of beginning the analysis, but it took months to get a picture of her acting out and much longer to understand it analytically in terms of her unconscious fantasy.

Things are not often so easy. Another patient, previously described (Stein, 1973), was a young woman who came because of repeated infatuations and disappointments in her personal life, which she sensed she had brought about herself. This behavior, which showed marked impairment of judgment with respect to her highly masochistic love life, did not on the other hand significantly affect her very active professional career, in which she functioned with consistent intelligence and impressive responsibility. After consultation, my initial impression, which turned out to be correct, was that she suffered from a character neurosis marked by a pronounced tendency toward acting out.

As soon as she began her analysis, her acting out stopped; she manifested all the characteristics of the "good patients" I have described elsewhere (1983). At the same time, she developed the most intense admiration for me, my skill as an analyst, my standing in the profession, and my personal qualities. I decided that this was one situation in which I would be justified in holding off interpretation of this clearly developing transference phenomenon, until we knew more of the structure of her neurosis. It would hardly have done, at the moment, to point out bluntly that she had substituted a new infatuation for the old ones. For one thing, it was being *experienced* in the context of an analysis, but was not acted out, being confined to words rather than carried out in behavior. For another, we needed more time to be able to face her with the unconscious aspects of her feelings toward me, so that the interpretation would come as a useful clarification, rather than simply another in a long series of rejections.

Eventually, when I indicated, gently to be sure, the need to subject this development to analytic scrutiny, she reacted with intense anger and threatened to resume her exciting, sad adventures in love. When I failed to react with dismay and anxiety—or jealousy—she threatened to refuse to leave my office. When I announced the end of the session, she stood up, gave me a wry smile, and left. Almost immediately however, she entered into another typical, fruitless love affair which, fortunately, did not get very far and resulted in no desperate unhappiness.

We soon discovered what she was reenacting in the transference and had acted out elsewhere. She had been sent off to nursery school when she was two years old (it was done in those days), but she cried so bitterly that she had to be taken home, and the attempt was abandoned. Two years later, a sibling was born, and she was sent off once more. Again, she tried to remain home, this time by complaining of illness, but after being declared well by the family pediatrician, she was carried off to school, kicking and screaming all the way. Once at school, having more or less accepted her fate, she became a model student. At home, however, she repeated her performance every school morning for some months.

Her elegant and narcissistic parents professed the highest and most up-to-date ideas of child-rearing "according to Freud and other authorities." In practice, however, they flouted these ideals and ignored the child except when they could show her off to advantage. This situation had profound effects in encouraging the development of her dramatic skills—she became a young charmer—favoring her choice of a profession, which was fortunate, and at the same time facilitated the less fortunate development of her most prominent neurotic symptom, acting out. In her work, she sought, and received, love from her audiences; but she also found herself seeking love from men who generally turned out to be incapable of giving it. Entering analysis fitted into the same pattern of idealization and hopeless infatuation. When she threatened to remain in my office, she had the fantasy that, like the pediatrician, I should have to remove her bodily. She found the idea a most exciting one but to my relief, she did not put me to the test by acting it out.

This young woman demonstrated discrepancies between verbalized thought and behavior to an extent which permitted self-destructive acting out to take place in an atmosphere of apparent rationality. Throughout life, she provoked rejections and desertions, each time being disappointed when the inevitable occurred. It affected her personal life very seriously; her work on the other hand suffered little, if at all. The latter absorbed much of her need for drama, but not enough to protect her against the need to act out in other aspects of her life. It is a phenomenon familiar enough in the life stories of talented performers.

Beginning her analysis required the greatest care in timing of interventions. It would not have done to point out the nature of her transference infatuation before she had been made aware that she had been living her life according to a repetitive pattern of infatuations and rejections, and that she was trying to repeat this pattern with me, hoping against her better judgment that I would be the idealized, loving parent. It would have been pointless at best to describe the content of her fantasy life before she could accept the degree to which her symptomatic behavior was organized around such a structure. A piece of verbalized insight at this phase could only have been used as a highly effective resistance.

Delay in pointing out the nature of such transference, "positive," only when regarded in a simplistic sense (Stein, 1981), is in some respects parallel to the advice of Kohut (1971), to let the idealizing transference in narcissistic patients go untouched for the sake of the therapeutic result. My point is a somewhat different one; such a transference reaction should be left without an attempt at interpretation *only* until it can be understood in the context of the illness, as a manifestation of the transference neurosis. When this point has been reached, the transference infatuation may be spelled out in terms of one of its most important functions, not only as repetition, but as resistance to understanding and remembering. The interpretation must be made with due regard for the pain it is bound to produce. To allow it to go on indefinitely is likely to result in a travesty of analysis, a prolonged stalemate, producing much greater difficulty in the long run.

I have also had the less satisfactory experience of working with acting out patients who only late in the analysis revealed how intransigent was the tendency to relapse. The symptom often remained manageable until termination was contemplated. Then serious outbreaks occurred in response to the prospect of parting. Usually, these events could be satisfactorily analyzed, and serious relapse avoided, although not without much painful struggle. But this was not always possible. Particularly when a patient whose previous pattern of substance abuse had been under control experienced a serious relapse, acting out which had been manageable became no longer so, and the analysis had to be terminated. It forced me to recognize that patients with a history of severe substance abuse, far more commonly met with now than in past years, are much more likely than others to present unmanageable problems of acting out. The danger of relapse into the enacting of one's fantasies is greatly enhanced by the accessibility and the acceptance of mind-altering drugs, and can render ineffective our most devoted efforts. The phenomenon of substance abuse, with alcohol, marijuana, cocaine, or hallucinogenics, has made the analysis of acting out a far more uncertain affair than it was some years ago.

And individuals who have extensive experience with these drugs may be less likely to seek the arduous path of analysis, when easy and quick relief, however temporary, can be obtained.

There are a few important differences in the way we proceed with patients who are especially prone to acting out, as compared with those who are not. We are more inclined to watch the level of anxiety very carefully, since a sharp rise may precipitate a major episode of acting out and put the analysis into jeopardy. The patient may destroy his treatment by means of a change of career requiring a move to a distant location, a disastrous love affair which creates enough havoc to make analytic treatment impossible, by arranging to lose all his money, or in a worse case, resuming a habit of substance abuse. I have no doubt that an insensitive confrontation or a too clever or premature interpretation (especially a "correct" one) can precipitate a disastrous episode.

This carefully disciplined mode of conducting the analysis exacts its own price. The patient who acts out is not likely to miss the fact that I am being so cautious and perhaps tactful in the beginning as to seem vague and indecisive. He may draw the conclusion, plausibly enough, that I am concealing my own anxieties over his behavior. If he senses that I am not only concerned about his acting out, but frightened of it, he is likely to manifest his resistance in the form of even more provocative episodes. In this case I may find him reexperiencing a time when his parents were frightened of him, constantly apprehensive about what he might do next in the way of mischief. He repeats instead of remembering.

This faces me with the need to examine and regulate my own anxieties. If I am ever to help my patient recall significant memories and substitute thought for action, I must retain, along with understanding and concern, a considerable degree of detachment. But if that concern beomes panic and I can no longer regard the tendency to act out as a matter to be understood and analyzed, I fall into the attitude of the anxious parent, and am tempted to express protective and moralistic attitudes which can be fatal to the analysis. The acting out patient is likely to be highly intelligent and extremely sensitive to the moods of others—that he cannot use these traits in his own best interests is another matter. If he senses insecurity, he is quick to take advantage, making use of subtle threats and often carrying them out by behavior which endangers the therapeutic goals. It is reminiscent of delinquent behavior in adolescence, and anxious warnings are about as useful as they are with excited adolescents, producing the usual negative results. Analyzing such patients has something of the quality of walking a tightrope.

It is evident, therefore, that countertransference complications are likely to be prominent in working with this group of patients. Considering their predilection for action, the combination of seductiveness and masochism, exaggerated sexuality and capacity to charm, provoke, frustrate, and threaten, they are capable of arousing powerful and complex reactions. Anxiety is the most common, taking the form of concern, justified or not, over outbreaks which threaten to destroy the analysis and even put the patient in danger, a countertransference reaction which may reawaken old uncertainties about one's own capacity for self-discipline, and raise doubts in us about our professional competence. When we propose taking a holiday, these patients give us the very clear impression that we are leaving them unprotected from their unruly impulses, thus making us feel like neglectful parents, and if we are susceptible, arousing old desertion fantasies out of our own pasts. They also threaten us persistently by making it clear how fragile is our control of the analytic process, which they have the power to wreck at any moment. And they endanger our sense of self-control. It is very difficult not to get angry now and then, a reaction which these patients are quick to detect; but unless we are so angry as to convey a threat (obviously something to be avoided), they will likely as not react with satisfaction at having gotten a rise out of us.

It is not unusual, therefore, to be tempted to respond to a patient's acting out by some acting out of one's own, whether it takes the form of reenacting rescue fantasies, or punitive ones. Either tendency, if unrecognized, can have unfortunate consequences for patient and analyst alike. In this situation, consultation with a colleague may be essential to attain a better perspective, perhaps by making clear such countertransference complications, and tempering one's own anxiety by the aid of a more detached view of the problem. I believe consultation to be indicated whenever we are faced with a patient's severe acting out, and we become sensible of extreme demands on our self-control, understanding, and objectivity.

In some cases these dilemmas, no matter what we do, turn out to be unresolvable in an analytic context, and active interference becomes unavoidable. It is necessary then to transfer the patient to another colleague, the sooner the better, since this may be the only way to resolve a transference impasse. This should be done only after frank discussion with the patient as to the reasons necessitating such a serious move. Whether analysis can be resumed by the new analyst, or some other procedure begun, is a decision to be made by the latter. What new procedure other than analysis will work is difficult to say. Warnings, prohibitions, and other such attempts to control behavior directly are likely to lead to exacerbation of symptoms, rather than improvement. We have learned by painful experience that if analysis doesn't help, it is likely to be unclear what will. Acting out patients do *not* learn by trial and error, nor by rewards and punishments—if they did, they wouldn't be acting out.

The tendency is rooted in a complex, deeply rooted personality organization, the understanding of which is necessary in order to treat such patients with any hope of success. We look for the origins of this character organization in the vicissitudes of preverbal development. Something has gone wrong there, probably in the form of disturbances in relations with the parents, most often perhaps, the mother. These are not necessarily conspicuous events, such as parental loss or illness, which are more likely to predispose to other forms of pathology, if any. In the cases with which I have worked, the term *peculiar* tended to come to mind when I thought about the patients' parents, as they were portrayed in their impressions of childhood. Whether they really were so strange, or whether they had to be perceived that way, it is hard to say. I suspect that both factors were operative.

It is also difficult in discussing this group of patients to avoid talking about "innate tendencies," "constitution" and the like. Are they born with a predisposition to acting out personal dramas? Do they have an unconscious attachment to magic and a belief in their own invulnerability? Is there a gene for the tendency to resort to fantasy-driven activity? We do not have the answers; meanwhile we must do the best we can to help the individual develop an effective degree of control over his own tendencies to periodic episodes of maladaptive, truly "thoughtless" behavior.

SUMMARY

To review the guidelines relevant to undertaking the analysis of acting out patients, it is necessary to make some judgment as to the severity of the symptom and the context in which it occurs, namely the other strengths and weaknesses of the personality; then to decide on this basis whether or not to recommend analysis.

Having agreed to begin the analysis (which assumes a degree of cooperation on the patient's part), and outlined the conditions, the analytic contract, it is necessary to listen attentively for some time, giving the patient the chance to recognize the analyst as a listener who is trying to understand and to make sense of his problems, to see them more clearly and to establish a context. It is of course necessary to help the flow of associations, but to do so in the least intrusive way. As in the case of children (Kabcenell, 1988), the transference here may be a rapidly growing, but very delicate plant. It takes a while for it to operate in a way consistent with analytic work, as opposed to mere superficial cooperation. With these patients especially, we may be led unsuspectingly, in an atmosphere of apparent cooperation and intellectual insight, into accepting a facsimile of analysis for the real thing.

Once the analysis is started and the transference neurosis well established, we may proceed for some time without seeing any evidence of acting out worthy of the name. But as soon as there is a rift, a rise in anxiety, precipitated by a holiday interruption perhaps, some acting out is likely to occur. When it does, and a description of it has been received from the patient, it is best to resist the temptation to interpret very extensively either its content or its transference implications. Instead, it is more useful and less risky to show the patient what he has been doing and how it reflects earlier patterns of behavior, the memories of which have remained in awareness. In this way he learns that his actions are part of a recurrent pattern, over which he has very limited control and even less useful understanding. I am tempted to call this the stage of *confrontation,* but that term gives a falsely harsh and moralistic tone, which is altogether inappropriate here. The approach must be unfailingly tactful and morally neutral. If that is impossible, for countertransference or other reasons, attempts to get an analysis under way are likely to be altogether futile. It is better to recognize this at the beginning and either resolve it or transfer the patient.

Once the analysis is well under way and patterns of behavior have been verbalized and outlined, it becomes possible to make significant transference interpretations, again firmly and tactfully, in such a way as to lessen the likelihood of further, and more troublesome, acting out. Later one can describe the underlying fantasies and foster the recall of the repressed memories which have played so crucial a role in the patient's pathology. This being done, we hope that the patient has achieved the kind of insight and working through he needs to establish control of his periodic impulses to reenact old fantasies in a stereotyped and maladaptive way.

Chapter 13

On Beginning with Patients Who Require Medication

Mortimer Ostow, M.D.

After years of rejecting the possibility of combining psychiatric drug therapy with psychoanalysis, our profession is becoming reconciled to its necessity. To a certain extent this reconciliation has been forced by the current dearth of patients considered appropriate candidates for psychoanalysis. By starting with a course of drug therapy, one can alleviate depression or even psychosis within a relatively short period of time, and bring a patient to a state of mind that will permit a normal psychoanalytic procedure.

Complementary use of medication literally widens the scope of psychoanalysis. The combined procedure implies that we acknowledge that for the treatment of psychosis, mania, and melancholic depression, psychoanalysis is an inefficient tool if it is effective at all. We are learning to face the fact that these conditions should not be treated with psychoanalysis, because even if it could be demonstrated in any given case that the analytic treatment resulted in the patient's recovery, it has become evident to everyone that drug treatment can produce the same relief in a much shorter period of time, not only saving the patient time and money, but sparing him months or years of unnecessary suffering.

What has not become well known yet is the fact that many conditions that we do not recognize as depression, and that seem to be the neurotic or character disorders that we consider appropriate for classical analysis, for example, masochistic character, or anxiety or panic disorder, may also respond dramatically to antidepression drug treatment. In many such instances, psychoanalysis becomes unnecessary, and in others it can be curtailed. It follows that although psychiatric drug treatment makes some patients available for psychoanalysis who would not otherwise be available, in other cases it makes psychoanalysis superfluous. We must conclude that there are common pathogenic processes that respond poorly, if at all, to insight treatment. Some of these respond easily to psychiatric drug therapy.

The profession's resistance to acknowledging the power of medication and its potential for complementing the analytic procedure in the treatment of some patients, was based, it seems to me, on two considerations. Psychodynamic drug therapy seemed, at first glance, to be another method for devaluing psychoanalysis and the unique contribution that it makes. Although every psychoanalyst knows that Freud anticipated the availability of psychiatric drug therapy and correctly related it to the humoral messenger system (Freud, 1933, 1940), nevertheless, most psychoanalysts have seemed to believe that if one took the possibility of psychoanalytic drug therapy seriously, one was betraying the psychoanalytic profession. I learned from Dr. Herman Nunberg that Freud spoke of anticipating a time when it would be possible to use chemical substances during a therapeutic analysis in order to direct the analysis into the most fruitful channels.

Second, the technique of psychoanalysis is carefully structured so as to minimize all influences upon the patient other than insight derived from his own free associations. The analyst is not to influence him by revealing to the patient more than a minimum amount of his own personal life, nor by making decisions for him, nor by advising him, nor by communicating with members of his family. By prescribing drug therapy, the psychoanalyst seems to violate this basic principle of treatment: he advises the patient, makes decisions for him, he steps inside his arm's length distance from the patient, and if he is a good physician, he encourages, instructs, and attempts to mobilize and motivate. All of this seems to threaten the "purity" of the analytic procedure itself, and to contaminate the transference irreparably.

The title of this essay, "On Beginning with Patients Who Require Medication," requires some discussion. One may begin a psychoanalytic procedure with a patient already being treated with medication. One may commence a treatment with a patient who requires medication at first, with the intention of initiating a psychoanalytic procedure as soon as the patient is ready for it. One may introduce medication in the course of an existing psychoanalytic procedure. The principles involved in all three situations are the same: one responds appropriately to the clinical state of the patient, but tries to avoid maneuvers that will irreversibly compromise analytic technique. One introduces each departure from classical analytic technique with a clear explanation of why it seems to be indicated at this point, what one hopes to accomplish, what are the prospects for its success, and, if the patient can tolerate such a discussion, what undesirable complications might ensue. If the clinical situation is not too urgent, one asks the patient to consider the recommendation and to bring back his views, which one then responds to, first on the basis of manifest content, and then where possible, on the basis of unconscious meaning. Ultimately, one attempts to analyze the meaning of the extra-analytic intervention to the patient.

THE INDICATIONS FOR COMBINED TREATMENT

The specific population of those who will profit from combined treatment must be distinguished from those who will profit optimally from either treatment alone. Patients who will profit from psychoanalysis but not from drug therapy include those with classical transference neuroses, and patients with personality disorders, except for borderline personality and various forms of depressive personality. Patients who will profit from drug therapy include those with conditions that appear on the manic–depressive spectrum, that is, melancholic depression, mania and hypomania, also panic disorder and nonspecific anxiety, and other syndromes when they are based upon a depressive diathesis. They include also schizophrenia, some but not all borderline patients, and according to some recent claims, some obsessive–compulsive patients.

Not all patients who profit from drug therapy are suitable candidates for psychoanalysis. Many patients are just not interested in anything but immediate relief of their most distressing symptoms, depression, or anxiety. Others really don't require any further treatment. Especially after the fifth decade, the successful treatment of a discrete episode of depression that is not based upon a personality disorder or an ongoing neurosis leaves the patient without evidence of any important neurotic disability and therefore no indication for analysis. Some patients with manic–depressive disease, when their excursions into illness have been controlled with lithium, exhibit neither indication nor desire for psychotherapy of any type.

Many patients who recover with proper drug therapy are poor candidates for psychoanalysis. For example, in the case of young schizophrenics, even the most skillful treatment with medication alleviates only the gross psychotic symptoms, but leaves the underlying personality disorder, the intense timidity, the paranoid attitude toward the world, untouched. For such patients, an insight-oriented therapy is a remote, if at all achievable goal. Many borderline patients, especially the most primitive among them, are too preoccupied with dealing with their frequent and painful mood swings to be able to take interest in underlying dynamic states. Though they may accept the format of an analysis, that is, treatment frequency of three to five times a week, lying on the couch and free association, no psychoanalytic process appears.

The indications for analysis in patients whose symptoms can be controlled with drug therapy include the following: a continuing personality disorder; neurotic symptoms that derive from early trauma rather than from constitutionally poor regulation of affective excursion; object relations and self-image that are impaired by the recurrent disruption of continuity in mood and affect caused by rapid or slow cycling manic–depressive excursions.

After my very first experiences with psychiatric drug therapy, it seemed to me interesting that those conditions that responded to medication were conditions that responded poorly, if at all, to any psychotherapy, and similarly, those that responded to psychotherapy were not likely to respond to psychiatric drug therapy. For example, an acute episode of schizophrenia will ordinarily be resolved easily with medication, but psychotherapy is relatively ineffectual and psychoanalysis is inappropriate. On the other hand, a patient with a neurotic problem with object relations will not be helped by medication, only by an intensive psychotherapy.

By and large, I consider that conclusion still valid. But then why do we consider treating any given patient with both modalities simultaneously? There are some patients who suffer acute breakdowns, most commonly depression, as episodes imposed upon a continuing personality disorder. One ascertains from the history that before the onset of the presenting bout of depression, the patient exhibited difficulty in his relations with others, parents, spouse, business associates.

Before one can commence a definitive psychotherapy or psychoanalytic treatment of this latter continuing problem, one must overcome the depression. For that drug therapy is initiated, and psychoanalysis as soon thereafter as the patient becomes available for it. Combined treatment is also indicated for those patients whose lives are seriously disrupted, whose object relations and identity are distorted by the affective fluctuations, by the conflicts between impulse and inhibition that constitute the primary illness. The most common of such patients are the relatively high level borderline patients that we encounter in our practice, the narcissistic personalities, the rapid cycling manic depressives, and the adult attention deficit disorder patients.

When medication first appeared, I hoped and expected that it would restore the equanimity necessary for analysis and that the analysis would eliminate the need for the medication (Ostow, 1960b). Thirty years later, that prediction seems to have been woefully incorrect. It seems to me that no psychotherapy can overcome the pathologic instability or impaired regulation of psychic "energies" that I believe to be the basis of the drug responsive mental illness. It is always striking to see rapid loss of insight, perspective, and objectivity when medication is abruptly withdrawn. I have seen a few patients who require medication only during the course of one or a few relatively brief episodes of depression or of schizophrenia, and I like to think that the psychotherapy or analysis that they had during the intervals contributed to the long periods of remission, but I cannot be sure that it did.

One does have the satisfaction of seeing patients whose neurotic needs seriously impair interpersonal relations and work improve in these areas, clearly in response to analytic therapy. But the analysis itself and the improvement in performance are contingent upon the concurrent control of mood with medication when a mood disorder or psychosis would have prevented analysis. Although there are exceptions, I find that many patients who require medication exhibit a surprising rigidity in analysis. They may follow the rules properly—although some have difficulty doing so—but the analytic process that we are able to cultivate in responsive patients fails to appear. Nevertheless the procedure has some value. For such patients the analyst functions as a guide, a teacher, a constant parental object in an otherwise remote and impersonal universe. Over a period of years, the analyst walks the patient through the crucial periods of his life, the challenges that he encounters, and tries to compensate for the absence of courage and self-esteem.

TECHNIQUE OF DRUG THERAPY

In the title of this chapter, who prescribes the medication is not specified. All nonmedical analysts who believe that a patient requires medication will refer the patient to a psychopharmacologist and leave the decision of whether to prescribe and what to prescribe and how much to the latter. Most will deal analytically with everything that the patient brings into the analysis that relates to the drug treatment. The nonmedical analyst has no choice. However, many medical analysts, too, prefer to refer their patients out for psychopharmacologic intervention; they do not wish to become involved in the treatment. Those analysts who do this do not know how to prescribe, but that is because they have not learned how to use medication, and they have not learned because, in most instances, they consider prescribing medication inappropriate for a psychoanalyst while conducting an analysis.

I should like to take a strong stand here in urging the analyst to prescribe the medication himself. I recall a conversation I had with Herman Nunberg in the 1950s, when the first psychiatric medications appeared, about the ultimate effect of such agents on the practice of psychoanalysis. No matter how effective medication might be, he argued, one would still need analysts to select medication and to regulate dose and combination. While analysts are not really necessary for this task, by virtue of their command of psychodynamics they can do it better than others once they have acquired mastery of psychopharmacology.

Medication cannot just be prescribed. For the medications that we currently possess, it is important to select, to monitor, to titrate, and to combine. The psychopharmacologist does these things on the basis of the clinical evidence that he accumulates during a fifteen- or thirty-minute conversation with the patient (after the initial workup examination), once a week initially, and then once a month or once every several months after a while. The psychoanalyst, on the other hand, is in a much better position to select, monitor, titrate, and combine, because he has access daily or almost daily to what is going on in the patient's mind. It is not uncommon, for example, to hear the patient report at the beginning of the session that he is feeling fine, but then to hear the recitation of a dream that discloses a worsening depressive state. The psychopharmacologist will hear only the conscious report; the psychoanalyst has the truly revealing data.

Splitting the treatment between a psychopharmacologist and a psychoanalyst can be compared to driving a car with one person steering and the other controlling the throttle, with little if any communication between them. It can be done, but badly. The psychopharmacologist has little access to the truly important clinical data, and the psychoanalyst never knows whether he is hearing the patient speak or the medication. It follows that even when the treatment is split, a psychopharmacologist who is psychoanalytically knowledgeable will do considerably better than one trained purely as a nondynamic, biological psychiatrist.

Of course, psychoanalysts who have not prescribed medication are concerned that doing so violates the classical arm's length position of the psychoanalyst vis-à-vis the patient. He is trying to influence the patient extra-analytically. I can only say that in thirty-five years of combining drug therapy with psychoanalysis, I have never encountered a situation in which I felt that the one treatment interfered with the other. Neither writing the prescription, asking about drug response, whether therapeutic or toxic, nor even occasionally checking blood pressure, recommending laboratory testing, or examining the patient for tremor, ataxia, or nystagmus, has evoked analytic fantasy or activity that could not be analyzed in session, frequently with profit. (Touching the patient is not required for any of these procedures except for placing a blood pressure cuff.)

As in unmodified analysis, the analyst must focus clearly on the transference, especially at the beginning of a drug therapy. A., a fifty-six-year-old man who came to me in a state of fairly pronounced melancholic depression, was treated with a monoamine oxidase inhibitor and daily psychoanalytic sessions on the couch. Twelve days after starting treatment (monoamine oxidase inhibitor treatment usually requires about four weeks before an adequate dose becomes effective) he reported:

> I got through okay. I'm about the same, but at moments I feel better. I may as well confess that I'm figuring out how to get out of New York. I am claustrophobic. New York frightens me.

> I keep wanting my brother-in-law to help me, to give me a job. I see my mother reaching out her hand to help me. I see my mother's face and she wants to help me. Sometimes I see a child's face near hers, like the infant Jesus. One time I had a vision of my mother and Jesus Christ both reaching out their hands to help me. The only happy time in my whole day is when I get into bed. It's killing me to pay that much money, but I have to do it. I think I am better in some ways; the panic is less. The thought I choke back is, "Thank God I've got you to come to." At least you gave me the medication, in which I have great hopes. I would like to go out and screw someone else's wife, someone nice. Too many people, fire engines, noise; it terrifies me. Christmas terrifies me. I have just gotten to be a big fat slob. I worry about cancer all the time. I have been making up lists for my wife, my safe deposit keys, etc. I suppose I have a fear of homosexuality. I used to sit in the office with my factory manager, and I would get a pain in my balls as I spoke to him. I'm in a state of fury that this should happen to me. I have lived a fairly decent life, except that I screwed a few women and evaded the draft.

Here it was clear that my providing medication was interpreted as being fed by mother. The infant is being rescued magically. However, that very anaclitic dependence invokes a fear of homosexual attack. That had to be interpreted to him to prevent his flight from treatment, which he was already considering.

The patient's response to the medication will strongly influence the transference. If the medication alleviates his distress, he will be grateful to the analyst and see him as a loving and protective parent. It is also frequently interpreted as impregnation in preparation for rebirth. At the end of the fourth week of treatment of this same patient, in order to encourage him, as he left, I said, "Maybe you'll have a surprise for me on Monday." He replied without hesitation, "A baby."

Again, B., a borderline young woman, was referred to me after her discharge from a psychiatric hospital on a large dose of antipsychosis tranquilizer. She seemed to me depressed and so I replaced the latter with an antidepression drug. As her depression lifted, she dreamed that her father was giving her pills that had holes in them.

When I asked what kind of pills had holes in them she replied, "Life Savers." Associated with the pills in the dream was a white, jellylike material, which clearly symbolized semen. Evidently the treatment had fulfilled her fantasy that an experience of fellatio with her father had effected rebirth by oral impregnation.

If the medication fails to alleviate the distress for which it was intended, or if it produces distressing side effects, as some medications do, the patient may come to feel that he is being poisoned by the analyst. If the patient is impulsive, he may on such occasion abruptly leave treatment, even if he had been warned that the procedure of selecting medication is one of systematic trial and error. Usually when the transference becomes negative as a result of untoward drug response, analyzing will have little therapeutic effect. The reality of the physiologic toxic change makes interpretation unconvincing. However, the situation and its analysis can be recalled on some subsequent occasion when they are relevant, and when the patient is capable of greater insight. The converse is also true; the transference will influence the patient's attitude toward the medication. If the transference is positive, the patient will report a positive response to the medication and minimize its side effects. When, on the other hand, the transference is negative, the patient will minimize the therapeutic effect of the medication and complain about side effects. The perception of medication and the effect of the medication make a reality contribution to the transference fantasy comparable to what day residue does in dreams. (I owe this formulation to Joseph Sandler.) When the drug has been effective, the transference is influenced to become more positive and to remain positive longer than otherwise. The patient becomes more forgiving toward the analyst. However, I have seen no evidence that the prescription of medication per se alters the transference or any other aspect of the psychoanalysis permanently and significantly.

While some patients will welcome the idea of medication readily, others will resist it. Resistance to medication is something that all psychopharmacologists encounter, but they have no real understanding of its nature, and no means of contending with it. The psychoanalyst may be able to deal with it analytically.

Some patients fear, as retribution for what they consider inappropriate oral–aggressive wishes, that they will be poisoned. Such a fear engenders a paranoid attitude, which can cause the patient to resist taking the prescribed medication. It is the same attitude that fuels the health food and natural food fad. Occasionally, such patients, while resisting therapeutic medication for fear of being poisoned, will at the same time use marijuana or alcohol or other dangerous drugs, thereby revealing their own tendency to poison themselves while projecting the wish onto those who are trying to rescue them.

Resistance is sometimes created by the patient's fear for his own physical integrity. We encounter this issue among those who are subject to recurrent attacks of panic and anxiety. They, like all phobic patients, fear that they will literally fall apart during an anxiety attack, and so they tend to avoid any experience over which they do not possess full control, or at least the illusion of full control. Medication represents to them an influence that is beyond their control, and therefore they resist it. Interestingly enough, these patients respond to doses of medication considerably lower than the doses ordinarily required. It is as if their lower threshold for anxiety is related to or caused by a low threshold for response to chemical agents.

Among those patients who resist psychiatric drug treatment, one finds those who come for help, but who nevertheless resist it out of a neurotic need to suffer. This need does not necessarily lead to seeking pain, but may easily create resistance against opportunities to be relieved from current distress. They seem to fear the rapid therapeutic power of medication more than the slow influence of a psychotherapy.

Some patients seem to recognize in themselves a tendency to become excessively dependent, and they react by resisting close relations which might become dependent relations. They seem to try to dilute the attractiveness of the analysis by keeping the frequency of visits as low as possible, and by looking for opportunities to discontinue treatment. These patients frequently displace their fear of dependency from the analyst to the drug that he prescribes, or that he arranges for someone else to prescribe.

In the minds of many patients, an illness that can be treated by psychologic means is less threatening and less shameful than one that must be treated with an organic modality. Drug treatment means brain dysfunction or permanent defect, while psychotherapy merely means temporary and reversible psychic perturbation. If the patient avoids the drug, he loses less self-esteem. A related resistance appears when a member of the family or close friend has been treated with medication either unsuccessfully or partially successfully. The patient feels that accepting drug therapy, and especially if the same drug is prescribed, means that he is just as unfortunate as the other.

Patients whose illness creates euphoria, such as hypomanic, manic, or "high" borderline characters, or certain incipient schizophrenics, enjoy their "high" and resist any procedure that threatens it. If their behavior becomes dangerous, medication may have to be administered against their wishes.

It is difficult to recommend a specific procedure since cases differ so much from one to the other, just as it is difficult to specify procedure for analysis in general. In what is perhaps the most common situation, the patient applies for treatment in a state of clear-cut, melancholic depression. From the history the analyst infers that the depression can be understood as an incident in the course of and prepared for by a continuing neurosis or personality disorder. He conveys this conclusion to the patient, and recommends that treatment start with an attempt at chemotherapy for the depressive episode, and that it continue, as the depression subsides, with analysis, giving the reasons for his proposal. If the patient concurs, the analyst opens the first phase of treatment by prescribing a specific medication and explaining why he has chosen that medication, what effect is desired, how soon it might come about, and what toxic side effects might be encountered on the way. It is important to reassure the patient that if this drug must be abandoned, prescribing it represents merely the first phase of what could be a systematic program for achieving relief. (I shall not here discuss the pharmacologic aspects of choice of medication, dosage, monitoring and titration, nor of combining medications, since these issues alone would require book length treatment. However, the psychoanalyst, whether or not he has prescribed the drug, should have this information because it enters into the day residue, not only of dreams, but of conscious fantasy and thought.) In most instances, during the first phase of treatment, only the most superficial psychotherapeutic maneuvers are appropriate—reassurance, comfort, support, offering hope and advice. Therefore, initially the patient need be seen less frequently than he might be seen later. There is little process in the presence of depression, and the sessions soon become dull and boring, and discouraging for the patient, except for those who need continuing contact.

The analyst must then look for responses to the medication, both desired therapeutic responses and undesired side effects. If the patient resists the medication, he will complain noisily about side effects and minimize evidence of improvement. If he welcomes the intervention, the opposite may occur; that is, he will minimize or fail to report side effects and exaggerate indications of improvement. In order to assess what is really happening, the therapist must evaluate all of the patient's statements in the light of his knowledge of the expected course of recovery and the common side effects of the medication being used, as well as their time course. Even if the analyst is not himself prescribing the medication, he must still evaluate the reports of the patient. For example, if the patient reports clear-cut improvement within one or two days after starting medication, the analyst must know how likely it is that improvement will be felt so soon. Is this a true drug effect, or a placebo effect? If it is the latter, then the patient must be protected against the disappointment that will follow when it disappears.

When the recovery that is hoped for actually starts, the patient is helped to recognize the specific changes in psychic function that have occurred. Recognizing the difference between the parameters of psychic function in recovery contrasted with depression is a form of superficial insight that gives the patient a sense of some mastery of his illness. When we are dealing with psychosis, but even to a certain extent in the case of depression, after recovery, the episode of illness appears as a gap in the patient's psychic function, and he appreciates the analyst's assistance in filling in that gap, in being helped to understand why the psychic continuity was disrupted, and what was the content of his thought during the interruption.

In only a very few cases will the first drug and first dose serve to achieve the desired results. In most cases dose will have to be increased gradually and one drug may have to be replaced by or combined with another, or the principal drug or drugs might require reinforcement by adjuvants. (These procedures require a sound knowledge of psychopharmacology and should be pursued with a light and sensitive touch. I say this not to discourage the analyst from prescribing medication, but to encourage him to inform himself really well before doing it, initially perhaps by consulting with competent psychopharmacologists when a difficult problem arises.) As each of these changes is made, the patient must be prevented from becoming disappointed and discouraged. The reason for each change should be explained clearly, and he should be reminded on each occasion that a systematic program is being followed—that the procedure is not random guesswork.

In most cases, sooner or later, a desired, or at least acceptable, result is obtained. It will be a few days or weeks before the extent of the recovery and its stability can be ascertained. During this period, the patient will be celebrating the improvement and the transference will become quite positive. During the period when the medication starts to become effective, but before a true stabilization has occurred, the patient will present with varying degrees of comfort or distress, with fluctuating symptoms and mental states. In unmodified psychoanalysis, the psychoanalyst is constantly challenged by such fluctuations to try to ascertain whether they are the result of spontaneous intrapsychic processes, whether they are responses to the analysis or the transference, or whether they have been elicited by external events, or whether two or three of these influences are simultaneously active. If a varying drug therapy is going on, the additional variable makes the assignment even more complicated. How much of this process of assessment and its results should be communicated to the patient is a matter of analytic judgment.

As the desired mental state and the medication regimen that has established it becomes stabilized, the true psychoanalytic process begins to develop. Now the psychoanalyst can address himself primarily to that, and to encourage free association, and the reporting of fantasies, dreams, and behavior. He becomes able to intervene and interpret in exactly the way that he would in an uncomplicated analysis. When he judges that the time has come, he may readjust the frequency of sessions and suggest the use of the couch. From the point of view of the analysis, the procedures of the drug therapy, and the various mental responses that it elicits, are all proper subjects for analytic scrutiny.

While many patients will do well on an appropriate dose and combination of medication for years, others exhibit mood swings and symptom fluctuations at intervals of days, weeks, or months. In that case, the analyst may have to vary the medication from time to time. In some such cases, lithium may induce some stabilization.

Not infrequently, a patient already in a conventional analysis for what has seemed to be a simple neurotic state or personality disorder becomes depressed, or less often, even psychotic. If this supervening state is not overcome by appropriate analytic work within a reasonable period of time, and especially if the condition precludes analytic work or threatens the life of the patient or those about him, then medication should be introduced. I usually introduce the idea of medication by citing the indications for it, describe what I expect it to do, what is the likelihood of its success, and what are the drawbacks. If the situation is not acute, I generally wait for a few sessions while the patient digests and accommodates to my recommendations and I try to analyze his response to it. The patient generally likes to be assured that the analysis will not thereby become jeopardized, and he can be assured that it will not. If the patient is frightened by what has happened to him, he may welcome this extra-analytic intervention and it will help him to overcome his resentment toward the analyst for permitting the deterioration to occur. When the medication is prescribed, and as its effects are developing, the sessions may become concerned with it, especially since the clinical state that has required the medication will usually prevent much analysis from taking place. As in the case of the new patient, with the attainment of a stable state of remission of the complicating episode, the analysis can resume its normal course. In most cases, neither the frequency of visits nor the use of the couch need be affected by the interruption.

Theoretically, we should also consider the case of the patient, already on drug therapy, who then applies for psychoanalytic treatment. I can imagine, for example, that a manic–depressive patient or a borderline patient, already stabilized on lithium, may wish to overcome problems with object relations and then seek analysis. In fact however, I have never been approached by such a patient. On the contrary, I have seen patients, after obtaining satisfactory results with drug therapy that was initiated only after a long and unsuccessful analysis, then leave the analysis that had failed over a period of years to bring the relief desired.

Because the psychoanalyst has immediate access to both the conscious and unconscious processes of the patient, he is in a much better position to monitor the parameters of manic–depressive disease and psychosis as well as other drug susceptible conditions, and the effect of medication upon them, than the psychopharmacologist who can assess, in a brief period of time or limited by the constraints of a fixed questionnaire, the conscious reports of the patient.

I accept Freud's suggestion (1933, 1940) that psychopharmacologic agents—which he merely anticipated—act to influence the psychic energy available to mental functions, because it seems clear to me that what these drug change is motivation, specifically libidinal motivation, as distinguished from aggressive motivation. (Aggressive energies are elicited by distressing perturbations in the supply of libidinal energies, as well as by actual external danger.) Under the influence of antidepression agents, subjects exhibit increased motivation, increased interest in seeking and exploiting opportunities for gratification, optimism, self-confidence, and enthusiasm. Contrariwise, under the influence of antipsychosis tranquilizers, subjects will display inertia, lack of interest, pessimism, diffidence, and discouragement. (Psychiatrically normal individuals respond to these chemical influences as well as to spontaneous internal changes with corrective maneuvers so that the drug effect is muted or suppressed. The drug effect becomes visible especially easily among those individuals who cannot correct for energy deviations spontaneously, and who are therefore easily driven to manic or depressive extremes by these chemical agents.)

My formulations are based purely upon clinical observation, but deal with fluctuation of clinically visible behavioral parameters. The term *psychic energy* as I use it, is not identical with, and may not even correlate directly with physiologic energies. The complexities of drug effect upon neural transmission within the brain, that fill the literature of psychopharmacology and the biochemistry of the brain, cannot yet be translated into clinically visible processes and cannot yet be used to make clinically useful predictions. The behavioral parameters that they affect and the effect that they have upon them are visible clinically, and certain patterns and sequences can be distinguished and used to prescribe and to monitor.

The chief advantage of this concept of psychic energy is that it links metapsychologic thinking to the kind of behavioral change that responds to medication and that is induced by medication. It makes it possible to organize one's thoughts and observations in relating behavior to drug therapy. The energy concept is out of favor nowadays among psychoanalytic theoreticians, but I anticipate that it will be resuscitated as psychoanalysts become more familiar with the action of psychopharmacologic agents (Loeb and Loeb, 1987).

Simply put, those conditions that respond to antipsychosis tranquilizers or antidepression energizers can be thought of as caused by excessive excursions of the energy level from a midpoint of a spectrum. One end of the spectrum is the position that induces a manic state, and the other end, a state of depression. A movement toward either end in the individual without disease will induce a corrective tendency. Those individuals whose ability to correct deviations is impaired will suffer from manic, depressive, or schizophrenic illness.

When the failure to regulate level is compounded by an instability of the system, we have conditions that favor borderline personality.

For example, conventional psychopharmacologic wisdom has it that the proper treatment for mania is lithium combined with an antipsychosis tranquilizer. But there is a problem: Many manics treated that way will become more agitated before they are overwhelmed by large doses of medication, while others will recover with relatively small doses of medication. Again, those in the first group will improve with an antidepression drug—paradoxically and against the rules—while those in the second group will become worse with an antidepression drug. The psychopharmacologist has no explanation for this paradox. I have seen no discussion of it in the literature. The dynamic psychiatrist on the other hand, familiar with psychic mechanisms of primary tendencies and secondary corrections, will infer that the mania of the second type is a primary mania, while that of the first type is a reactive mania, a secondary attempt to resist a threatening depressive state. While it may be difficult to distinguish between these two states before they have both been seen in the same patient, one will suspect a corrective rather than a primary manic state if the patient is more volatile, exhibits paradoxical weeping, expresses more anger than expected, and especially if he reports depressive dreams. In other words, the corrective manic state is more likely to resemble what DSM III-R (1986) calls Bipolar Disorder, Mixed. However in many instances, the depressive component of the mixture may be all but invisible to any but the psychoanalyst.

Similarly, the proper drug formula for treating an acute episode of schizophrenia, or schizoaffective disease, is not immediately self-evident. Some patients respond to antipsychosis tranquilizers alone, and others require the concurrent administration of an antidepression drug. A schizophrenic patient may exhibit a psychotic state under any of three circumstances: when he is at the "high" end of the spectrum, as the primary manic is; when he is at the "low" end of the spectrum, as a depressed patient is; or when he is trying to struggle against being overwhelmed by depression, as the secondary manic does. It follows that those patients who belong in the first category will, like the primary manic, respond well to treatment with an antipsychosis tranquilizer, while those in both the second and third categories should be treated with an antidepression energizer, usually together with the tranquilizer. Those in the first and third categories resemble each other in the same way that primary and secondary manics do.

For the purposes of monitoring, I have found the following parameters useful. The primary indicator of status is the patient's mood. A good mood indicates high position on the manic–depression spectrum, and a low mood, a low position. In other words, a good mood, if it is associated with a pathologic condition that requires treatment, indicates the use of an antipsychosis tranquilizer, and a bad mood, though somewhat less reliably, an antidepression energizer.

The patient's self-observation tells us about his status fairly sensitively. If the patient speaks ill of himself, he reveals that he is decending toward or is at lower levels of the manic–depressive spectrum, or a homologous "high–low" schizophrenic spectrum. One must allow, however, for defensive denial of a true depressive state. Again, if the patient reports on subjective feelings (primary self-observation) rather than reporting accounts of his activities (secondary self-observation), I infer that he approaches the lower end of this spectrum. Self-criticism, especially the expression of feelings of guilt, also suggests a low position.

A tendency to become involved with love objects and others suggests a "high" state, which I interpret as the consequence of a profusion of libidinal energy; while conversely, a tendency to withdraw to solitude suggests a "low" state.

The patient's outlook, whether optimistic or pessimistic, is usually consonant with his mood, and may reveal his status fairly transparently.

The degree of objectivity that the patient is able to maintain tells us how close to the midrange of the spectrum he can remain. Toward either end he tends to lose objectivity, perspective, and insight.

The problem of monitoring and assessing the patient's "energy" status is complicated by the fact that people do not move or drift directly toward either end of the spectrum without a struggle. Usually as extreme positions are approached, we see counteractive, corrective tendencies that create the impression of turmoil and struggle.

Most manics of the primary type seem to become euphoric without evidence of any corrective tendency. However, the schizophrenic differs from the manic in that as he becomes higher and higher, a corrective tendency sets which he interprets and projects out as a destructive force. The corrective tendency may express itself in attempts at self-destruction, self-mutilation, and/or rejection of the world of reality. When it is projected out, it becomes the basis of paranoid delusions and/or the perception that the world is being destroyed, a projection of his rejection of it. An antipsychosis tranquilizer suppresses the excess "energy" and thereby makes the pathogenic corrective tendency unnecessary. The hypochondria and narcissism of the schizophrenic may suggest a depressionlike, low "energy" syndrome. However, they may be phenomena created in reaction against the "high" state that instituted the pathogenic process.

As the patient descends toward the depressive position, we observe a number of maneuvers that seem intended to arrest the descent. (All of these changes, primary and corrective, can be observed not only when they occur naturally, but also, almost experimentally, when they are induced by the administration of one or the other of the medications that we have been discussing.)

Frequently, the earliest evidence of the struggle against depression is a paradoxical overactivity, which, when sufficiently intense, may become the secondary hypomania or mania that we discussed above. An early corrective maneuver is clinging to a protective love object. When that love object is lost, or threatens to become unavailable, anxiety may appear. I infer that in such cases the anxiety signals a loss of support against depression. The syndrome suggests separation anxiety or agoraphobia. As the patient descends further toward depression, he becomes angrier and angrier. Although some anger can be seen in the secondary manic and in the phobic, it becomes the primary presenting manifestation of illness when the descent to depression is not arrested. In many instances, the anger itself seems to be able to induce an organized campaign that aims to overcome what is thought to be the depressing influence, so that some paranoid characteristics might appear. If any one of these syndromes becomes symptomatically overwhelming so as to require drug therapy, the proper drug in each of these cases is an antidepression energizer. Sometimes, if the system is labile, it may swing too far to the up side, so that ultimately a combination of antidepression energizer and antipsychosis tranquilizer may be necessary. Lithium too may contribute to stabilizing this "psychic energy" system. My purpose in spelling out these corrective maneuvers here is to make it clear that it is not always easy to ascertain what the "energy" status is at the moment, and therefore which drugs are appropriate. The distinction between primary tendencies and secondary corrective phenomena is essential.

I have observed that the manifest content of dreams can frequently be used to monitor the patient's "energy" changes and therefore to guide one in drug selection and titration. Patients who require drug therapy for control are likely to report apocalyptic dreams, namely, dreams that portray, in manifest content, widespread destruction and/or death followed by a rebirth indicated by a reunion with mother. In my 1962 book, *Drugs in Psychoanalysis and Psychotherapy*, I reported in some detail the analysis of two patients who were receiving medication, one a patient with conversion and anxiety hysteria, and the second with paranoid schizophrenia. The latter patient, C., during her second visit, volunteered two dreams from the previous week:

> *Dream 1*
> One was a painting of a city that seemed dead—a "ghost city." It was painted in black and white and no human or animal figures appeared. All at once the doors of the houses opened and gaily dressed people came out, including my husband and me.
>
> *Dream 2*
> The patient was driving very fast in an automobile with her husband. She was afraid of a crash. Suddenly she was resting on a peaceful green meadow.

Sometimes the union with mother precedes the destruction. A schizophrenic young man, D., who maintained fairly comfortably on a combination of antidepression energizer and antipsychosis tranquilizer, one night omitted his medication and reported the following dream:

> I had a nightmare. I found myself in bed with my mother. We had no clothes on. She was insisting that I start sexual advances. I touch her breasts. I don't know whether she had anything on the lower part of her body.
>
> I watched a movie that became real life. Grand Central Station was about to explode and kill everyone inside. A great ball of fire. It would pass from that building onto Park Avenue. I ran for my life.
>
> I watched it again. People were being led into a theater innocently, without knowledge of what's to come. They would

> die. I watch from the second level. Chaos. No one had the authority to call the police. I ran out to 39th Street. Swimming for my life. As fast as possible. Tough enemies with machine guns were firing indiscriminately.
>
> You appeared in the station. I was assured that chaos wouldn't break out again.

I recognize in these dreams the conflict between primary and secondary movements. In dream 1 of patient C., the image of the world has been destroyed. Then a corrective rebirth occurs spontaneously. The depressing influence has been overcome by the rebirth influence. It is the latter that creates the psychosis and the delusional fantasy. Therefore an antipsychosis tranquilizer was indicated. After the psychosis subsided, the patient became depressed, since the depressing influence was now unopposed. Accordingly, an antidepression drug was added. The combination has kept the patient stable for thirty years now.

Dream 2 starts with the union of the patient with her caretaking spouse in a vehicle, which we commonly encounter in apocalyptic fantasies and dreams. Then the destruction occurs and it is followed by a rebirth. The destructive phase did not succeed in overcoming the pathogenic upward striving. The second dream then confirms the picture in the first dream, namely, that the upward movement must be suppressed.

D.'s dream starts with an oedipal approach to mother, impelled by the imbalance of medication caused by the omission of the scheduled dose of medication that evening. Note that there was no alteration of behavior and no new symptoms appeared. The effect of the omission of the medication appeared only in the dream. The inappropriate oedipal striving was promptly subdued, overwhelmed by an apocalyptic destruction. The upward and downward impulses are evenly matched here and, in the end, tranquility is restored by the analyst, a messianic rescuer. (I have discussed the apocalyptic characteristics of all of these dreams elsewhere [Ostow, 1986].) The omission of the medication released both upward and downward tendencies and created a potential for instability, rather than for relapse into their "high" or "low" pathologic states. What was indicated here was the resumption of both medications in order to restore mental stability.

Not uncommonly a patient will report that he is feeling well; he will deny depression. However, he may, during the same session, report a dream like this (patient E.):

> He saw someone suffering wounds all over his body. Then he saw and was impressed by a large house, but once inside, he discovered that it was supported by only very thin and insubstantial uprights. It could easily topple.

Here we find an unopposed depressive tendency, the falling of the house because the uprights are too fragile. (That detail suggests a problem with potency. All of these dreams can, and in an analysis, should be interpreted in the usual way, using associations, memories, fantasies, and day residue to uncover the meaning of the details of the dream for the individual. In this discussion, I am focusing only on the manifest dream, demonstrating how it can be used for the purpose of assessing "psychic energy" status and conflicts without the personal associations.)

A borderline, but now chronically depressed man (patient F.) who was taking large doses of antidepression medication, reported one day that his mother had returned home from visiting him, and that whenever she left, he would become more depressed. A few days later he reported the following dream:

> I was in Brooklyn on Eastern Parkway driving past the headquarters of the Lubavitch Rebbe. I was sitting in a room with Hassidim. They said, "This time it really happened.—No, it couldn't." What were they talking about? I walked out. They were all talking. It turned out that the Rebbe had died and these people believed that he was directly related to God. A number of times he'd been sick, but hadn't died. Now he had died. If he had had divine protection he should not have died. They paraded him around on a chair. He would ascend to heaven in a fire. They put me in the chair, which I thought was strange. They were rocking me back and forth. I fell off the chair. There was a fire. I fell into it.

The patient associated falling into the fire with going to hell, and being carried around on a chair to a common practice at Jewish weddings of elevating the bride and groom on chairs to be carried around on the shoulders of their friends. The man said, "After I awoke I thought, 'There's a depressive dream, death and rebirth.' "

In the dream, the patient invokes religious sentiments, which he never does in conscious life. We see evidence of a struggle upwards, in fact literally upwards, but a struggle that involves usurping the role of father. (The chair represents mother.) However, instead of the ascent, that is, the rebirth that he hopes for, he is cast down into the fires of hell. Clearly the depressive forces prevail.

This type of dream analysis can assist in following the progress of the patient's treatment. Before he came to treatment and while visiting his parents, a seriously depressed borderline young man, G., dreamed: He was on a roof eating a hot dog. As he finished it, he noticed a building nearby. There were some fire escapes crisscrossing, leading down from the roof. A young man was being restrained by some uniformed men. He was able to get away from them and jump. Here the patient attempts to find comfort in oral gratification with his parents. An oral aggressive tendency accompanies that effort. But the downward pull asserts itself, literally represented as a compulsion to jump off the roof.

When he started to recover as a result of both antidepression medication and psychotherapy, the quality of his dreams changed. He had started treatment on January 4th and on the 15th he reported: "I was floating down a river, away. My mother saved me, pulled me out." The following day he dreamed:

> I was with my two sisters. We were walking over a walkway over a highway to get to some sporting event. We went over a bridge. There were three: one, another, and then a third. We went over it. We would come back. The third one was only a plank of wood. Going back I go first. I had trouble. I was scared I would fall. My sisters went over it. Then I was able to. One of them showed me how to do it.

The water and the bridges represent separation anxiety and death. The fear of falling off the bridge reproduces the pretreatment fear of jumping off the building. However, now he is rescued by his mother or his sisters. As a result of treatment, the rebirth tendency is powerful enough to counteract the destructive tendency. It was almost a week later before the patient was able to acknowledge that he actually did feel better.

Examination of apocalyptic death and rebirth tendencies that appear in dreams and fantasies can reveal the dynamics of the conflicting forces and their relative strength at each point in the treatment.

POTENTIAL AND LIMITATIONS OF COMBINED TREATMENT

Although we are focusing on the opening phases of analysis when it is combined with psychiatric medication, let us glance at the outcome of the procedure. The methods that I have described and the approach apply to the combined procedure in general, but the results depend to a large extent upon the patient and on his clinical problem.

First let us note that while we would expect the concurrent use of psychoanalysis and psychopharmaceutical modalities to permit a greater degree of success than we obtain with either alone, it seems to me that many patients who require medication to permit analysis to proceed exhibit a surprising rigidity, a greater resistance to the offering of free associations and to the incorporation of insights offered. While they seem to make a genuine effort to comply with instructions and they dutifully accept and repeat interpretive interventions, nevertheless the enlightenment is accepted only superficially and influences behavior only to a relatively small degree.

Patient G., the suicidally depressed young man, started psychotherapy on a three-times-a-week schedule. He accepted medication, though reluctantly. I tried to engage him in an analytic procedure but obtained only rigidly limited reports. At first I attributed his lack of interest in psychodynamic formulations and understanding to his depressive pain. However as he improved and overcame his depression and engaged joyously and hopefully in many activities, his interest in treatment dropped even further. These activities themselves revealed serious inhibition in selecting and pursuing age-adequate goals. Nevertheless he produced almost no analytic material, restricting his reports to poor descriptions of daily events in a stereotyped way, unaccompanied by reflections, thoughts, fantasies, or dreams. He insisted on reducing the frequency of sessions to twice a week and then once a week. (He had left a number of previous psychotherapists completely, after brief attempts at psychotherapy.) Within a few months he discontinued the medication without telling me, certain that he had no need for it. Over the course of the next several months his depression returned insidiously and he gave up one activity after another. He acquiesced to resuming medication only after it became obvious that he was deteriorating rapidly and that he had no control over the situation. He was no more amenable to an analytic procedure when he recovered again.

Yet the treatment is indeed very helpful to such patients to the extent that it offers them guidance in the sense of instructing them in appropriate responses to social situations that they seem incapable of coping with on their own, and support against the frequent occurrences of despair that they incur by virtue of their illness, and to which they are so sensitive. The analyst functions as a companion and guide and the patient regards him as a kind of messianic rescuer with whom he ultimately identifies as he gradually begins to look after himself. Profound insight into unconscious dynamics and the reconstruction of childhood experience seem to play little role in the improvement that is obtained. One may with some justice conclude that what has started out as an analytic procedure becomes a supportive psychotherapy.

I find it surprising that the patient who, with proper medication control, becomes so self-possessed, so self-critical, and so insightful, nevertheless when the medication is inappropriately altered, quite abruptly loses his objectivity and insight and relapses into profound neurosis or psychosis. One is impressed to a greater degree than one is in the case of unmodified psychoanalysis, with the fragility of the normal mental state and its dependence upon fairly precise regulation of affects and "energies."

Let us look at the individual syndromes. The situation of the patient who presents in a state of depression that is superimposed upon a personality disorder, someone whose difficulty with object relations creates distress for others and defeat for himself, is probably least complicated. Overcoming the depression permits the conduct of a psychoanalytic procedure that is not remarkable in any way other than its being accompanied by a fairly constant regimen of drug therapy. The analysis can be quite successful by both internal criteria of a satisfactory analytic process and external criteria of improved functioning. Yet the susceptibility to recurrent depression may be unaffected.

The manic–depressive patient whose illness is controlled by lithium or other medication or both may be able to participate in an analytic procedure in a quite unexceptional way. In the course of the treatment it will be useful to discuss previous manic and depressive episodes, how they have influenced the patient's life, how they were perceived by others and by himself, and what effect they might have had on his self-esteem. But the psychoanalyst should not expect that the analysis will prevent subsequent episodes of illness. In most instances one will have to rely on the medication for that.

A group of patients exhibits rapid, successive, or alternating manic–depressive attacks, or at least highs and lows. Psychopharmacologists speak of them as "rapid cyclers." When this rapid cycling is accompanied by an unusual degree of aggressiveness, of overt hostility, whether directed inward as suicidal or self-mutilating behavior, or whether directed outward toward others and when it is accompanied by impulsiveness and an inconstant sense of personal identity, we speak of borderline personality disorder. However, I'm not sure how often rapid cycling occurs without the other qualities of the borderline personality. I attribute the volatility of the borderline, the poor sense of identity, and perhaps some of the anger to the "energy" instability. However, my experience with drug therapy suggests that there may indeed be two different syndromes. It is simply that some borderline patients respond with impressive improvement to the administration of lithium, while others do not. It may be that the latter are just nonresponders to the drug, as some manic–depressives are. On the other hand, it may be that an additional factor may be at work. I was impressed by one borderline patient who failed to respond at all to medication or whose responses were short lived. However medication affected her when it did, it did nothing to deter her insistent self-destructive drive, which ultimately succeeded. The rapid cyclers who respond well to medication lend themselves to concurrent analysis. Those who do not respond can scarcely be engaged in a true analytic procedure.

Schizophrenics, of course, cannot be considered a homogeneous group. There are those whose psychosis can easily be contained with relatively small doses of medication and who can then engage in a psychotherapeutic procedure. Perhaps these should be considered instances of schizoaffective disorder. Some can participate genuinely in a true analytic exploration, in search of insight that they can utilize for therapeutic purposes. Others, on the other hand, find it difficult to comply with the formal requirements of psychoanalysis, that is, to give free associations and even to report accurately their mental state and recent experiences. Therapy serves the purpose merely of guiding them, encouraging them to continue with medication which they may resist, and being alert for changes in mental state that would require changes in the medication regimen.

One encounters also schizophrenics, many of whom are no less involved affectively, who respond only incompletely to medication despite one's best efforts to titrate dosages carefully and to seek optimal combinations. While the most prominent signs of illness, for example, hallucinations, may be suppressed, the patient may remain quite paranoid and therefore difficult to deal with psychotherapeutically. Obviously an analytic process is impossible. In these patients one must infer pathogenic processes other than the spectrum shift that I described above. Here the primary tendencies and corrective processes are determined dynamically rather than "energetically." For these the outlook must be considerably more unfavorable than for the group that responds well to medication.

CONCLUSIONS

The possibility of combining psychiatric drug therapy with psychoanalysis opens the opportunity to treat patients otherwise inaccessible to psychoanalysis, and to continue psychoanalytic treatment despite intercurrent episodes of depression or even psychosis.

Experience demonstrates that the departure from what has become "classical," abstinent psychoanalytic technique need not affect the analysis adversely. Responses to accepting medication and experiencing its various desired and undesired effects must be treated as "day residue" in the analytic material, especially in assessing the transference.

When a new patient requires drug therapy before he becomes ready for analysis, the analytic procedure can be begun gradually as the patient's mental state stabilizes and he acquires sufficient self-control and perspective to participate.

While the combined treatment opens doors hitherto closed to

many patients, a good number of them demonstrate a surprising rigidity that makes their compliance with instructions only nominal, insight only superficial, and true behavior change limited.

In my opinion the drug therapy should be administered by the same person who does the analysis, and it should be informed by true psychopharmacologic sophistication.

Chapter 14

Possible Technical Modifications in the Beginning Phases of the Psychoanalytic Treatment of Patients with Psychosomatic Symptoms

Charles C. Hogan, M.D., D.Med.Sc.

INTRODUCTION

Conventional psychoanalytic wisdom teaches us that treatment and its modifications are dictated by the nature of the underlying neurosis or psychosis regardless of the symptom. Certainly, when one begins to deal with a patient with psychosomatic symptoms, the analyst discovers a psychoneurosis, a character disorder, a borderline condition, or a psychotic regression as the treatment evolves. Tradition-

Acknowledgments. I want to express my gratitude to the members of the Psychosomatic Study Group of the Psychoanalytic Association of New York, founded by Melitta Sperling in 1965 and chaired by C. P. Wilson since 1973. Their support and critical comments have facilitated the development of my work.

ally, we would expect that the appropriate approach would depend on the evaluation of such underlying disorders.

Psychosomatic symptoms are frequently accompanied by certain defensive constellations that make such an evaluation difficult in the earlier phases of therapy. I hope to demonstrate that certain patients adapt quite readily to what we might call traditional classical psychoanalysis. However, there are some cases who display denial to such a degree that a hierarchy of emotional conflicts in all their severity may be hidden and subsumed in the organic symptom. Any clear evaluation of the psychiatric diagnosis or the defensive processes is impossible in the beginning phase of therapy. Only when the denial is relinquished (and/or at times, when the psychosomatic symptom is temporarily given up) are we able to begin to understand the nature of the psychopathology. One such subgroup has been called pensée opératoire (Marty and de M'Uzan, 1963; Marty, de M'Uzan, and David, 1963) and was later designated as alexithymia (Sifneos, 1972, 1973). I mention these labels only because they seem to have attained a position of importance in discussing psychosomatic patients. I shall address these concepts later when I discuss specific clinical material.

We have observed a wide variety of somatic symptoms which are representations of internal emotional conflicts. Among the most common are headaches, both tension and migraine; anorexia nervosa, both abstaining and bulemic; mucous colitis; ulcerative colitis; Crohn's disease; bronchial asthma; atopic dermatitis, as well as a wide variety of vascular and allergic reactions such as hives. Briefly, I want to make clear that there are undoubtedly certain genetic predispositions to these conditions. We are well aware that the mechanisms of the precipitation and maintenance of such symptoms deserve study, whether approached from the viewpoint of gross anatomy and physiology; biochemistry; immunology; molecular biology; neurophysiology, or other disciplines. Such studies have and will allow for a variety of therapeutic initiatives. Naturally, not all such patients are appropriate for psychoanalytic or psychotherapeutic treatment. All of these considerations are not pertinent to the focus of this chapter and have been discussed elsewhere (M. Sperling, 1946, 1961, 1967, 1969, 1978; O. Sperling, 1978a, b; Wilson, Hogan, and Mintz, 1983; Wilson, and Mintz, 1988).

It is apparent that in this work the psychoanalyst is frequently dealing with patients suffering with potentially life-threatening symptoms. This demands certain parameters, unnecessary in the treatment of the psychoneuroses. I will demonstrate that it is possible to combine good medical and psychiatric investigative procedures with a clinical setting that will allow for interpretable psychoanalytic work and an interpretable transference relationship.

As a background for our discussions I will present three brief clinical vignettes that I feel will illustrate three varieties of clinical problems that we face as we initiate psychoanalytic treatment.

The first patient adapted herself to what we would view as a classical analysis with few parameters. The second patient falls into that category of patient described earlier with a hierarchy of defenses supporting his denial. The third is a patient with a medical and psychiatric emergency, who although suffering from a severe illness of long duration was able to lend himself to psychoanalytic investigation with relatively little difficulty.

CLINICAL MATERIAL:[1]

Case Example 1

This young woman had a history of migraine headaches of ten years duration and of abstaining anorexia since shortly after puberty.

What does distinguish this patient for our purposes is that she displayed immediate adaptability to psychoanalytic treatment. After the minor parameter imposed by sessions for evaluation, she enthusiastically involved herself in psychoanalytic work on the couch. In a very short time, spontaneity and free flowing associations were available for study. Except for the expected resistances and the predictable acting out that is always present in patients with pregenital defenses this patient's analysis progressed to completion with no unusual modifications or incidents. Today, many years later, this young woman is married, has a family, and remains asymptomatic.

Case Example 2

This young man with ulcerative colitis offered an interesting contrast to the patient presented above. I will spend a little more time in the

[1](NOTE: A more complete report of the following case histories can be found in Hogan [1985, 1986b, 1988, in press].)

discussion of the particular resistance presented in the beginning of treatment.

This patient seemed ostensibly cooperative and communicative in a rather formal detached manner. There was little spontaneity. He seemed capable of only a shallow presentation of emotional and fantasy life. A paucity of dreams accompanied his obvious difficulty or reluctance in verbalizing feelings. Early in treatment, if I occasionally had some contributing information from an infrequent dream, he might allow as how he had had an emotional reaction to psychoanalysis. Less frequently, after interpretation, he might even acknowledge some annoyance at treatment, but not at the analyst. Some modifications to the traditional approach seemed indicated.

Parenthetically, as I have previously indicated, this massive withdrawal of affect and the detachment has been singled out and labeled "alexithymia" (Sifneos, 1972, 1973). The concept evolved from observations by two French psychoanalysts, Marty and de M'Uzan. They had given this constellation of defenses the name pensée opératoire (Marty and de M'Uzan, 1963; Marty, de M'Uzan, and David, 1963). At first observers closely associated these clinical states with psychosomatic illness. Some of the early work is summarized in the chapters of the 11th European Conference on Pychosomatic Research (Bräutigam and von Rad, 1977). However, over the intervening years a large body of literature has accumulated in which attempts have been made to define and test for this presumed entity. As this literature has expanded, this form of denial has been associated with so many clinical conditions that, to me, it has little meaning, and indeed may be misleading and harmful. It distracts from careful delineation and interpretation of specific defenses while giving the illusion that there is no need for such work.

Returning to Case 2, the psychoanalyst's handling of an external life experience precipitated a profound change in the clinical picture. The patient's father died, and as is my practice, I charged for the two missed sessions. The patient's hurt and rage were immense. He sought out consultations with other psychiatrists. At least one of them agreed with him about his unfeeling physician and recommended a change of therapists.

He did not, however, change therapists. His slowly improving but episodic attacks of colitis went into complete remission for some months. Now that he felt justified and free of doubts and shame he began to verbalize the hostility that he had consciously felt and denied over the previous months of treatment. He reviewed every real and fantasied neglect or slight that he had experienced since his first day of therapy. Each new remembrance seemed to further support and justify his judgments as to my coldness and incompetence. The so called "alexithymia" disappeared. The denial and splitting occasioned by his primitive superego and superego precursors became an understandable subject for analysis. The rich but primitive fantasy life was available for psychoanalytic understanding. The treatment proceeded over a period of time to completion with a resolution of his physical and emotional problems.

The resolution of defenses can be dramatic, and related as in this case, to an external event. This is certainly not always the case and when it does occur it is a response made possible by the preparatory work described below. It is of interest that such important work at times begins with such a hostile response.

Freud, in his descriptions of the beginning of a psychoanalysis (Freud, 1912; 1913, p. 139) noted that the emergence of a positive transference was necessary for the work to progress. How, in this case, did the appearance of anger herald the beginning of a positive transference? First, there was a newly found trust that had evolved from the patient's experience of the constancy and honesty of the analyst. As we will also note below, the previous interpretations of the patient's sadistic superego had helped to allow the freedom for the expression of feeling.

In effect, Case 2 for the first time separated his perceptions of the psychoanalyst from his experience with the introjected fragments of primitive perceptions of the primary object. These incorporated superego demons had continually attacked his impulses with their own sadistic contempt. His lapses in control, his presumed childish verbalizations, the pratfalls he felt he made when he attempted to assert himself, were all material for this mocking internal dialogue. It is not difficult to understand how such a patient must keep up his guard and constant self-control to avoid his self-imposed shame and humiliation.

One place where this control is almost universally demonstrable in the transference is in the termination of the session. Such patients maintain an awareness of the time so that they can metaphorically "leave" rather than "be left." They defend themselves against experiencing the humiliation of rejection with its anticipated confrontation, with control not only of their own impulses, but in the fantasied control of the object (the analyst).

Spontaneity becomes possible only after the patient is aware of the mechanisms he utilizes in his conscience to dodge a conflict with his shameful and disowned impulses and fantasies.

This type of massive denial and control is not unusual in psychosomatic patients and makes up the second subgroup in the arbitrary groupings that I am making in this chapter. The extent of the denial is frequently correlated with the severity of the psychosomatic symptomatology, but this is certainly not always the case.

I will demonstrate that such correlation is not universal by proceeding to the third subgroup of patients with psychosomatic symptoms.

Case Example 3

This patient is included because his symptoms were among the most serious and life threatening of any patients that I have successfully treated. Also, he allows me to illustrate how one can handle a perceived emergency without endangering the patient's welfare or compromising a future psychoanalytic position.

This young man had a history of Crohn's disease of the colon and rectum going back many years with repeated episodes of bacteremia. He had had numerous hospitalizations. There was a history of repeated attempts at hyperalimentation and prescriptions of every conceivable medication.

The present exacerbation went back a number of months and had included one hospitalization. He ran a fever, was emaciated, was unable to walk without help and could not sit. He was brought to my office on a mattress in the back of a station wagon.

I had obtained a preliminary history and a knowledge of the laboratory findings from his parents before the consultation. They desperately wanted to avoid surgery. Despite the generally gloomy outlook for surgery in a patient with Crohn's disease, he had been told that he would die without a colectomy.

As to the details, I had no choice but to use the couch. He could not sit. I did not separate out the early sessions for an investigative phase to evaluate the situation.

I did contact a cooperative internist for a future consultation.

Also this colleague could make arrangements for hospitalization, should we deem it necessary.

I told the patient that I saw no reason that he couldn't handle his illness and that I thought I could be of help. I was quite clear about the obvious—that we were going to try. I emphasized that what we were trying to do depended upon him. I made no promises.

The patient acknowledged that he had little hope of help from psychiatric treatment. He had been involved in three attempts at supportive psychotherapy in the past. I have often noted that if a patient expresses his skepticism it is a plus. It indicates a degree of spontaneous honesty not always present in patients with psychosomatic illness. It obviously represents a tolerance for his or her own doubts and hostilities. He was quite verbal, and unlike Case 2 he was aware of the emotional nature of his illness. Within the first week, he started to explore the conflict in which he had been involved before the current exacerbation of the illness.

The patient was quite conscious of the ruminations that had troubled and frightened him. They had been in response to a humiliating experience at the hands of a former friend. He had been afraid that he might physically attack and injure this individual. Within a very short time he discussed the brutally sadistic dialogues that went through his mind with reference to this individual as well as to others. Interestingly enough, no physician had really taken the time to listen without verbally interfering.

Very shortly this patient was driving himself to treatment and within a matter of months he was gainfully employed for the first time in years.

MODIFICATIONS

Time

If I decide to see the patient in what I hope will be a successful psychoanalytic treatment, I institute the usual psychoanalytic schedule of four or five sessions per week. I am as careful in questioning and interpreting breaks in this schedule as I would be with any other patient. I think that the manner in which I handled the missed sessions with Case 2 is a good illustration of the importance of such attention to psychoanalytic concerns.

Couch

The question always arises in seminars and group discussions as to whether it is better to see these patients vis-à-vis or on the couch. Some of my colleagues feel that the more severely disturbed patients should be seen vis-à-vis. A few feel that any psychosomatic patient is regressed enough that very destructive transference reactions (or defenses against them) can occur when the patient is on the couch.

I have respect for these opinions, but I am inclined to place any psychoanalytic patient on the couch unless the patient objects strongly. I feel that the patient's reaction to the separation can be valuable and interpretable. I feel that any refusal to lie on the couch is loaded with potentially useful material.

Formal Organization (Medical History)

I here wish to repeat that with some psychosomatic patients we are dealing with life-threatening symptoms. Practically all patients with psychosomatic symptoms have important medical histories with painful debilitating symptomatology.

While some feel that this may differ from more traditional psychoanalytic approaches, it is obviously important to obtain a careful medical and psychiatric history. Surprisingly, we have found that the interference with an analyzable relationship is minimal and interpretable. It is of no greater moment than the introductory histories we obtain from clinic patients to evaluate them for analysis by candidates.

I do believe that we would be challenging the credulity of a patient, as well as compromising his or her reality testing, if we did not indicate our serious interest in, and our desire to investigate, the background of any serious symptomatology.

To be more specific, these patients have often been seen and treated by practitioners who neglect the importance of emotional conflict in the genesis and continuation of somatic symptoms in patients, or are downright hostile toward any intervention by a physician interested in the role of such conflicts. It is important that the patient tell us about such attitudes of previous clinicians and that we obtain some verbalization of such a patient's feelings about past experiences. It is not wise to challenge directly or argue about past professional recommendations. However, the psychoanalyst may raise some tentative questions.

We also need the history of treatment, medications, and hospitalizations with whatever relevant documentation that may be available.

Usually is it neessary to establish contact with a consultant internist and/or surgeon for future consultations should they be needed.

Formal Organization (Primary Physician)

This brings us to a frequent and most important point of controversy with our medical and surgical colleagues on the one hand and with our nonmedical psychological colleagues on the other. The psychoanalyst must be the primary physician who decides with the patient on the treatment decisions and the appropriateness of consultations and medications.

It obviously follows that the psychoanalyst must be a well-trained physician who is not only involved in the psychotherapy of the neuroses, but who has maintained an active interest in and study of the medical problems and complications which may be found in the diagnosis and treatment of these disorders. He has to be well acquainted with the benefits and drawbacks of the use of any medications, as well as the possible dangers and complications possible in the use of such drugs. He has to be aware of the signs and symptoms that may indicate a serious exacerbation of physical manifestations of the illness.

Both the patient and the psychoanalytic physician should be aware of the importance of competent consultation, medical evaluation, and laboratory studies. The consultant, on the other hand, must have some understanding of the psychoanalytic process and be willing to function in that particularly important auxiliary advisory role. The patient will, of course, become more and more aware of how he utilizes his particular symptoms for his own masochistic and sometimes provocative needs.

The importance of this therapeutic posture cannot be overemphasized. If an analyst believes that the clinical responsibilities should be shared, that the analyst will analyze the emotional problems while the internist manages the medical problems, the trio is faced with what they started with—an irreparably split transference which is uninterpretable and physical symptoms which are unanalyzable.

There is a secondary and very important aspect to this. In our experience it is frequently possible to reduce the medications very early as the patient's physical symptoms improve. It is essential that the primary physician be able to interpret the magical longing for the medications, and their placebo effect, even of those active drugs which may temporarily ameliorate the physiological symptoms. This is feasible in practical terms only when a cooperative consultant is willing to remain in the background and not get too disturbed and involved when the patient begins to test the psychoanalytic physician with a mild exacerbation of symptoms. In order for such a complicated transference situation to remain in the realm of analyzable psychic reality, the prescribing or withholding physician must be the psychoanalyst.

Formal Organization (Specific Maneuvers)

I have indicated the importance of a thorough medical and psychiatric history in psychosomatic cases. In some of these patients a complete workup with laboratory studies is an absolute necessity.

Since this is so clearly separated from treatment, I generally devote one, and usually more, sessions to this investigative phase. Ordinarily, I withhold any promises of treatment until after an evaluation is completed. There are some exceptions, as I indicated in Case 3 above.

If I decide on psychoanalysis (or for some reason psychoanalytic psychotherapy) I tell the patient so, and begin treatment as a specific event. As in any analysis, I make no promises, but indicate in one way or another that there is no reason why these problems can't be worked through. I do my best to indicate that the conflicts and associations are the responsibility of the patient.

It is here, however, that modifications or psychotherapeutic maneuvers may be necessary. If the patient is involved in massive denial as was patient 2, it is important to educate the observing self by indicating that the patient had symptoms at a time that others might get hurt or angry. It is important to stress the patient's fear of his feelings and interpret the ways in which he avoids them.

Content of Interpretations

It is very crucial to interpret the defenses of these patients early in treatment rather than emphasize the aggressive or sexual wishes.

Specifically, we direct attention to the punishing superego or conscience that is intolerant of any aggressive or libidinal impulses. The self-punishment and suicidal activities are pointed out in these early weeks of treatment (Hogan, 1985d, pp. 199–206). The need for control and the fear of loss of control are repeated themes for interpretation as they are verbalized or demonstrated by the patient. In patients such as Case 2, behavior is utilized for such interpretations, if interpreting the particular piece of behavior does not humiliate the patient. In the initial phases of treatment, these patients are exquisitely sensitive to any observation that they experience as contemptuous, that highlight anything they feel may be considered childish, or subjects them to the shame of loss of control.

Usually such an approach allows the patient to mobilize some hostility, and eventually aggression becomes more interpretable (Hogan, 1985c).

Libidinal, especially oedipal, conflicts are usually left for late in the analysis. The early interpretation of such material can produce such shame and humiliation that the patient may run.

Despite the care that we take to avoid interpretation, triadic oedipal material may erupt spontaneously early in treatment and must be handled. When it erupts in the transference it may be more primitive in origin—a means of trying to control the psychoanalyst (Hogan, 1985c, pp. 134–137; 1985d, p. 158). In such an event attempts at seduction may be disguised manipulations for control.

As I have noted in Case 3, conflicts over aggressive material may be conscious and can also make their appearance early in analysis. Here, this patient's conscious conflicts over sadistic and sexual impulses were not suggested, defined, or interpreted. Naturally, when such material does appear it must be accepted and its importance acknowledged.

It is absolutely necessary to recognize in these situations that reassurance is of no help. As anxious as these patients may become, it is destructive to attempt to be the reassuring parent. One does well to remember Boyer's observation (1980) that "the best substitute for parenting one can afford the patient is to hew closely to the analytic model" (p. 206).

However, there are some relevant aspects of psychic reality that the analyst can point out. The patient's fear of taking action is easily interpretable and should be accompanied by the obvious observation that a fantasy or wish differs from action. One does not have to act on a wish if it is not to his or her benefit to do so.

This leads to another ubiquitous and threatening conflict in the unconscious of these patients. They are constantly defending themselves against their need for immediate gratification (and action). Early in treatment this conflict is usually interpretable, but the analyst must be conscious of the exquisite sensitivity of such patients. The psychiatrist has to be careful to avoid precipitating the overwhelming sense of humiliation that these patients are capable of imposing upon themselves. In the early stages of treatment, if there is an indication to the patient that he or she is inordinately demanding or greedy, then such a patient will frequently retreat to a prolonged protective period of denial (alexithymia?) which only prolongs the psychoanalytic process. Obviously, later in treatment patients with pregenital regressions will discover that such primitive demands for immediate gratification (their greediness?) are really a fundamental problem in the genesis of their illness. However, at this later date one hopes he or she will be able to take a less judgmental and contemptuous attitude toward the self. The sadistic superego will have been examined and the introjects illuminated as demons from the past rather than being present-day persecutors.

Countertransference

As a final observation on the beginning phases of the psychoanalysis of psychosomatic patients, I have noted how difficult it can be to work with a patient who is trying to politely shut you out, who wants to deny any importance the analyst may have for him. This is particularly true in cases like Case 2.

The psychoanalyst finds his mind wandering. He may become drowsy and disinterested. Such symptoms should give rise to a period of self-examination on the part of the physician.

A more unfortunate result may occur when the helplessness and hopelessness engendered in the analyst leads to rationalized terminations or initiations of other therapies. It is easy to proclaim such patients untreatable due to any one of a dozen rationalized causes: "alexithymia," "psychological ineptitude," "oganicity," "lack of transference," and so on (Hogan, 1985d, pp. 213–214; 1985c).

With few exceptions, we have found that when these patients show their interest in continuity of treatment, they do analyze their defensiveness and allow themselves freedom and spontaneity. At this point both patient and physician are aware that work has really begun.

Definitions

I trust that it is apparent in my use of parenthesis that I am not sure whether this early work should be called "psychoanalysis" or "preparatory psychotherapy." While this is of no consequence in Case 1, it might possibly be considered so in Cases 2 and 3.

Nevertheless, I hope that it is also apparent that I feel that such definitions are relatively unimportant if the stance is a nonreassuring analytic one, and if the ultimate work evolves into psychoanalysis, with a clear analyzable transference neurosis.

To reiterate, my colleagues and I have found that many patients with organic psychosomatic symptomatology lend themselves to successful psychoanalytic treatment when certain precautions are recognized and handled appropriately.

SUMMARY

Some of the specific problems posed by patients with psychosomatic symptoms were introduced.

Three patients, each illustrating one particular aspect of these problems presented by psychosomatic patients were briefly described. The first presented a few particular problems and progressed to a rather uneventful traditional psychoanalytic experience. The second presented a picture of detachment and shallowness with a noticeable dearth of observable fantasy life early in treatment. This massive denial and its resolution were described. The third patient presented a medical emergency. He was verbal and insightful despite the severity and chronicity of his symptoms.

An attempt was made to indicate the special parameters and techniques necessary to safely and productively initiate treatment, particularly in patients such as those illustrated by Cases 2 and 3.

These special problems involved are occasionally of a life-threatening nature. The need for a sound medical and psychiatric history along with appropriate consultative help was emphasized. It was demonstrated that such attention was not incompatible with psychoanalytic treatment.

The necessity for the psychoanalyst to remain the primary physician was stressed. Otherwise there is no possibility of analyzing symptoms or maintaining an interpretable transference.

The need to interpret the masochistic derivatives of the aggression in these patients early in treatment was emphasized. Lack of control and impulse interpretations are left for later work. Libidinal needs, particularly those relating directly to oedipal material, are so tied up with shame and disorganization that they must not be approached in the beginning phases.

Lastly, certain dangers inherent in the countertransference reactions to some of these patients were mentioned. In particular it was noted that the sense of hopelessness and helplessness engendered in the analyst can result in an undeserved rationalized termination or change of treatment.

With certain precautions many patients with often severe psychosomatic symptoms lend themselves to successful treatment with psychoanalysis or psychoanalytic psychotherapy. This chapter is an attempt to underline some of the problems in the initiation of such a treatment.

Chapter 15

On Beginning with Patients with Eating Disorders

C. Philip Wilson, M.D.

There is a wide range of eating disorders (Blinder, Chaitin, and Goldstein, 1988). Shifting unconscious conflicts can be manifested in a single patient's life span by a variety of different psychosomatic diseases as well as other symptoms. As we have demonstrated (Wilson and Mintz, 1989), the basic problem in psychosomatic disease is the treatment of the underlying personality disorder. If an eating disorder appears as a symptom in a neurotic patient, it may often be resolved in the course of the analysis of the patient's nuclear conflicts and may not be a problem for the therapist in the initial phase of treatment. The focus of this chapter is on the initial phase of analysis of restrictor and bulimic fat phobia (Moore and Fine, in press) (anorexia nervosa) in cases where the eating disorder is a major presenting problem. (We have detailed our technique of analysis in over forty cases [Wilson, Hogan, and Mintz, 1983]. I have elsewhere [Wilson 1988b] also outlined an analytic approach to the treatment of obesity.)

INITIAL CONSULTATION

Although the psychiatric diagnosis ranges from neurotic to psychotic and the symptoms and behavior of the patients offer dramatic evidence of conflict, usually restrictor and bulimic fat phobic (anorexic) patients deny their conflicts. Most often it is the unhappy parents or concerned friends, roommates, or spouses who bring the eating disorder patient to the therapist. In cases where fat phobic (anorexic) patients come for consultation themselves, their motivation is ambivalent and their wish for a magical cure is intense. Consultation techniques with adolescents will be reviewed because the majority of cases are in this age group and because with older patients the same basic approach is utilized with modifications dictated by such factors as the diagnosis, the psychodynamics, the capacity for insight, the life situation, and object relations.

Most of the points made in this chapter apply to obese patients. However, it should be kept in mind that underneath the genial, kind, cooperative, often joking facade of most overweight people, there is the same guilt, ambivalence, impulsivity, and wish for a magical cure that we find in the anorexic patients. Most obese patients do not come for the analysis of their obesity but for neurotic conflicts and symptoms such as depression and phobias. My research (Wilson, 1988b) shows that the obese individual has the same fear-of-being-fat complex (Savitt, 1980) as the anorexic but with variations in the body image, personality structure, and object relations caused by differences in functioning of the ego and superego.

CONSULTATION TECHNIQUE IN RESTRICTOR AND BULIMIC FAT PHOBIC CASES

It is important to understand the motivation, the source, and the method of referral for eating disorder patients. Although some patients come because they are aware of emotional conflict, others are referred by their physicians because behavior modification, medication, or other treatments have not effected a symptom cure. The source of referral is important: unless the internist (adult patients) or pediatrician (children) understands an analytic approach, a split transference between the medical and psychoanalytic specialists can block treatment.

In many cases, with adults as well as children, the parents bring the patient for consultation. These parents are usually highly motivated, well-meaning people who will do everything they can for their sick child. These parents are often *over*conscientious; a character trait that manifests itself in their efforts to control their anorexic children. The adolescent child, and frequently the adult anorexic patient who evidences conflicts in separation–individuation, is in a situation of realistic and neurotic dependence on the family, so that changes in the parents' behavior and attitudes can be crucial for therapeutic success. Parents may try to terminate treatment when the first strivings toward independence emerge, which may first be manifested by rebelliousness and acting out. Other adult patients may have transferred separation–individuation conflicts to the boyfriend, girlfriend, or spouse, so that cooperation, understanding, and in some cases the therapy of the parent surrogate may be necessary.

With respect to their understanding that symptoms are emotionally caused, patients fall into three groups. One group has no idea that their symptoms have any connection with emotional conflict. The second group has some understanding that stress plays a part in the precipitating symptoms. The third, relatively small group is psychologically sophisticated and understands that conflicts cause or precipitate symptoms. The therapist should inform the parents and the patient that his or her symptoms are emotionally caused and acquaint the patient with the therapist's experience in the treatment of psychosomatic disorders. The fact that other patients have been cured of their symptoms by psychodynamic treatment should be emphasized. The analyst should proceed from a position of authority, thereby permitting the development of the intense pregenital relationship in which the therapist is a new and different object, besides being a transference object. Neither trial analysis nor having the patient consult a number of different analysts is advisable with these regressed, ambivalent patients.

The therapist should be well acquainted with the symptoms and clinical picture of anorexia nervosa. Ample time should be set aside to see the parents and the anorexic child. Most often, the parents are frightened and bring the child for consultation. Usually the anorexic is seen first, then, with the patient's consent, the two parents are seen together, and, finally, if it seems advisable, they are seen separately. It can be useful prior to consultation to ask the parents to write up and send a history of their daughter's psychological development and medical treatment and any relevant family problems. It is crucial to explain to the parents both the serious, possibly fatal nature of the disease and the treatment aims—to clear up the anorexic symptoms and resolve the underlying personality disorder. Parents must be prepared for aggression, hostility, and criticism from their daughter; they can be reminded that, to a considerable extent, these attitudes are normal adolescent manifestations. The therapist should explain that rebellious acting out, as well as suicidal preoccupations or gestures, may occur.

While explaining these probable developments, the therapist also assesses the parents' capacity for psychological understanding, their knowledge of people, and the nature of their transference. This assessment helps the therapist to decide whether the parents need and will consent to psychotherapy concurrently with their child. No matter what degree of psychopathology the parents may exhibit, they should be asked to undergo psychotherapy themselves only for the sake of their sick child. Otherwise, because they are perfectionistic and deny conflict, they may become angry, refuse therapy, and obstruct their daughter's treatment. A review of the medical findings with the attending pediatrician or other specialist, with the family's permission, is important. It is not advisable to criticize the parents; suggestions as to ways they should change their relationship with their daughter should be carefully explained. A frequent parental question is, "Should we encourage eating?" It is most important to explain to the parents that emotional conflicts cause the eating disturbance and that eating should be left up to the patient.

If the patient has been in previous therapy, the parents should be forewarned that she may soon be hostile and critical of the therapist and want to stop, and that the parents will have to back up the treatment. The therapist should take emergency calls from anxious parents and quiet their anxieties by interpretation. In some cases, the therapist needs to explain carefully how and why his or her treatment method differs from the patient's previous one.

In the initial interview with the adolescent, a developmental history is taken. It is very useful to ask the girl what kind of conscience she thinks she has. Questions about the family's religion, ethical and moral values, rules, regulations, and attitudes about social issues may reveal cogent information. Although the ego structure, diagnosis, and motivation for treatment vary from one patient to another, all anorexics are very guilty people who deny conflict and control emotions. They withhold information and lie about their habits (i.e., fasting, gorging, vomiting, and taking laxatives). The therapist may be aware that a patient is not giving a straight answer, but should not pressure her with more questions. Anorexics also withhold and lie about their object relationships and sex life. Many have had no boyfriends and are virgins, and they usually will state this. Others will say they have no sexual conflicts and are orgastic. They must be allowed to tell their story, as it is only after months, or even years, of analysis that they will level with themselves and the therapist about their sexual conflicts.

It is best to begin by asking the least conflict-laden questions. It is helpful to inquire about the past first: Did you have boyfriends in adolescence? How intense were the relationships? Did you go steady? Were you engaged? The therapist then can ask about the patient's sexual experiences. Next, the therapist should concentrate on current experiences, such as fears of pregnancy, which can be intense in these patients, and the use of contraceptives (many anorexics do not use contraception of any kind, because they deny pregnancy). Another important line of questions involves the birth of siblings. Particularly important is whether the patient was prepared by the parents for the coming birth of a younger brother or sister. Likewise, the therapist should ask whether the patient was given information about puberty and menstruation. For adolescent patients, all these areas should be explored with the parents as well.

Masturbation and sexual fantasies should be brought up. However, the therapist has to realize that the superego of the fat phobic can be so strict that she may never have masturbated or permitted sexual fantasies. The gorging, vomiting patient usually has had sexual experience with masturbation, sexual fantasies, necking, and intercourse. The restrictor is frequently afraid of thoughts and fantasies and only wants to talk about dieting and food. Questions about homosexuality should be asked, although the latter is rare among fat phobics. One of the fifty cases studied had had homosexual experiences. She was a bisexual gorger–vomiter whose much-older homosexual lover was a maternal object.

It is important in obtaining the medical history to ask about other psychosomatic symptoms such as asthma, migraine, and spastic and ulcerative colitis, because these diseases may be alternate manifestations of the same underlying personality disorder that causes the eating disorder.

Amnesia for childhood events is frequent. Some fat phobics, particularly certain restrictors, are silent and negativistic. The best approach is to interpret the need to control emotions and deny conflict.

The therapist may decide, based on knowledge of the girl's history, to detail her real problems to her. It is not wise to accept a patient for therapy shortly before a vacation because there is a serious risk that she will express her unconscious anger at the separation by symptom exacerbation or self-destructive acting out. The adolescent is told that she will be informed of any conversations and communications with the parents.

The characteristic family psychological profile that was found in the great majority of fat phobic cases should guide the therapist's interviews with the family and the later therapeutic process[1] (Bruch, 1978; Minuchin, Rosman, and Baker, 1978; Wilson, Hogan, and Mintz, 1985). A useful acronym for the profile is PRIDES. P = perfectionism; R = repression of emotions; I = infantilizing decision making for the anorexia-prone child; D = parental overconcern with dieting and fears of being fat; E = parental sexual and toilet exhibitionism which is denied; S = the unconscious selection of a particular child for the development of anorexia. Another psychological situation that should be kept in mind in consultations with anorexics is the split in their ego. One suicidal, gorging, and vomiting anorexic told me very rationally about a book she was writing and her interesting editorial job and the next minute talked of how she should die because she was an awful person.

THE ROLE OF THE FAMILY PHYSICIAN IN THE THERAPY OF ANOREXIA NERVOSA

The family physician usually makes the diagnosis of restrictor or bulimic fat phobia (anorexia nervosa) and can play an important supportive role in therapy. It is important that he emphasize to the parents and the anorexic patient the serious, possibly fatal, nature of this disease while advising psychodynamic treatment for the members of the anorexic family unit. In the course of therapy, the family physician can fulfill an invaluable role in backing up treatment, quieting the parents' fears about their child's health by appropriate examinations, and deciding in consultation with the psychiatrist when hos-

[1]There are some exceptions to this profile.

pitalization is necessary if the anorexic patient induces a starvation crisis.

The family physician should understand that the restrictor or bulimic fat phobic anorexic patient is in intense conflict about eating and that unless the patient's weight is at a dangerous level, it is best to prescribe a reasonable diet but to leave the issue of eating or not eating for the patient to bring up in her psychotherapy. Attempts to coerce or force the patient to eat can result in a sadistic refusal to eat. These patients can be most deceptive and provocative. They will ask for diets or for special foods themselves but then will not eat or, if bulimic, will throw up the food.

Since they deny their illness and the danger of their self-starvation, they are brought to consultation by their parents, husband, lover, concerned friends, or family physician. Because of the anorexic's extreme denial and weak ego, whoever brings or influences the patient to come for consultation should be viewed by the therapist as the patient's auxiliary ego.

SITUATIONS INVOLVING SEPARATION–INDIVIDUATION

In taking a history from both the anorexic patient and the parents, the therapist should focus on situations that involve separation–individuation, which is when fat phobic symptoms or their prodromata first appear. The first major separation is birth. Breast-feeding and weaning should be asked about in detail. Because of their overconscientiousness, many mothers of anorexics have trouble dividing up their time. One mother, who worked as her general practitioner husband's secretary and bookkeeper, could not relax for breast-feeding. The daughter was bottle-fed and mother's feedings were compulsive and pressured. In the daughter's later anorexic behavior, she took revenge on her parents by keeping them at the table endlessly watching her cut up food that she did not eat.

Bladder and bowel control, walking, and talking all involve separation–individuation. The birth and death of siblings and relatives, particularly the death of grandparents, involve profound separation conflicts. One anorexic recalled in her analysis that her grandmother's death had been denied by the parents. She was not taken to her beloved grandmother's funeral when she was four years old, but was told that "grandmother went to sleep."

The first school experience is also very important; frequently there is a history of school phobia in nursery school, kindergarten, or first grade. Any geographical moves of the family provoke separation–individuation conflicts. Because their egos are immature, anorexia-prone girls usually do not adjust well to new surroundings, new schools, and new friends. Each school graduation involves conflict. Frequently, anorexics do well in high school, but procrastinate on the major maturational step of graduating from college. It is important to inquire about all situations that involve separation from the family, such as sleep overs, camp, and college. Questions should be asked about whether the girl could handle things on her own or telephoned home often. Also, how did the parents handle the separation? Daily phone calls to and from daughters away at college are common in families of anorexics.

The first love affair can provide very useful information, but the nature of all the patient's object relations is important. The first job and marriage involve other separations. Frequently, the anorexic girl's best friend is her mother and she is not close to her peers. Another conflict-laden event is illness in either the patient or her parents. Later in life, the loss of a mate or a parent may be significant in precipitating the separation conflicts, which may manifest themselves in anorexic symptomatology. Anorexic symptoms mask and defend against depression, and most anorexics are dry-eyed; it is a sign of therapeutic progress when they become depressed and cry.

THE FEAR-OF-BEING-FAT COMPLEX

An understanding of what I have termed *the fear-of-being-fat complex* (fat phobia) is necessary for the treatment of the eating disorders. I define the fear-of-being-fat complex as that cluster of orally rooted unconscious conflicts whose conscious manifestation is the pathological anorexic body image characterized by an irrational fear of being fat and an obsessive overconcern with being thin.

The unresolved preoedipal fixation on the mother contributes to the difficulty in psychosexual development and the intensity of the oedipal development. Restrictor and bulimic fat phobia (anorexia nervosa) can be considered to be specific pathological outcomes of unresolved oedipal conflicts in patients whose preoedipal relationship to the mother has predisposed them to this particular reaction under precipitating circumstances. Along with Mintz (1983, chapter 13), I include males under the diagnostic category of restrictor and bulimic fat phobia (anorexia nervosa).

CLINICAL CASES[2]

An Adolescent Patient

In the following case, restrictor fat phobic symptoms were resolved and the underlying personality disorder was analyzed. The parents were in conjoint therapy with colleagues.

A Restrictor Fat Phobic and Her Family

The R. family came for consultation about their seventeen-year-old daughter Sally, who recently had lost thirty pounds and become anorexic. Sally was a typical fat phobic "good" girl, obsessed with proper behavior, studying, and social achievement. Her father was a dissatisfied workaholic, successful businessman. The mother, a social worker, was overconcerned with ladylike behavior, manners, and proper behavior for her daughter.

Sally's brother, Robert, two years her senior, was an easygoing dolescent boy, who had a succession of girlfriends, smoked, drank, and enjoyed parties, dancing, and rock music. Although the mother weakly argued with Robert and chided him for his poor performance in school, most of her attention was focused on her daughter. She did everything she could for Sally, helping her with her studies, reviewing her homework, and barraging her with advice and criticism.

The R.'s followed a strict routine: meals were always on time, television was rationed to one hour a day, and the major form of relaxation for the parents was intellectual discussion and reading of

[2]Some aspects of these cases were published previously (Wilson, Hogan, and Mintz, 1983, 1985).

a serious nature. They never quarreled in front of their children and, in general, they shared the same ethical, social, and political views.

Memories of having witnessed parental intercourse (primal scene) emerged in the course of Sally's analysis. At three years of age, she woke up screaming with nightmares and, in order to quiet her, her mother had her sleep the rest of the night in the parents' bed. It was then that Sally heard the heavy breathing of intercourse, which she fantasied was an attack by her father on her mother. Other occasions of her witnessing parental intercourse, at four and six years of age, increased Sally's fear of sexuality. There were no operable locks on the doors in the R.'s home. Parental nudity and toilet activities were also observed frequently by Sally, who became inhibited and afraid of boys.

Analysis: As with all anorexics, many different conflicts were displaced onto and masked by Sally's anorexic symptoms. The focus of therapy was upon showing Sally the nature of her overly strict conscience, which demanded perfect behavior in herself and others. In her treatment behavior she was hypercritical; memories and dreams revealed that she had developed this attitude by identifying with her mother's perfectionism.

EXAMPLES OF INTERPRETATIONS

In the early sessions Sally came on time, sat quietly, and only talked about eating or not eating; for example, that she had gone off her diet and eaten half a blueberry muffin instead of yogurt and a carrot for lunch. I confronted her with her denial and displacement, pointing out that she had other conflicts, not just eating or not eating. She replied in a snappy tone of voice, "I don't even want to go to the school dance." The interpretation was made that she felt she should have no conflict so that she avoided anything that upset her, that, as she had mentioned before, going to a dance meant choosing a dress and having to go with a date who was not the most popular boy in school. Sally replied that she guessed she'd go to the dance with Billy, even though he did not dance very well. The interpretation was made that she demanded that she and Billy be perfect in everything.

The next session, which was after the dance, Sally announced that she was starting a new diet and was not going to have any lunch at all. The interpretation was made that the dance must have upset her, that since she could not control her emotions, she could control eating. She snapped angrily, "You are so stupid, I am just dieting." The interpretation was made that she felt she could avoid all conflicts of any kind by not eating. Sally then said that actually she felt very depressed, had suicidal thoughts, and ideas of stopping all eating after the dance, that she had been jealous of her friend Jane, whose date was handsomer than Billy. The interpretation was made that she paid a price if she tried to avoid feeling lonely, suicidal, and bitter (depressed) by not eating and socializing. She replied that "maybe you [the analyst] were right; Billy called to ask me to a rock concert and I decided to go."

Both Mr. and Mrs. R. were referred for psychotherapy. Mrs. R. came to understand that she was treating Sally very differently from Robert, and that she had been pressuring her daughter to carry out certain of her own unfulfilled aspirations in life. The R.'s moderated their overconcern with dieting and weight loss, and they learned how to tolerate and understand the emerging rebellious, depressed, critical adolescent behavior that Sally manifested when her anorexic symptoms subsided. Mrs. R. interrupted her intrusive controlling attitude toward her daughter. The parents also took some vacations without their children for the first time and began to quarrel in front of their children. Operable locks on the bedroom and bathroom doors were installed, and Sally was given a degree of privacy appropriate to her age.

Sally's acute restrictor anorexic symptoms subsided in six weeks and she resumed eating, achieved normal weight levels, and began to menstruate again. Two years of analysis were required to resolve her underlying personality disorder and her fat phobia.[3]

A Bulimic Anorexic Case

The patient was a twenty-one-year-old single woman living with her family and working as an editorial assistant in a publishing firm. She had been gorging and vomiting for six years. Overweight since early

[3]Shorter periods of analysis may be sufficient for eating disorder symptoms that can be treated in statu nascendi in adolescence; longer analyses are usually necessary for the personality disorders that underlie chronic adult eating disorders (Wilson, 1986).

childhood, she went on a Weight Watchers diet at age fifteen, shortly after her first menstrual period. She lost thirty pounds, then a friend taught her how to vomit, and she had been dieting, gorging, and vomiting ever since. She would gorge and vomit up to five times a day. She was on a perpetual diet of salads, cottage cheese, and diet food. When she gorged she consumed prodigious quantities of rich food, candy, cake, pastry, ice cream, cereals, and spaghetti, until she felt she'd burst. Then, overwhelmed with guilt and intense fat phobia, she'd vomit repeatedly. She also used laxatives and exercise (jogging up to twenty miles a day at times) to get rid of her "fat." Her parents were of Irish Catholic background. The mother, a church-going housewife, was ten to fifteen pounds overweight. She chronically complained of being too fat and unsuccessfully went on and off diets. The father was a controlling, perfectionistic, workaholic insurance executive whose "only vice" was cigarette smoking. The patient, Martha, was their only child and the center of their attention. Martha was inhibited sexually until her teens, when she had many dates, permitting herself some necking and petting, but developed a phobia about travel and found that the boys she liked took other girls out. Her periods were irregular and prior to consultation she had been amenorrheic for six months.

In the fifteenth session of her analysis she was late to her session for the first time. Her associations were that she missed the bus because she had been enjoying talking to her friend. She thought about not being efficient and not allowing time to get to appointments. She also does not take care of things. She lost her bag when she went skiing. She procrastinates about sending in her medical health insurance forms that will get her payment for sessions. She realizes that she does not do the things she should do. Her car needs to be taken in for an oil change, but she does not do it. She knows she waits until her parents and others get impatient with her. The interpretation was made that chores and details of living are not exciting; that one part of her wants immediate pleasure and resents tasks; that it was more fun to talk to her friend than to come for her sessions.

Her associations were to childhood: her father was a perfectionist who would make up chores for her to do. He would save up his anger when she did not do the things he wanted her to do, then he would explode. "Even now when I'm an adult," she said, "he yells at me." The interpretation was made that she was angry with me, fearing that I was a perfectionist like her father, but that she keeps her anger to herself, having a secret valve for it: her bingeing. The patient said, "It is funny, I don't think about what I am doing when I binge." The interpretation was made that her strict conscience does not let her know about things that she is angry about and that she feels she has to get rid of conflicts by bingeing. At this point, for the first time, she became upset and cried. She said that she had never realized before how unhappy she was.

In subsequent sessions her associations and dreams unfolded aspects of her neurosis, her dependence on her parents (her parents were in conjoint psychotherapy), her agoraphobia, and various age-appropriate realities that she avoided (such as having a bank account and checkbook of her own). A number of dreams revealed her wish to be back in high school, to remain a teenager with no adult responsibilities. She talked about age and time; she hated the idea of anyone growing old; she refused to accept the possibility of her parents ever dying. As she faced more and more of her conflicts she also began to exert willpower to interrupt her bingeing. The frequency of her bingeing decreased to every other day from five times a day.

The underlying depression that is masked by fat phobic symptoms began to emerge. She cried in sessions and expressed feelings of hopelessness. She wondered if anything could be done for her and asked if analysis would be forever. She had suicidal ideas and was aware of wishes to not come to sessions. She wanted medication to relieve her depressed feelings. As a result of confrontational interpretations she acknowledged that she gorged when she was depressed and that her upset feelings disappeared when she gorged. Repeated interpretation emphasized that if she could think about what upset her, she might not have to gorge.

She remembered that as a girl she used to be called "princess" by her father, that she knew she could get anything she wanted from him. Feelings of hopelessness emerged as she thought about the fact that she did not have many friends, and those few she had, she felt, used her. She talked of not wanting to grow up. She ignored the idea of people dying; her parents were ageless to her. Recently she had refused to go to the funeral of her cousin's grandmother. Her family was angry with her but told the others that she was sick with the flu. Although she was twenty-one, she said she thought of herself as a preteen girl and dreaded the idea of her next birthday. With further maturation of ego capacities to face and tolerate conflicts and affects, particularly depression, bingeing frequency decreased to once a month. Four years of further analysis resolved the underlying personality disorder and the bulimic symptoms.

TRANSFERENCE AND THE TECHNIQUE OF INTERPRETATION

Analytic technique has to be adapted to the varying defenses of the ego (Wilson, Hogan, and Mintz, 1985; Schwartz, 1988). During the first phase of treatment, as Blos (1987) emphasized in discussing the technique of analysis of adolescents, every type of "parameter," such as educational approaches, suggestions, and advice, may be used, usually in a dyadic context.[4] The technique of interpretation is determined by multiple factors such as the transference and the quality of object relationships.

Initial technique involves the interpretation (often confrontational) of the defenses against acknowledging and understanding the masochistic conflicts (Mintz, 1988) that are displaced onto the eating disorder; that is, restrictor self-starvation masks and expresses compulsive conflicts, and bulimic gorging and vomiting mask and express hysterical and compulsive conflicts.

Only when the patient's archaic superego has been modified, and when the ego has matured so that there is a capacity to face and tolerate libidinal and aggressive conflicts, and when there has been a shift from part object relations toward whole object relations, can the analyst interpret triadic oedipal material.

TECHNIQUES FOR INTERPRETING THE IMPULSE DISORDER

Another crucial aspect of technique is to interpret defenses against the patients' understanding their need for immediate gratification (the impulse disorder, i.e., the primary narcissism) early in treatment (Wilson, Hogan, and Mintz, 1983). Thus, the patient comes to see

[4]In some healthier (i.e., neurotic) anorexics a more classical oedipal approach may be used from the beginning.

that the symptoms are manifestations of a split-off, impulsive part of the ego,[5] one aspect of which is the fear-of-being-fat complex. If the ego's defenses against the acknowledgment of this primitive aspect of their personality are not interpreted in the patient's dreams, associations, body language, treatment behavior, and object relations from the beginning of therapy, acting out, particularly sudden premature termination, will occur.

For example, at the end of my first interview with a seventeen-year-old anorexic, I told her the time was up and we would continue the following day. She covered her face with her hair as if to hide from me and made no sign of leaving or hearing me. I sensed that she wanted to provoke a fight and knew from her history that she had often provoked her father into losing his temper and sometimes hitting her. I hazarded the interpretation that she seemed to have a princess in her who wanted all my time and that we would find out about this princess in therapy. She responded by getting up and leaving. I had hit the target with my educated guess; later in treatment she revealed layered narcissistic fantasies that she really had been the child of a wealthy, aristocratic, noble family.

TRANSFERENCE AND COUNTERTRANSFERENCE

The restrictors tend to be more faithful and consistent in their analytic behavior than the bulimics, whose acting out causes difficult problems. However, with all fat phobics the analyst has to withstand perpetual testing, be aware of nuances and changes in the transference feelings, and, most important, preserve the analyst role and avoid falling in with patients' wishes to turn the analyst into the image of the omnipotent mother. These patients can pick up almost imperceptible nuances in the tone of voice, facial expression, movements, and even feelings of the analyst. Annoyance or irritation on the part of the analyst is taken to mean rejection and intensifies the need for control of the object (analyst) and situation (analysis) at any cost (exacerbation or return of illness). Worry or anxiety on the part of the analyst is taken as an expression of love—the kind of love patients have received

[5]This split-off archaic ego is related to Volkan's (1976) "little person" and Niederland's (1956, 1965) "little man" phenomenon.

from their mother, which means a reward (anxiety, worry) for being sick. Like the mother, the analyst is worried and expresses love toward the patients when they are sick. Correct, well-timed interpretations are crucial. The transference cannot be split with another medical specialist; rather, the analyst must be basically in charge of treatment. The projections and projective identifications of these patients range between two extremes: alternate attempts to turn the analyst into the complete source of pleasure (the breast–food–all–giving mother) and into the critical, punishing mother who demands perfection. The specific countertransference problems with anorexics are even more complex and difficult than those with other patients because part of their conflict is conscious, which means that, in addition to the development of a transference neurosis, there is a conscious battle with the analyst.

The transference of the fat phobic patients is characterized by their projecting their inner world of masochistic submission to powerful, omniscient maternal and paternal introjects onto the analyst. The analyst has to understand and be tolerant of intense provocation, overt hostility, self-destructive, intimidating manipulation, and contemptuous if fearful withholding of material, as well as acting in and acting out.

THIRST, HUNGER, AND SAND SYMBOLISM IN ANOREXIA NERVOSA

The anorexic's defensive asceticism (Wilson, Hogan, and Mintz, 1983, pp. 252–254; Wilson, 1986) is represented in the associations and dreams of these patients by sand representations, which symbolize thirst and asceticism. The analysis of sand symbols in the dreams of anorexics is of great importance. The level of regression in anorexics is to the early infantile stage and it is thirst and hunger that the patient is trying to control, not just hunger, as the literature implies. The developing capacity to control oral sucking impulses results in asceticism and the defense of altruistic surrender (A. Freud, 1946, 1974; Kaplan, 1984). Altruistic surrender (masochism) is characteristic of eating disorder patients.

Stone symbolism dreams, which I found symbolize oral incorporative, cannibalistic conflicts (Wilson, 1967; Wilson, Hogan, and

Mintz, 1983, 1985) (i.e., the teeth and hunger), only appear in the terminal phases of analysis.

To understand and treat eating disorder patients, it is necessary to understand the impulse disorders, the addictive personality structure, and the habits of childhood which are frequently the developmental forerunners of restrictor and bulimic anorexia nervosa. As regards medication which is currently being used with bulimic anorexics, in my experience (Wilson, 1985, 1986, 1988a), the conjoint use of drugs and therapy usually is contraindicated. Among the negative consequences of medication are acting out, alternate symptom formation including toxic psychosis, vitiation of motivation for therapy, the use of drugs for suicidal attempts, split transference to the psychopharmacologist, and psychological addiction to the drug. Drugs can be resorted to because of countertransference conflicts of the therapist. It is emphasized that while there may be situations where the use of medication, particularly antidepressants, is appropriate (Panel, 1988a) (i.e., medical crises, treatment stalemates, or when patients cannot be motivated for psychotherapy, or where cost and therapist availability are problems), the use of drugs may be a trade-off, with potentially dangerous consequences. Psychoanalysis or psychoanalytic psychotherapy without the use of medication are the treatments of choice for bulimic anorexia nervosa.

SUMMARY

Eating disorders, like other psychosomatic symptoms, are manifestations of an underlying personality disorder. The focus of this chapter is on the technique of analysis in the beginning of treatment with restrictor and bulimic anorexics.

A review of the extensive psychoanalytic literature shows that most psychoanalysts view restrictor and bulimic anorexia nervosa as emotional disturbances that emerge as a retreat from developing adult sexuality via regression to the prepubertal relation to the parents. The technique of consultation with the anorexic was detailed with a review of such problems as family psychopathology and conjoint parental therapy, the anorexic's ambivalent transference and wishes for a magical cure, split transference to other professionals, and the problem of medication.

(1) *Fat phobia* should replace anorexia nervosa as a diagnostic term. (2) While the underlying conflicts, their fear-of-being-fat complex, are similar, the ego of the bulimic is not as perfectionistic and controlling as that of the restrictor so that it is periodically overwhelmed not only by impulses to gorge but impulses of other kinds. (3) Family psychodynamics which are viewed as etiologic were detailed. (4) Techniques of treatment focus in the first phase of analysis on the dyadic transference, the failure to free associate, the patients' impulsivity, and their use of denial and projective identification. The importance of understanding sand and stone symbolism in anorexia was emphasized as they reveal these patients' conflicts over thirst, hunger, impulse control, and asceticism. Psychoanalysis or analytic psychotherapy is the treatment of choice for anorexia nervosa. Most patients are seen vis-à-vis in the first dyadic phase of treatment. The parents of adolescent anorexics are usually seen in conjoint therapy by a colleague. The analyst is in charge of treatment, with hospitalization reserved for true emergencies. Medication usually is contraindicated if analysis is feasible.

Chapter 16

On Beginning with an Elderly Patient

Wayne A. Myers, M.D.

In this chapter, I will describe a number of issues which are relevant to beginning an analysis with an older patient. While most of these differ little from those involved in the treatment of younger patients, some may necessitate actual modifications in analytic technique.

Two of the factors to be discussed below are more frequently of importance in older patients than in other age groups. One involves the consideration of the actual physical health of the patient at the start of the treatment, and the second deals with the likelihood of a need for antidepressant medication early in the treatment. An additional factor revolves around gathering the specific information pertinent to the assessment of suitability for analysis in this age group. A final factor to be considered involves the analyst's need to recognize countertransference responses as early as possible in working with older patients. Following the exposition of these issues, I will present some clinical examples to illustrate the principles described.

Before turning our attention to the issues which seem relevant to beginning an analysis with an older patient, it behooves us to define what we mean by the term *older*. In Freud's early writings (1898, 1904, 1905), he suggested that people over the age of fifty were not suitable for treatment by the psychoanalytic method. He felt that the large amount of material to be covered in such treatments would make them inordinately long and impractical because of the "advanced" age of the patients at the end of the analyses. He was also concerned about the presumed "inelasticity" of the mental processes in such individuals.

Over the years, this viewpoint has been called into question both by the general advances in medicine and surgery which have enhanced overall life expectancy and the quality of life for older people, and by the work of a number of psychoanalytic investigators (A. M. Sandler, 1978; Myers, 1984; Nemiroff and Colarusso, 1985) which demonstrates the success of the analytic method with patients in their fifties and sixties. As a consequence of these findings, the patient's chronological age may not be the best method for determining whether he or she is "too old" for the analyst to contemplate recommending analysis.

Thus the question of just how old is "too old" for an individual to begin an analysis is one that cannot be answered with any exact degree of precision. A teenager of sixteen may be more psychically rigid than a grandmother of sixty-six. As a consequence, the degree of psychic resiliency of the patient is a more reasonable guide to the issue of who is analyzable, than the exact chronological age of the individual.

In my own experience, I have begun analyses with a number of individuals in their fifties and sixties. The oldest age at which I have started an analysis in a patient is sixty-eight, though I see no reason to hesitate beginning analyses on patients in their seventies, should the conditions warrant doing so.

PHYSICAL HEALTH

One issue of importance in deciding whether to undertake an analysis with an older patient involves the patient's physical health. While this is obviously of importance for a younger person as well, it is more frequently an issue in patients who present for treatment in their fifties to seventies. Many people in this age group will have been referred for treatment by their physician because of feelings of depression secondary to some intercurrent life situation, such as the loss of a spouse or a life-threatening physical illness. In such instances, some comment on their physical well-being is frequently given as part of the referral process.

When this is not the case, and there is cause to be concerned about the state of the patient's physical health, one modification to be considered is to ask the patient to see their physician for an overall physical checkup. This modification may be called into use when patients present with physical complaints, such as painful headaches, which, while they may be psychogenic in origin, may also be a symptom of a physical illness, such as malignant hypertension.

In such instances, what generally happens is that I will question the patient about whether they have seen their physician in order to investigate their physical complaints. When they have not done so, I probe as to what they think might be involved in their not having pursued this problem medically. While this rather direct confrontation with the patient's denial of their anxiety over recognizing the possibility of their own mortality may be somewhat premature, it seems imprudent not to pursue the very real possibilities of actual medical illness which exist in patients of this age group.

MEDICATION

Another issue which frequently differentiates patients in this age category from their contemporaries is that they often present for treatment either while receiving antidepressant medication or in need of receiving such medication. In my experience, in both this age group and with younger patients as well, the possible or probable need for the use of medication somewhere during the course of an analysis should not preclude our suggesting psychoanalysis as the treatment of choice for a given patient.

To be specific, many of the patients whom I see in the late fifties to early seventies age group are individuals who (as I noted above) are referred to me because of feelings of depression secondary to object loss or loss of self-esteem attendant upon insults to their physical well-being. It would be negligent not to treat these individuals with antidepressant medication.

When the immediate presenting symptoms have been relieved, however, we frequently find individuals whose lifelong character pathology is in need of modification by means of psychoanalytic intervention.

ASSESSMENT OF ANALYZABILITY IN THE OLDER PATIENT

While the overall assessment of suitability for analysis is not really different in the older individual than in younger patients, several factors of particular importance enter into such decisions. One involves what Pearl King (1980) has referred to as the "last chance" syndrome. This is essentially an assessment of the intensity of motivation for change in the older patient.

What I look for is some expression of the fact that the "time left to live" is regarded by the patient as finite, as Neugarten (1970) has observed, and not infinite. For example, most of the patients whom I see in their fifties to seventies have had some form of psychotherapeutic or psychoanalytic interventions earlier in their lives. More often than not, these treatments have not been eminently successful in outcome. This time, however, the patient recognizes that the biological clock is ticking and time is running out. This is the "last chance" to change things in the patient's life. I have found this modification in motivational intensity to be particularly meaningful to patients when they approach the age at which a parent died, especially when they have a strong identification with that parent and feel that the parent did not achieve a meaningful realization of their own potential (Myers, 1987a). If the patient does not voluntarily offer any expression of the recognition of the fact that the time left to them is finite, I will frequently direct their attention to this issue in the initial evaluative sessions in order to see what their response may be.

Another factor of importance in the initial assessment phase is one which deals primarily with the patient's potential for pursuing ongoing object relatedness, but which also gives us a measure of what might be referred to as the "elasticity factor," as well. To be more specific, I like to know if the individuals whom I see in this age group still retain the capacity to form new and meaningful object relationships. While this is also a factor of obvious significance in evaluating the suitability for analysis in younger individuals as well, in older patients it often gives us a hint of the presence of early organicity. To be able to form new object relationships, one must be able to deal with new concept formation, which is obviously difficult for the person suffering from an organic mental syndrome, even in the early stages of such a problem. A limitation in using the information gathered in this area is that people who are depressed when we see them initially also have a diminished capacity for object relatedness, particularly during the periods of acute depression. Here, we have to wait until the initial symptomatology has cleared, in order to make a realistic evaluation of the elasticity of such people's potential object relatedness capacity.

A further area of importance in evaluating analyzability in the older individual involves an assessment of whether or not the patient has achieved a reasonable modicum of acceptance of his or her own life and of the important objects therein. The more one is able to accept one's life and one's significant objects, without an undue amount of rage or envy toward them, the more one is apt to be found to be analyzable, regardless of age. In assaying this in an older patient, what is of especial importance is measuring the envy titer directed by the patient toward his or her own children and/or younger colleagues.

The concept being espoused here is similar to Erikson's (1959) idea that the achievement of integrity is one of the major tasks of the mature individual and to Klein's (1963) ideas about the interferences which undue envy poses toward successful adaptations to old age. It is also in keeping with ideas promulgated by Jaques (1970) and by Kernberg (1980). To wit, both of these latter observers noted that if a patient is able to accept his own personality, with its particular imperfections, without a need to globally devalue prior accomplishments, there is a diminution in narcissistic defenses and an increased potential for being analyzable.

A final facet of interest in evaluating the analyzability of older patients is the ease of access they possess to unconscious material, such as dreams and fantasies. Again, while this is something which we would want to evaluate in a potential analysand of any age, it is of considerable interest in our older patients. In my own work (Myers, 1987b; Myers and Solomon, 1989a), older patients offer a lower percentage of spontaneous dream reports than do younger individuals. While my work leads me to believe that the ultimate outcome of analysis correlates strongly with the frequency of dreaming, in both older and younger patients, the lack of spontaneous reports of dreams by older patients in the evaluative phase is probably of less importance than in a younger patient group. When older patients do, however, spontaneously report dreams or fantasies during the evaluative phase, I feel more sanguine about the possibility of their ultimately being analyzable.

COUNTERTRANSFERENCE RESPONSES

A final area to be cognizant of from the earliest moments of the evaluative phase in dealing with the older patient (especially if the analyst is considerably younger in age than the patient) involves the need for attunement to one's own countertransference responses to the patient. It is important that the analyst become aware of both displacements of positive rescue fantasies toward a parent (Lower, Escoll, and Huxter, 1972; Myers, 1984, 1986) or of negative feelings meant for a parent or for one's former analyst (Meerloo, 1953; Grotjahn, 1955; Myers, 1984, 1986) are of importance for the analyst to become aware of. They may positively or negatively influence our initial decision to either recommend or reject the idea of an analysis for an older individual, irrespective of the reality factors which may point toward the opposite decision.

CLINICAL DATA

Mr. A. was referred to me by a mutual acquaintance who knew of my interest in working with older patients. Mr. A. was sixty-three years old at the time that I first saw him and his presenting complaint was one of feeling "down in the dumps" since the death of his wife some six months earlier. He also complained of pains in his left arm and shoulder, especially during exercise, and of a lack of energy, concentration, and sexual desire. His sleep pattern included both early morning awakening and some frequent awakening during the course of the night. There was also some mild anorexia and a modest five- to ten-pound weight loss in the month prior to coming to see me.

When I found out that he had not been examined by his internist for nearly three years, I questioned him as to why this was so. His responses were vague and defensive and since I had some concern that the pains in his left arm and shoulder might be related to underlying cardiac disease, I finally suggested that he seek out medical consultation to clear up this matter. I also wanted to be certain that there were no contraindications to my treating him with antidepressant medication. While we later had to spend considerable time analyzing the meaning of my intervention, both in terms of its intrusive and its protective ramifications, it seemed imprudent to conspire with his denial and to run the risk of missing a potentially serious underlying organic disease. Needless to say, if prominent coronary artery disease had been discovered, then I might not have made the recommendation at that time for him to commence an analysis.

Once having determined that there was no serious underlying physical disease, it soon became incumbent on me to administer tricyclic antidepressants in order to alleviate the prominent depression which the patient was suffering from. Again, the use of medication was a second parameter which had to be analyzed later on, in terms of its multiple meanings for the patient. The presence of these two parameters, however, did not preclude my making the recommendation to the patient, some seven weeks after the initial consultation, that he undertake an analysis with me. My suggestions at this later date were based on his fears of entering into any new object relationships because of his fears of being abandoned once more, and upon his wish to achieve something "meaningful" with the life he had left to live, to have an impact on his children of a kind which his own father had never managed to have on him.

In this brief vignette, several issues of importance in beginning an analysis with an older patient are illustrated. To wit, the importance of having an accurate assessment of the patient's state of physical health is underscored, even to the point of recommending that they see their physician. While I have heard of occasional analysts and of at least one Treatment Center facility in the United States requiring that all potential analytic patients of any age undergo a thorough medical checkup before commencing an analysis, this is more often the exception than the rule with younger patients. With the older individual, though, it is probable that it should be the rule rather than the exception.

Another pertinent issue illustrated by Mr. A.'s case is the frequency with which older patients either present for treatment while taking antidepressant medication or require the administration of such medication early in the course of their treatment. Consequently, the decision as to whether or not to suggest an analysis to such individuals is one that is often delayed for weeks or months after the initial consultative appointment. Again, this is something which is done much less commonly in younger patients.

A third factor of importance in this patient's retinue of complaints after his depressive symptomatology had lifted was his desire to achieve a more meaningful "impact" with his life, than his own father had achieved. In my experience, this is one of the most important facets involved in assessing analyzability in the older patient. There is a profound motivational thrust to change, seen in certain older individuals (especially those who enter treatment at, or around, the age at which a parent with whom they are strongly identified died) by virtue of their awareness that this may be the "last chance" in their lives to effect any real modifications in their character structures. Perhaps this is best illustrated in the words of another man whom I treated many years ago, who responded to my inquiry as to how he might be different from the person whom he had been in his earlier life, who had responded unsuccessfully to a variety of psychotherapeutic interventions. He said:

> I was more closed up in the past. But now that I'm going to be 60, there isn't any more time to hold it all in. My father died when he was 60 and the only reason that he didn't live any longer was that he held his feelings all bundled up inside of him all of his life. I've done the same thing for most of mine. If I'm ever going to be happy, now's the time to open up and change things [Myers, 1984, pp. 23–24].

Mrs. B. entered analysis with me nearly two years ago at the age of fifty-six, following recovery from a brief depressive episode which she suffered after the death of her long-standing lover. While she was quite angry at her paramour for having abandoned her by dying, and though she acknowledged some reluctance to enter into a new relationship which posed the possibility of exposure to yet another object loss, she readily acknowledged that she did not wish to live the rest of her life alone. Her comment that she had to relearn how to "bite the bullet" and "take a chance with new people" was one of the factors which convinced me that she would be an apt candidate for analysis.

Another aspect of her personality which emerged in the evaluative phase was her willingness to serve as a mentor to younger people in her job. She held a senior position in a public relations firm and experienced a considerable degree of pleasure in helping younger assistants develop a growing sense of expertise in working with the firm's clients. In addition, she was proud of the beauty and success of her own daughter, who had achieved renown in the world of fashion.

A final factor of relevance was that she spontaneously offered a dream in one of the early sessions after she began to experience a lifting of her feelings of depression. In the dream, she is in mourning at the gravesite of the dead lover. As she rises from depositing a bouquet of flowers on the grave, she turns and sees another man standing nearby and takes the arm which he extends to her and walks off with him. In her associations to the dream, she wonders if the other man offering his hand to her is me and she is pleased that she has not been timid about accepting his helpful gesture.

This brief example illustrates the elasticity factor. Mrs. B. is open enough, despite her past hurts and losses, to risk attempts at forming new object relationships in the future. In this regard, her mourning dream (Myers, 1984, 1987b) also illustrates her capacity for forming a new object relationship with the analyst, which is an index of her overall potential as an analysand. The dream also shows that she has a ready access to her unconscious life, which is a good predictive variable regarding the ultimate outcome of treatment (Myers and Solomon, 1989a, b).

In addition, Mrs. B.'s ease of assuming the role of mentor in the lives of her younger colleagues, and her ability to take pride in the beauty and success of her own daughter, without experiencing an undue amount of anger or envy, are also indications of an acceptance of her own life and of the important objects in her past and present life. This capacity to accept the self and the important love objects of the past is also a good indicator of potential as an analysand in this age group.

The final case to be described is that of Mrs. C., a fifty-four-year-old widow, who came for treatment because of increased alcohol intake following the death of her husband. She was a bright, attractive woman, who reminded me in a number of ways of my former female analyst. Although this enhanced certain positive feelings which I had toward the patient, some of the unresolved negative transference feelings which I felt toward my former analyst also began to be displaced onto the patient. I became aware of desires to lash out at her, when I perceived her as being competitive and castrating. My understanding of these feelings crystallized, however, after I dreamed about the patient early in the course of the treatment.

> In the dream, the patient and I were dressed in fencing clothes. Each of us held foils and were moving down the mat toward each other. Then we engaged our foils and began to duel. For a number of moments, she parried my every thrust and I felt quite frustrated. Then she thrust at me with her foil and I parried and immediately riposted. With that movement, I scored

> a touché and she fell down on the mat. I stood over her with my foil poised, and she gazed up at me with an imploring look on her face. I felt a sudden surge of warmth for her and put my foil down and offered her my hand to help her up [Myers, 1984, p. 232].

From my analysis of the dream, I was able to understand the roots of my irritation with the patient and to be able to deal with her in a more effective manner. As a consequence, I was able to divorce my decision to analyze her from any unresolved feelings toward my former analyst.

While the handling of strong countertransference responses to patients is of importance in analyses with patients of all ages, I have found it to be of especial importance in dealing with older patients (Myers, 1986, 1987c). This is true, because older patients are more apt to evoke responses relevant to one's parents or one's former analyst(s) in younger analysts.

SUMMARY AND CONCLUSIONS

The analysis of patients in the fifty- to seventy-year-old age range (and perhaps older) is both a feasible and a rewarding pursuit. While most of the issues involved in assessing the suitability of individual patients for analysis, and most of the steps involved in beginning an analysis, are the same with older people as they are with younger ones, there are certain differences which I would like to underscore here once again.

One specific difference involves making an assessment of the patient's awareness of the finiteness of the time limitations on his or her life. When this awareness is present, it tends to add an intensity to the patient's motivation to change. In addition, while the capacity to form new object relations is important to assess at any age, it is of especial importance to assess in the older patient, inasmuch as it may give us some indication of potential organicity.

It is important also to study the patient's acceptance of his or her own life and of the important objects in it. When this acceptance is present without undue increments of rage or envy, we are likely to feel more comfortable about suggesting analysis for the patient. In addition, the presence of moderate degrees of depression in older narcissistic personalities is a hopeful sign regarding their potential analyzability. Finally, the ease of access to unconscious material is also vital to assay in this age group.

Two further factors of importance to take into account, before beginning an analysis with an older patient, are the physical well-being of the patient and the possible need for antidepressant medication. It may be necessary to directly suggest to a patient with physical symptoms that he or she see a physician before commencing an analysis. This is a parameter that will have to be analyzed later on, but it cannot be avoided for fear of missing significant organic illness. The need to utilize antidepressant medication is also a parameter that may later have to be analyzed, but its use should not preclude the suggestion of beginning an analysis after the depression has lifted.

One final area to be noted is the importance for the younger therapist working with older patients to be acutely aware of countertransference responses with the earliest phases of the treatment. Both positive rescue wishes and unresolved hostile feelings toward one's parents or former analyst(s) can affect one's recommendations regarding starting or avoiding an analysis with an older patient.

Conclusion

Arnold Rothstein, M.D.

When contributions to this book are considered, this editor is impressed by the importance of the analyst's interest in particular types of patients and problems. This no doubt influences their ability to modify the "standard" technique and their success in being able to begin analyses with subjects many colleagues might consider beyond the scope of collaborative potential. This perspective emphasizes that, particularly at the periphery of "the widening scope," the match is at least as important as the assessment of the patient's ego strengths and diagnosis. I believe this is what Stone (1954) had in mind when he stated "a therapist must be able to love a psychotic or a delinquent and be at least warmly interested in the 'borderline' patient" (p. 592) . . . "the therapist's personal tendencies may profoundly influence the indications and prognosis" (p. 593).

It is worth reiterating the editors' purpose in organizing this book. We believe that there is heuristic value in addressing the discrepancy between what candidate analysts are taught (and/or wish to believe) and what experienced graduate analysts actually do in their practices. This discrepancy derives, in part, from an exclusive emphasis on interpretation and insight in conceptions of analytic process and mode of therapeutic action as well as a corollary aversion for considering what else, in addition to interpretation, takes place in well-conducted analyses.

In addition, the seemingly interminable search for the good analysand with whom the candidate analyst can employ an uncontaminated analytic model contributes to an inhibition in many colleagues' efforts to begin analyses and develop analytic practices. As a rule admission services of analytic institutes are much more particular in considering a subject's suitability for analysis with a candidate than are graduate analysts working in their private practices. Bachrach's chapter on research on analyzability clearly demonstrates the difficulty, if not impossibility, of predicting outcome at the beginning of an analysis. Bachrach states "analyzability is . . . no more than marginally predictable . . . at the initial evaluation" and he adds "the studies also suggest that it is necessary to wait until a case is terminated before a true assessment of analyzability can be meaningfully made." His contribution suggests to this editor that all beginnings are in a sense "trials" of analysis. Because analysis may be the optimal treatment for selected subjects in most nonpsychotic diagnostic categories the emphasis in an initial consultation should be on the contraindications to a trial of analysis.

Because interpretation is not the only or even the predominant activity of analysts at the beginning of analyses, it is probable that idealized conceptions of analysis which exclusively emphasize interpretation interfere with helping some patients who might *become* suitable subjects for an analytic collaboration.

Both Eissler's (1953) and Stone's (1954) important papers attempt to explore just this issue. Eissler (1953), from a more idealized perspective, explored the technical management of neurotics for whom correct verbal interpretation was insufficient to effect the integrative balance of their egos. He states, "in the *ideal* case the analyst's activity is limited to interpretation" (p. 108; emphasis added). He discussed the possibility of "advising the patient" (p. 109) in the midphase of a "stalemated" (p. 109) analytic situation in order to facilitate the use of interpretations. He defines this advice as a "parameter of a technique" (p. 109), and sees it as "a deviation . . . from a technique which requires interpretation as the *exclusive* tool" (p. 109; emphasis added). He proposed the validity of parameters as long as their influence was analyzed before termination. In addition Eissler noted that in delinquents: "the basic rule is inapplicable because of the patient's intentional and adamant refusal to follow it . . . and insight cannot be conveyed to these patients by verbal interpretation . . . at least not in the initial phase of treatment" (p. 113). The characteristic behavior of patients Eissler designates as "delinquents" may also be found in other patients, particularly those whose phase of development and/or personality organization is characterized by action. Thus, many adolescents and some young adults as well as subjects who might be labeled today as "borderline," "frozen," "antianalysands," and/or "narcissistic" may find it very difficult to collaborate within "the basic rule."

Stone (1954) seems to consider a number of patients sicker than those discussed by Eissler. From what I am stressing is a more realistic, rather than idealized, perspective, Stone (1954) broadens the concept of parameter to "modifications" (p. 573) in technique. He emphasizes modifications necessary to facilitate a "positive transference" (p. 588) that can withstand the inevitable hostile transference.

In Brenner's anchoring chapter the basic principles of the standard analytic techniques are stressed. The analyst works from a neutral perspective toward the data to understand it. The analyst interprets with tact at an appropriate time in the process. To do otherwise is to modify the analysis. When this is done in the beginning Brenner considers it reasonable preparatory psychotherapy. The contributions that are organized in the second section of the book emphasize the centrality of understanding and subsequent interpretation to the standard analytic method and process.

The final section of the book explores the application of modifications of the standard technique in the beginning of analysis. These modifications are of two different types: In one the analyst, based on his understanding of the patient's character organization, describes to the patient events that the analyst anticipates may disrupt and/or destroy the proposed trial of analysis; in the other the analyst functions as a psychiatrist and/or primarily as a physician who prescribes psychotropic drugs and/or other forms of medical treatment. In both situations it is the analyst's aim to analyze the meanings of these activities at later stages of the analysis.

From a historical perspective on the development of technique Brenner emphasizes that in spite of Freud's (1923, 1926) and A. Freud's (1936) important emendations of theory and their implications for technique it was not until the 1950s that analytic work focused on the analysis of defense. In Abend's, Horowitz's, and Applegarth's contributions the analyst actively pursues the exploration of the analysand's conscious fantasies about analysis in general and his prior experience with analysts and analysis in particular. This focus can be understood as an aspect of the analysis of the subject's resistance.

Blum's contribution can be viewed as a bridge to the last section of the book. His chapter's emphasis is on selection and the "patient's ego strengths and overall personality resources" in mitigating the tendencies of the traumatized patient to disrupt a trial of analysis with acting out. However, although he states that "ordinarily instructions are not necessary" the traumatized "patient can be . . . *cautioned* against impulsive action" (editor's emphasis).

Stein suggests that "in order to decide whether to advise analysis, we must rely on intuition tempered by experience." A similar combination of factors inevitably influences an analyst's decision concerning the cautioning of a traumatized patient against impulsive action. Stein reiterates his important technical contribution concerning the analysis of impulsive action: at the beginning of an analysis the acting out analysand is only able to focus attention on the action "after each episode." Therefore, the first technical task of the analyst with such patients is description. The aim of this work is the facilitation of the development of the analysand's observing ego. Stein states:

> First . . . place the history of acting out behavior in a verbal context, describe it, point out its periodicity, its compelled quality, its dramatic features and its correlation with lapses in reality testing and judgment. . . . Only after the symptom has been described . . . is it advisable to proceed with . . . analysis proper, the interpretation of transference, the description of the underlying fantasy and the reconstruction of significant infantile events.

Stein's contribution emphasizes that with enactment prone patients the analyst must be able to tolerate the unpleasure evoked within him by his patient's enactments so that subsequent to the enactments they can be better understood and more adequately interpreted.

In a similar fashion to Blum and Stein, Chused, Rothstein, and Porder focus on their analysands' penchants for action. In this regard Chused states "I begin 'an analysis' of our exchange almost immediately" . . . [and] To name the battle yet not participate goes a long way to preventing it from becoming an insurmountable resistance to treatment."

Porder appreciates his analysands' sensitivity. He anticipates their tendency to experience frustration in the transference as a narcissistic injury which may be associated with paranoid ideation and/or self-destructive behavior. Therefore he describes and explains a good deal about the work and possible future disruptions while not insisting on the implementation of all the parameters of the analytic situation at the beginning of the work.

Although I suspect that the reluctant patients I describe are not as sick as some of Porder's borderline analysands, our attitudes toward their resistances are quite similar. I have stressed that it is the analyst's neutral attitude toward these analysands' "enactment resistances" that is the essential characteristic of the analytic method. This neutral attitude toward their reluctance facilitates the analyst understanding it as analogous to a symptom best understood as a compromise formation. It is this attitude rather than the immediate implementation of the use of the couch, or the four or five times per week frequency of visits, that defines the analytic method.

In a similar fashion to Porder and this editor, Shane responded to his patient's mistrust and past history of failed prior analytic attempts when he decided to go slowly and to be particularly sensitive to small details of their interaction. Although this editor has significant differences with the Shanes' conceptions of mode of therapeutic action, these differences are less important when considering issues of the beginning of an analysis. Anything that facilitates the analyst's sensitive attunement to his patient's unpleasure in general and mistrust in particular is helpful in understanding the patient and in the subsequent establishment of the analytic relationship.

In reading the contributions of Ostow, Hogan, Wilson, and Myers it is clear that these colleagues have a special interest in particular groups of patients. Their interest and experience results in the suggestion that the analyst functions as both analyst and as primary physician. They propose that the meanings of their extra-analytic interventions should and can be analyzed. Their perspectives are in synchrony with the general principles of the management of modifications. Analysts modify the standard technique because their experience and intuition results in a judgment that interventions other than interpretation are required to help their patients and to proceed with their analyses.

As with the subject of modifications in general, colleagues question with varying degrees of skepticism, whether significant modifications irreparably distort the transference.

However Ostow, Hogan, and Wilson stress specific disadvantges in delegating nonanalytic functions to other physicians. In implementing this point of view Wilson stresses that "the analyst should proceed from a position of authority." From this vantage point he educates his prospective analysands. He tells them that he is experienced treating their condition and assures them that patients are cured of psychosomatic disorders with psychodynamic treatments. From a similar perspective Ostow cautions that the analyst who does not prescribe "never knows whether he is hearing the patient speak or the medication." In a similar fashion Hogan, Wilson, and Myers will prescribe medications for their patients and subsequently analyze these modifications of analytic function.

More specifically the contributions of Hogan and Wilson conceive of their patients' physical illnesses, in part, as analogous to symptoms. As such they stress the importance of the analyst's primary involvement in the overall care of their patients' illnesses. To do otherwise, they suggest, is to distance oneself from the data. Although many colleagues may differ with aspects of these colleagues' hypotheses most would agree that they deserve careful study.

References

Abrams, S. (1987), The psychoanalytic process as a schematic model. *Internat. J. Psycho-Anal.*, 68:441–452.

Abend, S. (1979), Unconscious fantasy and theories of cure. *J. Amer. Psychoanal. Assn.*, 27:579–596.

——— (1986), Some problems in the evaluation of the psychoanalytic process. In: *The Science of Mental Conflict: Essays in Honor of Charles Brenner*, ed. A. Richards & M. Willick. Hillside, NJ: Analytic Press, pp. 209–228.

——— Porder, M., & Willick, M. (1983), *Borderline Patients: Psychoanalytic Perspectives*. New York: International Universities Press.

Adatto, C. P. (1966), On the metamorphosis from adolescence into adulthood. *J. Amer. Psychoanal. Assn.*, 14:485–509.

——— (1980), Late adolescence to early adulthood. In: *The Course of Life*, Vol. 2, ed. G. Pollock & S. Greenspan. Washington, DC: U.S. Department of Health & Human Services, pp. 463–477.

Adler, G. (1985), *Borderline Psychopathology and Its Treatment*. New York: Aronson.

——— (1989), Transitional phenomena, projective identification, and the essential ambiguity of the psychoanalytic situation. *Psychoanal. Quart.*, 58:81–103.

——— Buie, D. H. (1979), Aloneness and borderline psychopathology: The possible relevance of child developmental issues. *Internat. J. Psycho-Anal.*, 60:83–96.

Alexander, F. (1956), *Psychoanalysis and Psychotherapy*. New York: Norton.

Alpert, A. (1959), Reversibility of pathological fixations associated with maternal deprivation in infancy. *The Psychoanalytic Study of the Child*, 14. New York: International Universities Press.

Altschul, S. (1968), Denial and ego arrest. *J.Amer. Psychoanal. Assn.*, 14:141–153.

American Psychiatric Association (1980), *The Diagnostic and Sta-*

tistical Manual of Mental Disorders, 3rd ed. (DSM-III). Washington, DC: American Psychiatric Press.

——— (1986), *The Diagnostic and Statistical Manual of Mental Disorders*, 3rd ed., revised (DSM-III-R). Washington, DC: American Psychiatric Press.

Applebaum, S. (1977), *The Anatomy of Change*. New York: Plenum Press.

Arlow, J. A. (1981), Theories of pathogenesis. *Psychoanal. Quart.*, 50:488–514.

Bachrach, H., & Leaff, L. (1978), Analyzability: A systematic review of the clinical and quantitative literature. *J. Amer. Psychoanal. Assn.*, 26:881–920.

——— Weber, J., & Solomon, M. (1985), Factors associated with the outcome of psychoanalysis (clinical and methodological considerations): Report of the Columbia Psychoanalytic Research Center Project (IV). *Internat. Rev. Psycho-Anal.*, 12:379–389.

Baekeland, F., & Lundwall, L. (1975), Dropping out of treatment: A critical review. *Psychol. Bull.*, 82:738–783.

Balint, M. (1954), Analytic training and training analysis. *Internat. J. Psycho-Anal.*, 35:157–162.

Benedek, T. (1969), Training analysis—Past, present and future. *Internat. J. Psycho-Anal.*, 50:437–445.

Berk, R., Ouker, R., Goldart, N., Swerdloff, B., & Wolf, L. (1964), A profile of the study of the applicant not accepted for treatment at analytic clinics. *Psychiat. Quart.*, 30:1–17.

Bernfeld, S. (1962), On psychoanalytic training. *Psychoanal. Quart.*, 31:453–482.

Berzins, J., Bendar, R., & Severy, L. (1975), The problem of intersources consensus for measuring therapeutic outcome: New data and multivariate perspectives. *J. Abnorm. Soc. Psychol.*, 84:10–19.

Bibring, G. (1954), The training analysis and its place in psychoanalytic training. *Internat. J. Psycho-Anal.*, 35:169–173.

Bion, W. R. (1959), Attacks on linking. *Internat. J. Psycho-Anal.*, 40:308–315.

——— (1967), *Second Thoughts. Selected Papers on Psychoanalysis*. London: Heinemann.

Blinder, B. J., Chaitin, B. F., & Goldstein, R. (1988), *The Eating Disorders*. Jamaica, NY: S. P. Scientific Books, pp. 433–446.

Blos, P. (1963), The concept of acting out in relation to the adolescent process. *J. Amer. Acad. Child Psychiat.*, 2:118–143.
——— (1967a), The second individuation process of adolescence. *The Psychoanalytic Study of the Child*, 22:162–186. New York: International Universities Press.
——— (1967b), Keynote address on treatment of adolescents. Meeting of the Association for Adolescent Analysis, Miami, FL, April 4, 1967.
——— (1972), The epigenesis of the adult neurosis. *The Psychoanalytic Study of the Child*, 27:106–135. New Haven, CT: Yale University Press.
——— (1980), The life cycle as indicated by the nature of the transference in the psychoanalysis of adolescents. *Internat. J. Psycho-Anal.*, 61:145–151.
——— (1985), *Son and Father*. New York: Free Press.
Blum, H. P. (1983), Splitting of the ego and its relation to parent loss. *J. Amer. Psychoanal. Assn.*, 31 (supplement): 301–324.
——— (1986), The concept of the reconstruction of trauma. In: *The Reconstruction of Trauma*, Monograph 2, Workshop Series of the American Psychoanalytical Association, ed. A. Rothstein. Madison, CT: International Universities Press, pp. 7–27.
——— (1987), The role of identification in the resolution of trauma. *Psychoanal. Quart.*, 56:609–627.
Boyer, L. B. (1980), Working with the borderline patient. In: *Psychoanalytic Treatment of Schizophrenia, Borderline and Characterological Disorders*, ed. L. B. Boyer & P. L. Giovacchini. New York: Aronson, pp. 171–208.
Bradlow, P. (1971), Murder in the initial dream in psychoanal. *Bull. Phila. Assn. Psychoanal.*, 21:70–81.
——— (1973), On reporting an initial dream in psychoanalysis of undisguised sexual activity between family members. *Bull. Assn. Psychoanal. Med.*, 12:18–22.
——— (1987), On prediction and the manifest content of the initial dream reported in psychoanalysis. In: *The Interpretation of Dreams in Clinical Work*, Monograph 3, Workshop Series of the American Psychoanalytic Association. ed. A. Rothstein. Madison, CT: International Universities Press, pp. 155–178.
——— Coen, S. (1975), The analyst undisguised in the initial

dream in psychoanalysis. *Internat. J. Psycho-Anal.*, 56:415–425.

Bräutigam, W., & von Rad, M. (1977), *Toward A Theory of Psychosomatic Disorders: Alexithymia, Pensée Opératoire. Psychosomatisches Phänomen.* Proceedings of the 11th European Conference on Psychosomatic Research, Heidelberg, September 14–17, 1976. Basel: Karger.

Brenner, C. (1982), *The Mind in Conflict.* New York: International Universities Press.

Bruch, H. (1978), *The Golden Cage: The Enigma of Anorexia Nervosa.* Cambridge, MA: Harvard Univ. Press.

Buie, D. H. (1985), Book Review: *Borderline Patients: Psychoanalytic Perspectives*, by S. M. Abend, M. S. Porder, & M. S. Willick. *Internat. J. Psycho-Anal.*, 66:375–379.

——— Adler, G. (1982–1983), Definitive treatment of the borderline personality. *Internat. J. Psycho-Anal. Psychother.*, 9:51–87.

Calef, V., & Weinshel, E. (1973), Reporting, non-reporting and assessment in the training analysis. *J. Amer. Psychoanal. Assn.*, 21:714–726.

Chused, J. (1988), The transference neurosis in child analysis. *The Psychoanalytic Study of the Child*, 43:51–81. New Haven, CT: Yale University Press.

——— (1990), "Neutrality in the analysis of action-prone adolescents." *J. Amer. Psychoanal. Assn.*, 38 (in press).

COPER Report (1974), In: Goodman, S. (1977), *Psychoanalytic Education and Research.* New York: International Universities Press.

Eissler, K. R. (1953), The effect of the structure of the ego on psychoanalytic technique. *J. Amer. Psychoanal. Assn.*, 1:104–143.

Eitingon, M. (1926), Preliminary discussion of the question of psychoanalytic training. *Internat. J. Psycho-Anal.*, 7:129–135.

Erle, J. (1979), An approach to the study of analyzability and analyses: The course of forty consecutive cases selected for supervised analysis. *Psychoanal. Quart.*, 48:198–228.

——— Goldberg, D. (1979), Problems in the assessment of analyzability. *Psychoanal. Quart.*, 48:48–84.

——— ——— (1984), Observations on assessment of analyzability by experienced analysts. *J. Amer. Psychoanal. Assn.*, 32:715–737.

Erikson, E. H. (1959), Identity and the Life Cycle. *Psychological Issues*, Monogr. 1. New York: International Universities Press.

Esman, A. H. (1971), Consolidation of the ego ideal in contemporary adolescence. In: *Psychology of Adolescence*, ed. A. H. Esman. New York: International Universities Press, 1975, pp. 211–218.

Feldman, F. (1968), Results of psychoanalysis in clinic case assignments. *J. Amer. Psychoanal. Assn.*, 16:274–300.

Firestein, S. (1978), *Termination in Psychoanalysis*. New York: International Universities Press.

——— (1984), The dilemma of analyzability. In: *Psychoanalysis: The Vital Issues*, Vol. 2, ed. J. Gedo & G. Pollock. New York: International Universities Press, pp. 227–248.

Flemming, J. (1973), The training analyst as an educator. *The Annual of Psychoanalysis*, 1:280–295. New York: Quadrangle.

——— (1978), Assessment of progress in a training analysis. *Internat. Rev. Psycho-Anal.*, 5:33–43.

Fraiberg, S. (1955), Some considerations in the introduction to therapy in puberty. *The Psychoanalytic Study of the Child*, 10:264–286. New York: International Universities Press.

Freud, A. (1936), *The Ego and the Mechanisms of Defense*. New York: International Universities Press, 1966.

——— (1946), The psychoanalytic study of infantile feeding disturbance. In: *The Writings of Anna Freud*, 4:39–59. New York: International Universities Press, 1968.

——— (1965), Normality and pathology in childhood. In: *The Writings of Anna Freud*, 6. New York: International Universities Press.

——— (1968), Acting out. *Internat. J. Psycho-Anal.*, 49:165–170.

——— (1976), Remarks on problems of psychoanalytic training. In: *The Writings of Anna Freud*, 8:186–192. New York: International Universities Press, 1981.

Freud, S. (1898), Sexuality in the aetiology of the neuroses. *Standard Edition*, 3:263–285. London: Hogarth Press, 1962.

——— (1900), The Interpretation of Dreams. *Standard Edition*, 4 & 5. London: Hogarth Press, 1953.

——— (1904), Freud's psycho-analytic procedure. *Standard Edition*, 7:249–254. London: Hogarth Press, 1953.
——— (1905), On psycho-therapy. *Standard Edition*, 7:257–268. London: Hogarth Press, 1953.
——— (1912), The dynamics of transference. *Standard Edition*, 12:97–108. London: Hogarth Press, 1958.
——— (1913), On beginning the treatment. (Further recommendations on the technique of psycho-analysis I.) *Standard Edition*, 12:121–144. London: Hogarth Press, 1958.
——— (1914), Remembering, repeating and working-through. *Standard Edition*, 12:147–156. London: Hogarth Press, 1958.
——— (1917), Introductory Lectures on Psychoanalysis. *Standard Edition*, 15 & 16. London: Hogarth Press, 1963.
——— (1918), From the history of an infantile neurosis. *Standard Edition*, 17:7–123. London: Hogarth Press, 1955.
——— (1920a), Beyond the pleasure principle. *Standard Edition*, 18:1–64. London: Hogarth Press, 1955.
——— (1920b), The psychogenesis of a case of homosexuality in a woman. *Standard Edition*, 18:145–172. London: Hogarth Press, 1955.
——— (1923), The ego and the id. *Standard Edition*, 19:1–59. London: Hogarth Press, 1961.
——— (1926), Inhibitions, symptoms and anxiety. *Standard Edition*, 20:75–174. London: Hogarth Press, 1955.
——— (1928), Letter to Sándor Ferenzi. *Internat. Rev. Psycho-Anal.*, 13:271.
——— (1933), New introductory lectures on psychoanalysis. *Standard Edition*, 22:5–182. London: Hogarth Press, 1964.
——— (1937), Analysis terminable and interminable. *Standard Edition*, 23:209–253. London: Hogarth Press, 1964.
——— (1939), Moses and monotheism. *Standard Edition*, 23:1–37. London: Hogarth Press, 1964.
——— (1940), An outline of psychoanalysis. *Standard Edition*, 23:144–207. London: Hogarth Press, 1964.
Frosch, J. (1964), The psychotic character: Clinical psychiatric considerations. *Psychoanal. Quart.*, 38:81–96.
——— (1970), Psychoanalytic considerations of the psychotic character. *J. Amer. Psychoanal. Assn.*, 18:24–50.
Garfield, S., & Bergin, A. (1978), *Handbook of Psychotherapy and*

Behavior Change: An Empirical Analysis. New York: John Wiley.

Gitelson, M. (1948), Problems of psychoanalytic training. *Psychoanal. Quart.*, 17:198–211.

——— (1954), Therapeutic problems in the analysis of the normal candidate. *Internat. J. Psycho-Anal.*, 35:174–183.

Glover, E. (1955), *The Technique of Psycho-Analysis*. New York: International Universities Press.

Greenacre, P. (1941), The predisposition to anxiety. In: *Trauma, Growth and Personality*. New York: International Universities Press, 1969, pp. 17–82.

——— (1950), General problems of acting out. *Psychoanal. Quart.*, 19:455–467.

——— (1963), Problems of acting out in the transference relationship. In: *Emotional Growth*. New York: International Universities Press, pp. 695–712.

——— (1968), The psychoanalytic process, transference and acting out. *Internat. J. Psycho-Anal.*, 49:211–218.

Greenson, R. (1965), The working alliance and the transference neurosis. *Psychoanal. Quart.*, 34:155–181.

——— (1967), *The Technique and Practice of Psychoanalysis*. New York: International Universities Press.

Grotjahn, M. (1954), About the relation between psychoanalytic training and psychoanalytic therapy. *Internat. J. Psycho-Anal.*, 35:163–168.

——— (1955), Analytic psychotherapy with the elderly. *Psychoanal. Rev.*, 42:419–427.

Grubrich-Simitis, I. (1986), Six letters of Sigmund Freud and Sándor Ferenzi in the interrelationship of psychoanalytic theory and technique. *Internat. Rev. Psycho-Anal.*, 13:259–277.

Hartmann, H. (1956), Notes on the reality principle. In: *Essays on Ego Psychology*. New York: International Universities Press, 1964.

Heiman, P. (1954), Problems of the training analysis. *Internat. J. Psycho-Anal.*, 35:254–262.

Hogan, C. C. (1985a), Psychodynamics. In: *Fear of Being Fat: The Treatment of Anorexia Nervosa and Bulemia*, ed. C. P. Wilson, C. C. Hogan, & I. L. Mintz. New York: Jason Aronson, pp. 115–128.

——— (1985b), Object relations. In: *Fear of Being Fat: The Treatment of Anorexia Nervosa and Bulemia,* ed. C. P. Wilson, C. C. Hogan, & I. L. Mintz. New York: Jason Aronson, pp. 129–149.

——— (1985c), Transference. In: *Fear of Being Fat: The Treatment of Anorexia Nervosa and Bulemia,* ed. C. P. Wilson, C. C. Hogan, & I. L. Mintz. New York: Jason Aronson, pp. 153–168.

——— (1985d), Technical problems in psychoanalytic treatment. In: *Fear of Being Fat: The Treatment of Anorexia Nervosa and Bulemia,* ed. C. P. Wilson, C. C. Hogan, & I. L. Mintz. New York: Jason Aronson, pp. 197–215.

——— (1986a), The analysis of the mother of a case of bulimic anorexia nervosa. Presentation to the Psychosomatic Study Group. Chairman: C. P. Wilson, co-chairman: C. C. Hogan. The Annual Meeting of the American Psychoanalytic Association, May 7, 1986.

——— (1986b), Inflammatory disease of the colon. Presentation to the Psychosomatic Study Group, Psychoanalytic Association of New York, February 27, 1986, and March 30, 1986.

——— (1987a), The adolescent crisis (in anorexia and bulemia). Presentation: Psychosomatic Study Group. Psychoanalytic Association of New York, Inc., November 12, 1987.

——— (1987b), The psychoanalysis of the mother of a female anorexic. Presentation: Psychosomatic Study Group. American Psychoanalytic Association, December 1987.

——— (1989), Inflammatory disease of the colon. In: *Psychosomatic Symptoms: Psychoanalytic Treatment of Underlying Personality Disorders.* Northvale, NJ: Jason Aronson, pp. 367–399.

——— (in press), *Inflammatory Disease of the Colon.* Madison, CT: International Universities Press.

Horowitz, M. H. (1987), Some notes on insight and its failures. *Psychoanal. Quart.,* 56:177–196.

Huxster, H., Lower, R., & Escoll, P. (1975), Some pitfalls in the assessment of analyzability in a psychoanalytic clinic. *J. Amer. Psychoanal. Assn.,* 23:90–106.

Jacobs, T. (1986), On the opening phase. Paper presented at

the Mid-winter Meeting of the American Psychoanalytic Association, New York.

Jaques, E. (1970), *Work, Creativity and Social Justice.* New York: International Universities Press.

Kabcenell, R. (1988), Some aspects of the treatment alliance in child analysis. Lecture presented at the scientific meeting of the New York Psychoanalytic Society, 1989.

Kairys, D. (1964), The training analysis: A critical review of the literature and a controversial proposal. *Psychoanal. Quart.*, 33:485–512.

Kantrowitz, J. (1986), A prospective study of suitability for psychoanalysis: A follow-up of twenty-two cases. *Yearbook Psychoanalytic Psychotherapy*, 2:403–415, ed. R. Lang. New York: Gardner Press.

——— Katz, A., Paolitto, F., Sashin, J., & Solomon, L. (1987a), Changes in level and quality of object relations in psychoanalysis: Follow-up of a longitudinal predictive study. *J. Amer. Psychoanal. Assn.*, 35:23–46.

——— ——— ——— ——— ——— (1987b), The role of reality testing in psychoanalysis of twenty-two cases. *J. Amer. Psychoanal. Assn.*, 35:367–385.

——— Paolitto, F., Sashin, J., Solomon, L., & Katz, A. (1986), Affect availability, tolerance, complexity and modulation in psychoanalysis: A follow-up of a longitudinal predictive study. *J. Amer. Psychoanal. Assn.*, 34:525–555.

——— Singer, J., & Knapp, P. (1975), Methodology for a prospective study of suitability for psychoanalysis: The role of psychological tests. *Psychoanal. Quart.*, 44:371–391.

Kaplan, R. W. (1984), Of empathy or altruistic surrender. *Dynamic Psychotherapy*, 2:123–131.

Karush, A. (1956), People who seek help. A diagnostic survey. In: *Changing Concepts in Psychoanalytic Medicine*, ed. S. Rado & G. Daniels. New York: Grune & Stratton, pp. 69–84.

Kernberg, O. (1966), Structural derivatives of object relations. *Internat. J. Psycho-Anal.*, 47:236–253.

——— (1967), Borderline personality development. *J. Amer. Psychoanal. Assn.*, 15:641–685.

——— (1975), *Borderline Conditions and Pathological Narcissism.* New York: Jason Aronson.

——— (1976), *Object Relations Theory and Clinical Psychoanalysis.* New York: Jason Aronson.

——— (1980), *Internal World and External Reality: Object Relations Theory Applied.* New York: Jason Aronson.

——— Burstein, E. D., Coyne, L., Applebaum, A., Horwitz, L., & Voth, H. (1972), Psychotherapy and psychoanalysis: Final report of the Menninger Foundation Psychotherapy Research Project. *Bull. Menninger Clin.*, 36:3–275.

King, P. (1980), The life cycle as indicated by the nature of the tranference in the psychoanalysis of the middle-aged and the elderly. *Internat. J. Psycho-Anal.*, 61:153–160.

Klein, H. (1960), Changes in and after psychoanalytic treatment. In: *Current Approaches to Psychoanalysis*, ed. P. Hoch & J. Zubin. New York: Grune & Stratton, pp. 151–175.

Klein, M. (1946), Some notes on schizoid mechanisms. *Internat. J. Psycho-Anal.*, 27:99–110.

——— (1963), *Our Adult World.* New York: Basic Books.

Knapp, P., Levin, S., McCarter, R., Wermer, H., & Zetzel, E. (1960), Suitability for psychoanalysis: A review of one hundred supervised analytic cases. *Psychoanal. Quart.*, 29:459–477.

Kohut, H. (1971), *The Analysis of the Self. A Systematic Approach to the Psychoanalytic Treatment of Narcissistic Personality Disorders.* New York: International Universities Press.

——— (1977), *The Restoration of the Self.* New York: International Universities Press.

——— (1984), *How Does Analysis Cure?* Chicago: University of Chicago Press.

Kris, E. (1951), Ego psychology and interpretation in psychoanalytic therapy. *Psychoanal. Quart.*, 20:15–30.

——— (1956a), The personal myth. *J. Amer. Psychoanal. Assn.*, 4:653–681.

——— (1956b), On some vicissitudes of insight in psychoanalysis. *Internal. J. Psychoanal.*, 37:445–455.

Kris, M. (1957), The use of prediction in a longitudinal study. *The Psychoanalytic Study of the Child*, 12:175–189. New York: International Universities Press.

Lampl-de Groot, J. (1954), Problems of psychoanalytic training. *Internat. J. Psycho-Anal.*, 35:184–187.

Laufer, M., & Laufer, M. E. (1984), *Adolescence and Developmental Breakdown*. New Haven, CT: Yale University Press.

Lazar, N. (1973), The nature and significance of changes in patients in a psychoanalytic clinic. *Psychoanal. Quart.*, 42:579–600.

Lewis, D. (1980), The phase of young adulthood, age eighteen to twenty-three years. In: *The Course of Life*, Vol. 2, ed. G. Pollock & S. Greenspan. Washington, DC: U.S. Department of Health and Human Services, pp. 523–529.

Loeb, F. F., & Loeb, L. R. (1987), Psychoanalytic observations on the effect of lithium on manic attacks. *J. Amer. Psychoanal. Assn.*, 35:877–902.

Loewald, H. (1960), On the therapeutic action of psychoanalysis. *Internat. J. Psycho-Anal.*, 41:16–33.

Lower, R. B., Escoll, P. E., & Huxster, H. K. (1972), Basis for judgements of analyzability. *J. Amer. Psychoanal. Assn.*, 20:610–621.

Mahler, M. S., Pine, F., & Bergman, A. (1975), *The Psychoanalytic Birth of the Human Infant*. New York: Basic Books.

Marty, P., & de M'Uzan, M. (1963), La "pensée opératoire." *Rev. Frac. Psychoanal.*, 27(supplement):1345–1356.

——— ——— David, C. (1963), *L'investigation Psychosomatique*. Paris: Presses Universitaires de France.

McLaughlin, J. T. (1973), The non-reporting training analyst, the analysis and the institute. *J. Amer. Psychoanal. Assn.*, 21:697–712.

Meerloo, J. A. M. (1953), Contribution of psychoanalysis to the problems of the aged. In: *Psychoanalysis and Social Work*, ed. M. Heimann. New York: International Universities Press.

Meissner, W. W. (1988), The borderline spectrum and psychoanalytic perspectives. *Psychoanal. Inq.*, 8:305–322.

Mintz, I. L. (1983), Anorexia nervosa and bulimia in males. In: *Fear of Being Fat: The Treatment of Anorexia Nervosa and Bulimia*, ed. C. P. Wilson, C. C. Hogan, & I. L. Mintz. Riverside, NJ: Jason Aronson, 1985, pp. 263–303.

Mintz, J., Luborsky, L., & Christoff, P. (1979), Measuring the outcomes of psychotherapy: Findings of the Penn Psychotherapy Project. *J. Clin. Consult. Psychol.*, 47:319–344.

Minuchin, S., Rosman, B. L., & Baker, L. (1978), *Psychosomatic*

Families: Anorexia Nervosa in Context. Cambridge, MA: Harvard University Press.

Modell, A. H. (1968), *Object Love and Reality.* New York: International Universities Press.

——— (1988), The centrality of the psychoanalytic setting and the changing aims of treatment: A perspective from a theory of object relations. *Psychoanal. Quart.*, 57:577–596.

Moore, B. & Fine, B. (in press), Analytic definition of anorexia nervosa. In: *Psychoanalytic Terms and Concepts.* New Haven, CT: Yale Univ. Press, co-published with the American Psychoanalytic Association.

Myers, W. A. (1984), *Dynamic Therapy of the Older Patient.* New York: Jason Aronson.

——— (1986), Transference and countertransference issues in treatments involving older patients and younger therapists. *J. Geriat. Psych.*, 19:221–239.

——— (1987a), Age, rage and the fear of AIDS. *J. Geriat. Psychiat.*, 20:127–142.

——— (1987b), Dreams of mourning and separation in older individuals. In: *The Interpretation of Dreams in Clinical Work*, ed. A. Rothstein. Monograph 3. American Psychoanalytic Association Workshop Series. Madison, CT: International Universities Press, pp. 224–280.

——— (1987c), Work on countertransference facilitated by self-analysis of the analyst's dreams. In: *The Interpretation of Dreams*, ed. A. Rothstein. Monograph 3. American Psychoanalytic Association Workshop Series. Madison, CT: International Universities Press, pp. 71–90.

——— Solomon, M. (1989a), The frequency of dream presentation in psychoanalysis and in psychoanalytic psychotherapy. *J. Amer. Psychoanal. Assn.*, 37:135–144.

——— ——— (1989b), Dream frequency and treatment outcome in psychoanalysis and in psychoanalytic psychotherapy. *J. Amer. Psychoanal. Assn.*

Nacht, S. (1954), The difficulties of didactic psychoanalysis in relation to therapeutic psycho-analysis. *Internat. J. Psycho-Anal.*, 35:250–253.

Niederland, W. G. (1956), Clinical observations on the "little man" phenomenon. *The Psychoanalytic Study of the Child*, 11:381–395. New York: International Universities Press.

——— (1965), Narcissistic impairment in patients with early physical malformations. *The Psychoanalytic Study of the Child*, 20:518–534. New York: International Universities Press.

Nemiroff, R. A., & Colarusso, C. A. (1985), *The Race Against Time. Psychotherapy and Psychoanalysis in the Second Half of Life*. New York: Plenum Press.

Neugarten, B. L. (1970), Dynamics of transition of middle age to old age. Adaptation and the life cycle. *J. Geriat. Psychiat.*, 4:71–87.

Nielsen, N. (1954), The dynamics of training analysis. *Internat. J. Psycho-Anal.*, 35:247–249.

Norman, H., Blacker, K., Oremland, J., & Barrett, W. (1976), The fate of the transference neurosis after termination of a satisfactory analysis. *J. Amer. Psychoanal. Assn.*, 24:471–498.

Nunberg, H. (1969), *Memoirs*. New York: Psychoanalytic & Development Fund.

Oberndorf, C. (1943), Results of psycho-analytic therapy. *Internat. J. Psycho-Anal.*, 24:107–114.

Ormeland, J., Blacker, K., & Norman, H. (1975), Incompleteness in a successful psychoanalysis: A follow-up study. *J. Amer. Psychoanal. Assn.*, 23:819–844.

Ostow, M. (1960a), Use of drugs to overcome technical difficulties in psychoanalysis. In: *The Dynamics of Psychiatric Drug Therapy*, ed. G. Sarwer-Foner. Springfield, IL: Charles C Thomas, pp. 443–458.

——— (1960b), The effects of the newer neuroleptic and stimulation drugs on psychic function. In: *The Dynamics of Psychiatric Drug Therapy*, ed. G. Sarwer-Foner. Springfield, IL: Charles C Thomas, pp. 172–191.

——— (1962), *Drugs in Psychoanalysis and Psychotherapy*. New York: Basic Books.

——— (1986), Archetypes of apocalypse in dreams and in religious scripture. *Israel J. Psychiatry & Rel. Discip.*, 2:107–122.

Panel (1960), Criteria for analyzability. S. Guttman, reporter. *J. Amer. Psychoanal. Assn.*, 8:141–151.

——— (1963), Analysis terminable and interminable: Twenty-five years later. A. Pfeffer, reporter. *J. Amer. Psychoanal. Assn.*, 11:131–142.

——— (1968), Indications and contraindications for psychoanalytic treatment. *Internat. J. Psycho-Anal.*, 49:254–275.

——— (1988a), Anorexia nervosa: Theory and therapy: a new look at an old problem. S. E. Risen, reporter. *J. Amer. Psychoanal. Assn.*, 36:153–161.

——— (1988b), Compulsive eating: Obesity and related phenomena, L. W. Reiser, reporter. *J. Amer. Psychoanal. Assn.*, 36:163–171.

Pfeffer, A. (1959), A procedure for evaluating the results of psychoanalysis: A preliminary report. *J. Amer. Psychoanal. Assn.*, 7:418–444.

——— (1961), Follow-up study of a satisfactory analysis. *J. Amer. Psychoanal. Assn.*, 9:698–718.

——— (1963), The meaning of the analyst after analysis: A contribution to the theory of therapeutic results. *J. Amer. Psychoanal. Assn.*, 11:229–244.

Porder, M. S. (1988), Projective identification: An alternative hypothesis. *Psychoanal. Quart.*, 56:431–451.

Rangell, L. (1967), The metapsychology of psychic trauma. In: *Psychic Trauma*, ed. S. Furst. New York: Basic Books, pp. 51–84.

Richards, A. (1980), Self theory, conflict theory and the problem of hypochondriasis. *The Psychoanalytic Study of the Child*, 36:319–337. New Haven, CT: Yale University Press.

——— (1988), Self-mutilation and father–daughter incest: a psychoanalytic case report. In: *Fantasy, Myth and Reality: Essays in Honor of Jacob A. Arlow*, ed. H. Blum. Madison, CT: International Universities Press, pp. 465–478.

Ritvo, S. (1971), Late adolescence: Developmental and clinical considerations. *The Psychoanalytic Study of the Child*, 22:241–263. New York: International Universities Press.

Rothstein, A. (1982), On the relationship of theory to conceptions and process of analyzablity of narcissistic personality disorders. Paper presented at the Annual Meeting of the American Psychoanalytic Association, Boston.

——— (1984), *The Narcissistic Pursuit of Perfection*, 2nd ed. New York: International Universities Press.

Sachs, H. (1947), Observations of a training analyst. *Psychoanal. Quart.*, 16:157–168.

Sandler, A. M. (1978), Psychoanalysis in later life. Problems in the psychoanalysis of an aging narcissistic patient. *J. Geriat. Psychiat.*, 11:5–36.

Sashin, J., Eldred, S., & van Amerongen, S. (1975), A search for predictive factors in institute supervised cases: A retrospective study of 183 cases from 1959–1966 at the Boston Psychoanalytic Society and Institute. *Internat. J. Psycho-Anal.*, 56:343–359.

Savitt, R. A. (1980), Discussion of C. P. Wilson's paper, "The fear of being fat in female psychology and anorexia nervosa." *Bull. Psychoanal. Assn. NY.*, 17:8–9.

Schlesinger, H. (1988), Historical review. In: *How Does Treatment Help?* ed. A. Rothstein. Madison, CT: International Universities Press, pp. 7–27.

Schlessinger, N. (1984), On analyzability. In: *Psychoanalysis: The Vital Issues*, Vol. 2., ed. J. Gedo & G. Pollock. Madison, CT: International Universities Press.

——— (1987), Evaluation of the outcome of psychoanalysis. Paper presented at the Mid-winter Meeting of the American Psychoanalytic Association, New York.

——— Robbins, F. (1974), Assessment and follow-up in psychoanalysis. *J. Amer. Psychoanal. Assn.*, 22:542–567.

——— ——— (1975), The psychoanalytic process: Patterns of conflict and change in ego functions. *J. Amer. Psychoanal. Assn.*, 23:761–782.

Schwartz, H. (1988), *Bulimia: Psychoanalytic Treatment and Theory*. Madison, CT: International Universities Press.

Shapiro, D. (1978), Survey of psychoanalytic practice 1976: Some trends and implications. *J. Amer. Psychoanal. Assn.*, 26:615–631.

Sifneos, P. E. (1972), *Short-term Psychotherapy and Emotional Crisis*. Cambridge, MA: Harvard University Press.

——— (1973), The prevalence of alexithymic characteristics of psychosomatic patients. In: *Psychotherapy in Psychosomatics*, ed. J. Reusch, A. Schmale, & T. Spoerri. White Plains, NY: Karger, pp. 255–262.

Sperling, M. (1946), Psychoanalytic study of ulcerative colitis in children. *Psychoanal. Quart.*, 15:302–329.

——— (1961), Psychosomatic disorders. In: *Adolescents: Psychoanalytic Approach to Problems and Therapy*, ed. S. Lorand & M. I. Schneer. New York: Hoeber, pp. 202–216.

——— (1967), Transference neurosis in patients with psychosomatic disorders. *Psychoanal. Quart.*, 36:342–355.

——— (1969), Ulcerative colitis in children: Current views and therapies. *J. Amer. Acad. Child Psychiat.*, 8:336–352.

——— (1978), *Psychosomatic Disorders in Childhood.* New York: Jason Aronson.

Sperling, O. (1978a), The concept of "psychosomatic" disease. In: *Psychosomatic Disorders in Childhood*, ed. O. Sperling. New York: Jason Aronson, pp. 3–10.

——— (1978b), Discussion of Chapter 1 at the meeting of the Psychosomatic Study Group of the Psychoanalytic Association of New York, March 16, 1978.

Spiegel, L. (1951), A review of contributions to a psychoanalytic theory of adolescence: Individual aspects. *The Psychoanalytic Study of the Child*, 6:375–393. New York: International Universities Press.

Spitz, R. (1956), Transference: The analytic setting and its prototype. *Internat. J. Psycho-Anal.*, 37:380–385.

Stein, M. (1973), Acting out as a character trait. *The Psychoanalytic Study of the Child*, 28:347–364. New York: Quadrangle.

——— (1977), A psychoanalytic view of mental health: Samuel Pepys and his diary. *Psychoanal. Quart.*, 46:82–115.

——— (1981), The unobjectionable part of the transference. *J. Amer. Psychoanal. Assn.*, 29:869–892.

——— (1983), Health—A psychoanalyst's view. In: *The Diary of Samuel Pepys*, Vol. 10, ed. R. Latham. London: Bell & Hyman, pp. 176–180.

——— (1984), Rational versus anagogic interpretation: Xenophon's dream and others. *J. Amer. Psychoanal. Assn.*, 32:529–556.

——— (1986), Acting out—Transference and countertransference: Technical considerations. In: *Between Analyst and Patient*, ed. H. C. Meyers. Hillsdale, NJ: Analytic Press, pp. 63–74.

——— (1987), The clinical use of dream interpretation in acting out. In: *The Interpretation of Dreams in Clinical Work*, ed. A. Rothstein. New York: International Universities Press, pp. 57–68.

Stern, D. N. (1985), *The Interpersonal World of the Infant.* New York: Basic Books.

Stone, L. (1954), The widening scope of indications for psychoanalysis. *J. Amer. Psychoanal. Assn.*, 2:567.

Strachey, J. (1934), The nature of the psychoanalytic action of psychoanalysis. *Internat. J. Psycho-Anal.*, 15:127–159.

Tartakoff, H. (1966), The normal personality in our culture and the Nobel Prize complex. In: *Psychoanalysis—A General Psychology*, ed. R. M. Lowenstein, L. M. Newman, M. Schur, & A. J. Solnit. New York: International Universities Press, pp. 222–252.

Thoma, H., & Kächele, H. (1985), *Psa Practice*, Vol. 1. New York: J. Springer.

Ticho, E. (1970), Differences between psychoanalysis and psychotherapy. *Bull. Menninger Clin.*, 34:128–138.

Tyson, R., & Sandler, J. (1971), Problems in the selection of patients for psychoanalysis: Comments on the application of the concepts of "indications," "suitability," and "analyzability." *Brit. J. Med. Psychol.*, 44:211–228.

Viederman, M. (1976), The influence of the analyst on structural change: A case report. *Psychoanal. Quart.*, 45:241–249.

Volkan, V. D. (1976), *Primitive Internalized Object Relations: A Clinical Study of Schizophrenic, Borderline, and Narcissistic Patients*. New York: International Universities Press.

Waelder, R. (1930), The principle of multiple function: Observations on overdetermination. In: *Psychoanalysis: Observation, Theory, Application*, ed. S. A. Guttman. New York: International Universities Press, pp. 68–83, 1968.

——— (1963), Psychic determinism and the possibility of prediction. *Psychoanal. Quart.*, 32:15–42.

Waldhorn, H. (1967), Indications for psychoanalysis. In: *Kris Study Group Mono.*, Vol. 2, ed. E. Joseph. New York: International Universities Press, pp. 3–51.

Wallerstein, R. (1986), *Forty-Two Lives in Treatment: A Study of Psychoanalysis and Psychotherapy*. New York: Guilford Press.

Weber, J., Bradlow, P., Moss, P., & Ellison, J. (1974), Predictions of outcome in psychoanalysis and analytic psychotherapy. *Psychiat. Quart.*, 40:1–33.

——— Bachrach, H., & Solomon, M. (1985a), Factors associated with the outcome of psychoanalysis: Report of the Columbia Psychoanalytic Center Research Project (II). *Internat. Rev. Psychoanal.*, 12:127–141.

——— ——— ——— (1985b), Factors associated with the outcome of psychoanalysis: Report of the Columbia Psychoanalytic Center Research Project (II). *Internat. Rev. Psychoanal.*, 12:251–262.

Werman, D. S. (1984), *The Practice of Supportive Psychotherapy*. New York: Brunner/Mazel.

Wilson, C. P. (1967), Stone as a symbol of teeth. *Psychoanal. Quart.*, 36:83–84.

——— (1985), Psychodynamic and/or psychopharmacologic treatment of bulimic anorexia nervosa. In: *Fear of Being Fat: The Treatment of Anorexia Nervosa and Bulemia*, ed. C. P. Wilson, C. C. Hogan, & I. L. Mintz. Riverside, NJ: Jason Aronson, 17:345–362.

——— (1986), The psychoanalytic psychotherapy of bulemic anorexia nervosa. In: *Adolescent Psychiatry*, ed. S. C. Feirstein, A. S. Esman, J. Ghoenly, A. F. Schwartzberg, A. D. Sarosky, & M. Sugar. Chicago: University of Chicago Press.

——— Hogan, C. C., & Mintz, I. eds. (1983), *Fear of Being Fat: The Treatment of Anorexia Nervosa and Bulemia*, rev. ed. New York: Jason Aronson, 1985.

——— Mintz, I. (1989), *Psychosomatic Symptoms. Psychodynamic Treatment of the Underlying Personality Disorders*. Northvale, NJ: Jason Aronson.

Winnicott, D. W. (1953), Transitional objects and transitional phenomena. In: *Collected Papers. Through Pediatrics to Psychoanalysis*. New York: Basic Books, 1958, pp. 229–242.

——— (1960), The theory of the parent–infant relationship. In: *The Maturational Processes and the Facilitating Environment*. New York: International Universities Press, 1965, pp. 37–63.

Name Index

Subject Index